Justice and Peace

Our Faith in Action

Author

Joseph Stoutzenberger

 **Harcourt Religion Publishers**

www.harcourtreligion.com

This first printing was manufactured prior to final ecclesiastical approval.

For permission to reprint copyrighted material, grateful acknowledgment is made to the following sources:

Costello Publishing Company, Inc.: From *Vatican Council II: The Conciliar and Post Conciliar Documents*, edited by Reverend Austin Flannery, O.P. Text copyright © 1975 by Harry J. Costello and Reverend Austin Flannery, O.P.

Division of Christian Education of the National Council of the Churches of Christ in the U.S.A.: Scripture quotations from the *New Revised Standard Version Bible: Catholic Edition*. Text copyright © 1993 and 1989 by the Division of Christian Education of the National Council of the Churches of Christ in the U.S.A.

Forest of Peace Publishing, Inc.: From *The Conspiracy of Compassion* by Joseph Nassal.

HarperCollins Publishers: From *The Long Loneliness* by Dorothy Day. Text copyright 1952 by Harper & Row, Publishers, Inc.; text copyright renewed © 1980 by Tamar Teresa Hennessy.

International Commission on English in the Liturgy, Inc.: From the English translation of the *Eucharistic Prayers for Masses for Various Needs and Occasions*. Translation © 1994 by International Committee on English in the Liturgy, Inc.

Patrick Regan: Adapted from "Maria's Story" by Carrol Joy and Patrick Regan in *World Hunger: Learning to Meet the Challenge.*

Fleming H. Revell, a division of Baker Book House Company: Adapted from *A Time for Compassion* (Retitled: "Two Fates") by Dr. Ron Lee Davis and James D. Denney. Text copyright 1986 by Fleming H. Revell Company.

Scribner, an imprint of Simon & Schuster Adult Publishing Group: From *Myth of the Welfare Queen* by David Zucchino. Text copyright © 1997 by David Zucchino.

United States Conference of Catholic Bishops, Inc., Washington, D.C.: From the English translation of the *Catechism of the Catholic Church* for the United States of America. Translation copyright © 1994 by United States Catholic Conference, Inc.—Libreria Editrice Vaticana. From the English translation of the *Catechism of the Catholic Church: Modifications from the Editio Typica*. Translation copyright © 1997 by United States Catholic Conference, Inc.—Libreria Editrice Vaticana. From "The Challenge of Peace: God's Promise and Our Response" by the U. S. Bishops, 1983. Text copyright © by United States Conference of Catholic Bishops. From "Economic Justice for All: Pastoral Letter on Catholic Social Teaching and the U. S. Economy" by U. S. Catholic Bishops, 1986. Text copyright © by United States Conference of Catholic Bishops. From "Sharing Social Teaching: Challenges and Directions," Reflections of the U. S. Catholic Bishops. Text copyright © by United States Conference of Catholic Bishops. From "Renewing the Earth," a Statement of the United States Catholic Conference. Text copyright © by United States Conference of Catholic Bishops. From "A Pastoral Message: Living with Faith and Hope After September 11" by the U. S. Conference of Catholic Bishops, November 14, 2001. Text copyright © by United States Conference of Catholic Bishops. From "One Family Under God" by the U. S. Catholic Bishops Committee on Migration. Text copyright © by United States Conference of Catholic Bishops. From "Putting Children and Families First: A Challenge for Our Church, Nation, and World," a Statement of the United States Catholic Conference, November 1991. Text copyright © by United States Conference of Catholic Bishops. From "Confronting a Culture of Violence: A Catholic Framework for Action," a Pastoral Message of the U. S. Catholic Bishops, 1994. Text copyright © by United States Conference of Catholic Bishops. From "Strangers No Longer: Together in the Journey of Hope" by the Catholic Bishops of Mexico and the United States. Text copyright © by United States Conference of Catholic Bishops. From "Responsibility, Rehabilitation, and Restoration: A Catholic Perspective on Crime and Criminal Justice," a Statement of the U. S. Catholic Bishops, November 15, 2000. Text copyright © 2000 by United States Conference of Catholic Bishops. From *To Live in Christ Jesus: A Pastoral Reflection on the Moral Life* by National Conference of Catholic Bishops. Text copyright © by United States Catholic Conference. From "Statement on Iraq" by United States Conference of Catholic Bishops. Text copyright © by United States Conference of Catholic Bishops. From *Society and the Aged*. Text copyright © 1976 by United States Conference of Catholic Bishops.

Writers House LLC, New York, on behalf of the Estate of Martin Luther King, Jr.: From "I Have a Dream" speech by Martin Luther King, Jr. Text copyright © 1963 by Dr. Martin Luther King, Jr.; text copyright renewed 1991 by Coretta Scott King.

ISBN 0-15-901674-6

Contents

Foundations For A Just World

Issues of Justice and Peace

CHAPTER 1

GOD'S LOVE
FOUNDATION OF JUSTICE

CHAPTER GOALS

In this chapter you will:

★ learn about the virtue of justice and Scripture's vision of a world in which people treat one another as images of God.

★ explore the Exodus story in which God establishes a covenant with his people.

★ understand that prophets speak for God about religious, political, and social injustices.

★ examine God's loving presence in Christ who proclaimed God's kingdom of justice, love, and peace.

What Is Justice?

what's your opinion?

Answer **agree, disagree, or uncertain** to the following statements. Explain your answers.

1. Injustice is a serious problem in our world.

2. Practicing the virtue of justice is very important to me.

3. I believe I can help bring about justice in my community.

4. In our country all people have their basic needs met.

5. Working for justice is a requirement of the Catholic faith.

FAITH ACTIVITY

Sense of Justice Imagine that a friend who is not taking this course picks up your textbook and reads the title of this chapter, *God's Love: Foundation of Justice*. How would you explain to your friend the meaning of these words? Do you believe that it is possible to have a sense of justice without belief in God? Explain.

Any study of Catholic action on behalf of social justice starts with the virtue of justice itself. To understand the virtue of justice, we need to look to our God who is just beyond human measure and to the way he shares his just nature with humans.

We learn about God's justice in Scripture: in the creation of all that is good, in his relationship with the first humans, in his persistent action on behalf of his people who continued to turn from him, in his promise of redemption and salvation spoken through the prophets, and, most especially, in the sending of his Son and later his Spirit to once and for all restore humans to their proper relationship with him. We will look in more detail at these biblical roots of justice later in this chapter.

The greatest insight we can get into God's justice is the revelation of God as Trinity: Father, Son, and Holy Spirit. For it is through the willingness of the Father to send us his only Son, the work of the Son, and the continued presence of the Holy Spirit, that we know and experience new life and the true meaning of the Great Commandment to love God above all else and to love our neighbor as ourselves. In many ways this is the most basic understanding of justice, giving God what is his due is giving him the love, faith, adoration, trust, and hope that he deserves as the most important person or thing in our lives, then giving others what we would expect from them. Thus, we can understand **justice** as giving God what is his due and our neighbors what is theirs.

The Trinitarian nature of God is the most important aspect of our faith. Revealed in Scripture and tradition, and central to Church teaching, we can come to understand relationships by the way the Persons of the Trinity relate to one another. This is important because in many ways justice is about relationships with God and others.

The Virtue of Justice

Above all, justice is a **virtue**. A virtue is a habit and firm disposition that helps us choose to do what is good. The virtues not only lead us to do good things but also to be the best we can be, pursuing what is good in all aspects of our lives. There are two types or categories of virtues: theological virtues and human, or moral, virtues. The theological virtues—faith, hope, and love (charity)—are gifts from God that focus us on having a relationship with the Trinity. They help us to believe in God and all that he has made known to us, trust in him and the promise of new life, and love him as he loves us.

The human virtues have to do with our intellect and our will. They guide our actions, help us keep our emotions in check, and prompt us to make reasonable and faith-filled decisions. We cultivate these virtues by our own efforts. Of the human virtues, the four cardinal virtues have primary importance, and from them, the other virtues are grouped.

- prudence, wise, careful, and sensible judgments in all circumstances

- justice, giving God and others what is due to them

- fortitude, courage to do what is right even if others disagree with or challenge us

- temperance, balancing your thoughts, actions, and feelings so that our desires don't rule your life

The virtue of justice, then, motivates us to put God first in our lives, to praise and thank him through prayer and the way we live, and to make choices that give God the honor and trust he deserves. Furthermore, justice is a disposition of the human heart that seeks to look upon others the way God sees them. It prompts us to respect the rights of others and to create human relationships that promote harmony and equality. In other words, justice doesn't simply mean that we have our heart in the right place. It implies taking steps to address injustices. And, as with all aspects of our faith, we don't do this alone; as members of the Church, we rely on one another to raise our awareness and challenge us to action. God's grace—our sharing in his life first received in Baptism and nourished in the Eucharist—strengthens us to live this life of virtue, to see the connections between believing in the Trinity and responding to the needs of others.

One of the most important ways we give God his "just due" is to worship him as the Body of Christ gathered together. In the opening words of the *Gloria*, which is sung most Sundays during the celebration of the Eucharist, we proclaim, "Glory to God in the highest, and peace to his people on earth." The two parts to the sentence are interconnected and have justice implications. That is, when we give glory to God, we long for all to know his peace and commit ourselves to making the world a more peaceful, livable place; when we work to help others experience the peace that comes from believing in Christ and following his example of just living, we give glory to God the Father.

The glory of God the Father is discovered in the world that reflects his beauty and goodness. His plan to have all humans share in his life and glory requires us to point out that goodness to others. He challenges us to work with him in maintaining a just world and, where necessary, in transforming it into the world he intended it to be. Jesus Christ, Son of the Father, embodies this message. He points the way toward justice and peace in this world, and through his death and Resurrection wins for us eternal peace.

GLOBAL PERSPECTIVE

Some Facts About Our World

★ In the countries of sub-Saharan Africa, **300 million people** live in poverty.

★ **100 million children**, more than 40 percent of all children in sub-Saharan Africa, are malnourished.

★ Life expectancy is falling to **40 years of age** in the poorest areas of Africa.

★ In the United States, **31 million people** live in poverty.

Catholic Relief Services, 2002–2003 catalog

After Jesus ascended into heaven, he sent the Holy Spirit so that his followers could be his witnesses and share the Good News of hope and new life that come from believing. As the Holy Spirit strengthened and guided the Apostles and first disciples, he gives us strength and guidance today. He makes it possible for us to share in God's life, to believe in all that the Father and the Son have made known to us and to act on that belief. Always with us, the Holy Spirit makes Christ present to us and the world, being with us in our struggles for justice and peace. The Church is a living reminder of the Holy Spirit's presence and the instrument of the Spirit at work in the world.

A Just World

We need to look at justice from two perspectives— that of the doers as well as that of the receivers of justice. The definition of the word implies that everyone has a right to justice. It flows from the very nature of human beings created in the image of God and therefore endowed with inherent dignity—worth, respect, and esteem due to each person because he or she is made in the image of God.

Human beings are religious through and through. We come from God and we are going toward God. A life of justice is not an add-on to our humanity. Rather, it flows from our very nature. We can work for justice because we participate in the wisdom and goodness of God himself! (*CCC* 1954) The "original moral sense" (*CCC* 1954) that we possess is called **natural law**. It is engraved on our soul. We can access natural law through the use of reason, a capacity that is proper to human nature. Along with reason, Revelation, particularly in the Decalogue, also makes the natural law, known to us. We cannot separate being moral from being just. The moral choices we make in our lives impact others and, directly or indirectly, society itself. Recent popes in particular have pointed out that in justice people have a right to access the means necessary for their basic welfare (for example, education, work opportunities and a living wage, and adequate health care). The popes have also listed the minimal requirements due all people (for example, adequate food, water, clothing, and shelter). A just person respects others and shows regard for their rights and needs.

Being the best, Martin and Angelo were always chosen as captains of the basketball teams. In a ritual duplicated on playgrounds around the world, each one in turn picked the players to fill out the team. After everyone else was picked, only Alexander and Brad remained. Seeing no other potential basketball players in sight, Martin reluctantly pointed to Alexander, leaving Brad for Angelo's team. As the game began, Martin barked directions to Alexander, "Cover Brad. Otherwise, stay out of the way." As is often the case, the "haves" ran the show while the "have–nots" were overlooked.

GROUP TALK

1. Have you ever been a Martin/Angelo or an Alexander/Brad in a similar situation during your life? If so, describe one.

2. This incident symbolizes power arrangements in our communities and the world. Name some world situations where power is also unequal.

3. How do you feel about the world of the basketball courts described in this story? Is it a just or an unjust system? Are there ways to make it more just? Explain.

We could easily become overwhelmed with justice-related problems that surround us. We need to set our sights on what a just world can be like. Consider the preceding story, and think about whether or not it described how power and privilege are commonly arranged in our world.

Winners and losers are okay in basketball. It's only a game. There will be another game or another season or at least pleasant memories of games well played. It's another matter when there are winners and losers in life. In life, losing can mean having insufficient food to sustain health, lacking the income needed to provide even basic necessities for a family, or being deprived of educational and work opportunities that would improve living conditions.

FAITH ACTIVITY

Life-Giving Encounter Think back on an encounter you had with someone—an encounter that turned out to be transforming or life-giving for you. Write a letter to that person, thanking him or her and explaining why the person was life-giving for you. Think about how the person would feel if you mailed the letter.

Christ offers a different reality. His actions show us *a just world is one in which no one is left out and everyone can flourish.* But Jesus' stand against injustice of the downtrodden, neglected, and cast aside started with his desire to bring them back into relationship with the Father. By healing people physically, spiritually, or emotionally, Jesus was helping them to have faith so that he could free them from the greatest problem: sin. Being both divine and human, he forgave people their sins and made it possible for them to participate in God's justice again. His just treatment of others was based upon his mission to reconcile people to God, restoring them to the righteousness for which God created them.

Jesus' invitation to turn to God and have life was not limited to any one class or type of person. All were welcome, but all were called to a change of heart and emphasis in their lives. This conversion of heart makes a person more just and precedes social change. It motivates the person to treat others as God does and to work against injustice.

The way to justice is people working together. There are no real winners when suffering and deprivation are commonplace and taken for granted. God wants a good life for all his people. He reminds us that everyone's life is interconnected with the lives of everyone else. Therefore, there can't be a just world without justice for everyone. A just world is one in which the well-being of each person is everyone's concern. Illness, death, and natural disasters cause pain and suffering. However, when people's choices and existing social structures cause unnecessary pain and suffering, then it is a matter of justice.

Ultimately, justice will be achieved only when Christ comes in his glory to judge the living and the dead and to bring God's kingdom to its completeness. Meanwhile, we need to call on the Father to bring about justice and peace. We need to cultivate our interior disposition toward justice in ways suited to our character strengths and responsive to the pressing needs of others. When we do our part, it is the Holy Spirit who works through us.

Creation and Liberation The Bible offers us the characteristics of a just world and the way we can work for justice. The Scriptures begin the story of God's saving actions with accounts of the **creation** of the world and the first humans. The Old Testament tells of God's promise to Abraham and the liberation of the Israelites. The New Testament recounts God's gift of Jesus, the Son of God, and the sending of the Holy Spirit. Though God the Father revealed himself fully by sending his Son, the history of salvation did not end there. Nor did it end when the work of writing the Scriptures was completed. The story is not yet finished; that's where we come in.

The Holy Spirit is still present and active today, inviting us to embrace a way of life that helps to bring more love and justice into the world. But what does this cooperation with God's plan for the world look like? This whole course is designed to help you answer that question. We begin, in this chapter, with an overview of salvation history drawn from the Old Testament, the New Testament, and the Church's Tradition. This is the foundation of the Catholic understanding of justice and the source of our hope that God—Father, Son, and Holy Spirit—with the cooperation of human hands, will one day transform the world into a place where love and justice reign.

Fundamental Truths The Genesis accounts of the creation and of Adam and Eve are examples of stories that use figurative language. The story of the Fall in Genesis 3, for example, "uses figurative language, but affirms a primeval event, a deed that took place *at the beginning of the history of man*" (*CCC* 390). These stories are true, though not necessarily in a literal sense. We tell these stories over and over again, because they express fundamental religious truths about who God is, where we came from, and how we relate to God. They also provide us with an understanding of justice and insights into some of life's biggest mysteries.

Natural Law We find order and design all through creation. The sciences and our human powers manifest a plan that discloses harmony and order. This harmony exists also in humans as natural law. Natural law "is *immutable* and permanent throughout the variations of history. . . . The rules that express it remain substantially valid [and provide] the solid foundation on which man can build the structure of moral rules to guide his choices" (*CCC* 1958–1959).

▲ Sistine Chapel ceiling detail *Creation of Adam* (1510) by Michelangelo Buonarroti

God's Creation of the World

Where did we come from? Catholics look to the Book of Genesis at the beginning of the Old Testament for insight into the mystery of creation. The very first words of Genesis are, "In the beginning. . .God created the heavens and the earth" (*Genesis 1:1*). The phrase the heavens and the earth is a way of saying "everything." All people and things exist because of God. When we read the first chapter of Genesis we are struck by the refrain, "And God saw that it was good," following every step of creation.

God created the world freely according to his wisdom. God did not have to create anything. He chose to do so in order to share his goodness and love. All of creation shares in his goodness. To say that people and things have inherent goodness implies a way of viewing and treating them. It requires that we show reverence for the earth and its creatures, including other people and ourselves. In the biblical refrain, God appears to be delighted and immensely pleased with creation. Similarly, we must develop a sense of wonder, awe, and joy for all God's creatures if we are to act justly.

People occupy a unique place in the universe. The Book of Genesis teaches us that "God created humankind in his image" (*Genesis 1:27*). Of all creatures, only humans are called to share in God's own life. We possess free will, are able to reason, and are capable of responding to God with faith and love. This is the reason the Church teaches that everyone—every single person—has dignity and worth that comes to him or her from God. Human life is sacred. Individuals can never lose this dignity and worth. Even if we don't recognize the sacredness in every person we meet, God does.

When God created the first man and woman, they saw things as God did. They had a share in his life, lived in harmony with him and all of creation. The paradise of the Garden of Eden symbolized the original state of holiness and justice for which God created humans. They knew no suffering, no pain, no sin. Their close union with God reflected in the way they treated each other and all of God's creatures. They collaborated with God to care for creation. But, they were free to choose, and we know the choice they made and the result it had for them and all of us who followed.

The Fall of the First Humans

If God is all-good and Creator of everything, why is there injustice and hatred in the world? Through the story of the Fall of Adam and Eve, the Book of Genesis reveals the reality of human sin and its painful effects. The first humans freely chose to reject God. Genesis depicts the seductive voice of a serpent luring them away from God. They disobeyed God's command not to eat from the tree of the knowledge of good and evil. As a consequence, they no longer lived in harmony and friendship with God and all creation. They lost the original holiness and justice for themselves and for all humans, and introduced sin into the world. Thus, this first disobedience of humans is called **original sin**. Since then every person has been born with a tendency to be drawn toward what is wrong and sinful.

Injustice and hatred are rooted in the free human choice to act contrary to God's will. Original sin refers to the fallen state of all humans, a state from which Jesus, as the new Adam, came to redeem us.

Original sin is a something with which every person is born. This is in contrast with the sin that we personally commit. **Sin** is a choice people freely make to turn away from God through what they say, do, or desire. It is a failure to love God and neighbor, an offense against God. In our work for justice and peace, we must grapple with the reality of sin in our own lives and its effects on the lives of others.

Despite their actions, God did not stop loving the first humans, nor does he stop loving us when we turn from him, disobey his commands, and fail to follow his will for us. God desires us to respond to his love by loving him back, making him the most important part of our lives, and honoring him by cooperating with his plan for creation. The Catechism of the Catholic Church explains that creation is "in a state of journeying" (CCC 302). When we freely choose to love, we are collaborating with God in this work of completing creation. When injustice exists, love means working to overcome it. Thus, creation by God lays the foundation for the work of justice.

GROUP TALK

1. Give examples to illustrate how the fact that God created everything and everyone has justice implications.

2. Explain how acceptance of injustice is a failure to love God.

3. What do you think is the relationship between original sin and injustice? Give examples to illustrate the connection.

The sacrifice of Isaac
(c.1551-1629)
by Camillo Procaccini ▶

God's Covenant with Abraham

We learn from the Old Testament that God never abandons his people. The Book of Genesis tells of God's **covenant** with Abraham. A covenant is a binding agreement or promise between parties. In the case of Abraham, God is the one who makes the covenant. Abraham is the recipient of a free gift— God's promise of land and many descendants. God enters into a special relationship with Abraham and his descendants, a covenant that is unconditional and unbreakable.

GROUP TALK

1 Justice means giving everyone what he or she is due. In light of this definition, discuss the following: What makes Christian justice unique

2 What are some aspects of U.S. society that indicate a lack of respect for the dignity and equality of all people?

3 What are the most serious sins today? What are some of the far-reaching results of these sins? Do they result in injustices?

The Exodus

The Exodus, the second great book in the Old Testament depicting salvation history, presents the Israelite's struggle for freedom and the subsequent **Exodus**. In the thirteenth century B.C., Abraham's descendants, the Israelites, were enslaved in Egypt. They cried out to God for help. God heard their cry and led them out of Egypt to freedom. The Exodus story combines universal themes with personal touches, such as trickery by the Hebrew women and Pharaoh's daughter—all behind the scenes of political power to save the lives of children. (To read the account of this story, see *Exodus 1:15—2:10*.) Through vivid images, Exodus tells of God acting in the lives of his people, of attempts at faithful living and trust and hope in God, of injustice overcome, of a fearful journey through the wilderness, and of a prize won. It shows us that God is a compassionate liberator.

> *"I have observed the misery of my people who are in Egypt; I have heard their cry on account of their taskmasters. Indeed, I know their sufferings, and I have come down to deliver them from the Egyptians, and to bring them up out of that land to a good and broad land, a land flowing with milk and honey. . ."*
>
> ✝ Exodus 3:7-8

If we examine the Exodus story symbolically, we can easily find parallels in our world. Today, too many people find themselves in "Egypt," that is, in the land of slavery. Jesus reminds us that first and foremost, we are all in slavery to sin, and he sets us free from this through our participation in Baptism and the other sacraments. However, because of the existence of sin and the poor moral decisions made by people, many in positions of authority, slavery exists in many forms.

For instance, too many people even in North America are enslaved in homelessness without much hope of escape. Too many people find themselves in low-paying jobs with little hope of advancement, while even those with decent jobs are constantly fearful of losing them. Too many people in our world go to bed hungry. The Egypt of their hunger continues to enslave them. In other words, for too many people, the slavery and oppression of "Egypt" are painful realities, not ancient history.

The black slaves in pre-Civil War United States who converted to Christianity found hope in the liberation message of Exodus:

> In their clandestine prayer meetings, held late at night in the slave quarters and hush harbors, the slaves participated in the transforming power of the age for which they hoped by petitioning God for deliverance from bondage. They believed that the same God who transformed the sinful status of their souls in the conversion experience would transform the sinful structures of the society. The God who had freed their souls from sin could certainly free their bodies from slavery.
>
> Cheryl J. Sanders, *Empowerment Ethics for a Liberated People*
> (Minneapolis, MN: Augsburg Fortress, 1955), p. 12

GROUP TALK

Liberation can appear to mean the same thing as freedom. However, the concepts are somewhat different as they are understood by many people.

1 Describe possible differences.

2 Based on your distinctions, is the God of Exodus a God of freedom or of liberation or both? Explain.

Liberation and Justice

While the first creation account affirms goodness, the stories of the first humans and the captivity of the Israelites in Egypt remind us of the reality of sin and challenge us to pay attention to its consequences in the world today. We know our lives and our world are not completely the way they should be. Too often people feel stuck and powerless. Many people are afraid to venture out at night. Suffering and injustice touch the lives of people in every nation.

As we face such sinful realities, personal and societal, we derive hope from God's love for his people revealed through the stories of creation and the Exodus. Creation is the first proclamation of God's love. His action on behalf of the Israelites reveals that he hears the cries of people seeking liberation. The cry for liberation or freedom arises from people seeking justice. Martin Luther King Jr., for example, joined with others seeking greater civil rights for African Americans and for people who were poor. He often referred to the struggle for civil rights in the United States as a freedom movement. As a matter of fact, in his stirring speeches, he frequently linked this movement with the story of the Exodus from Egypt to the promised land. On the night before he died, Dr. King said: "I have been to the mountaintop. . . . And I've looked over, and I've seen the promised land. I may not get there with you. But I want you to know tonight, that we, as a people will get to the promised land."

Another thrust for equality and liberation since the 1960s and '70s, has revolved around the rights of women, and what was popularly called the women's liberation movement. Progress has been made to benefit women's lives. The number of women seeking higher education has steadily increased, and more and higher-level jobs have begun to open up for them. On the home front, many husbands and wives see themselves as equal partners in caring for the home and raising children. While pay often is still unequal and many couples still struggle to share the ordinary tasks of life, many wives and husbands, mothers and fathers, have a greater opportunity to experience the freedom of shared responsibility.

The two examples above—the civil rights movement and the women's rights movement—have had a tremendous impact on social and political equality in North America. Many would argue that more progress is needed, and it's important to continue to evaluate the sinful structures and organizational aspects that allow such inequality   It's also important to remember that not all of the practices or positions of those who support movements such as these may be in line with Church teaching.

For those who struggle against the many forms of enslavement today, the nature of God as one who loves and brings liberation to the oppressed is a source of great hope. The faithful actions of many individuals we hear about in the Exodus story are also a source of hope for us. For instance, when the Egyptian pharaoh ordered midwives who assisted at the births of Hebrew women to kill all male babies, they refused. The mother of Moses, seeking to save her child, schemed to place her son under the protection of Pharaoh's daughter and even managed to serve as her son's nursemaid. These heroines possessed no apparent power. Yet, they followed God's law, not Pharaoh's. They used their ingenuity to help set in motion events that led the Hebrew people to liberation from slavery and entrance into the promised land. Their stories truly demonstrate the strength of the weak when they place their trust in God's saving power. These stories give encouragement to the seemingly powerless who must face the troubles of modern life.

FAITH ACTIVITY

Average Pay Research the average pay of various groups in U.S. society, such as men and women, people of African, European, Asian, and Hispanic descent. What conclusions can you draw?

God's Covenant with Israel After leading the Israelites out of Egypt, God formed a new covenant with them, a covenant often referred to as the "Sinai covenant." As the Book of Exodus recounts, God called to Moses from the mountain and instructed him to deliver this message to the Israelites:

> *You have seen what I did to the Egyptians, and how I bore you on eagles' wings and brought you to myself. Now therefore, if you obey my voice and keep my covenant, you shall be my treasured possession out of all the peoples. Indeed, the whole earth is mine, but you shall be for me a priestly kingdom and a holy nation.*

✝ Exodus 19:4–6

This covenant was binding on both God and the people of Israel. As part of this covenant, God gave his people the Ten Commandments. (See *Exodus 20:2–17.*) God's people were able to respond to his initiative and providential care by following the commandments. Thus, these commandments present the fundamental duties toward God, and others, and are a summary of the basic moral rules that were to guide the life of the ancient Israelites. They continue to guide the moral lives of Jews and Christians today. The covenant between God and Israel is summed up in this scripture passage: "Obey my voice, and I will be your God, and you shall be my people. . . ." (*Jeremiah 7:23*).

As we mature, our understanding of the expansiveness and intent of the Ten Commandments needs to grow, too. These laws are more than restrictive "do not" rules. They form the basis for our moral decision making and development of conscience as well as for the positive actions we need to take in order to love God, others, and ourselves. As we will see throughout this course, they have significant implications for social justice as well, particularly the fourth through tenth commandments.

GROUP TALK

1 In small groups, study the first fifteen chapters of the Book of Exodus. Divide the chapters among the groups. Describe how the people with little apparent power (for example, the midwives, Moses' mother, Moses' sister Miriam) did what they could to stand up to unjust power.

2 Continuing in your small group, name a group who possesses little apparent power in today's society. Analyze possible ways that this group exhibits "the strength of the weak," that is, how a people with little apparent power oppose or defeat unjust power. Present your work to the class.

3 Each of the Ten Commandments has justice implications. For each commandment, identify possible applications to issues of justice.

The Ten Commandments

1. I am the Lord your God: you shall not have strange gods before me.

   > Place one's faith in God alone.
   > Worship, praise, and thank God the Creator.
   > Believe in, trust, and love God.

2. You shall not take the name of the Lord your God in vain.

   > Speak God's name, and that of Jesus and the saints, with reverence.
   > Don't curse.
   > Don't call on God to witness to a lie.

3. Remember to keep holy the Lord's Day.

   > Gather to worship at the Eucharist.
   > Rest and avoid unnecessary work on Sunday.
   > Spend time with the family and participate in Works of Mercy.

4. Honor your father and your mother.

   > Respect and obey parents, and guardians.
   > Care for your parents and guardians and provide for their needs as they age.
   > Respect civil authority.
   > Participate in the political and social life of the community.
   > Promote the role of the family in society.

5. You shall not kill.

   > Honor the sacredness of life from conception to natural death.
   > Respect and protect your life and the lives of others.
   > Help others see that the inherent dignity of all people is the foundation of all social justice.

6. You shall not commit adultery.

   > Be faithful and loyal to spouses, friends, and family.
   > Respect God's gift of sexuality, and practice the virtue of chastity.
   > Learn to appreciate the gift of sexuality by practicing self-mastery.
   > Promote the role of marriage and the family as the basic unit of society.

Continued on next page

7. You shall not steal.

> Do not take what does not belong to you and share your belongings with others

> Promote the just sharing of goods on a more global scale.

> Respect the right to private property of others and thus the things that belong to others.

> Take seriously your responsibility to take care of creation and to be a steward of its resources.

> Treat all workers with respect, no matter what their profession or role.

8. You shall not bear false witness against your neighbor.

> Be honest and truthful.

> Avoid bragging.

> Don't say untruthful or negative things about others.

> Seek information in the media that is based on truth, freedom, and justice, and hold the media accountable to such truth.

> Practice moderation and self-discipline when using the internet and other forms of mass communication.

9. You shall not covet your neighbor's wife.

> Practice modesty in thoughts, words, dress, and actions.

> Encourage your peers to respect their own bodies and those of others by the way they dress, act, and show love.

10. You shall not covet your neighbor's goods.

> Rejoice in others' good fortune.

> Don't be jealous of others' possessions.

> Try to live a simple life in which you use what you need, not long for more than is necessary.

> Challenge others to see beyond cultural attitudes that emphasize possessions.

The Prophets

The Israelites had trouble following the commandments that God had revealed to them through Moses. They struggled to keep their part of the covenant with God by being faithful to the Ten Commandments.

They did acquire a system of government and a king to rule over them. And they established social systems, military power, and alliances with other countries.

Unfortunately, they also engaged in the conflicts, corruption, and injustices that all too often go with human society. During this period of Jewish history, a unique group of people arose to speak God's word. They reminded the people of their responsibilities to the covenant, and challenged them to honor God above all else. They loudly spoke a message of justice when power was abused and the Israelites strayed from God's commandments. Their message still has an impact today.

The Hebrew word for prophet—*nabi*— means "mouthpiece." A **prophet**, in the biblical sense, is a "mouthpiece" for God—a person who speaks for him. The prophets were divinely inspired to share God's will and plan with others. As a result, the prophets frequently challenged the people to turn back to God when they had gone astray.

◀ *Moses Receiving the Ten Commandments* (1960/1966) by Marc Chagall

For the Jews, Moses most clearly spoke God's message and therefore is their greatest prophet. For our purposes, we will focus on those prophets who lived during the eighth and seventh centuries before Christ. These were the prophets who called the Israelites to be faithful to their covenant with God.

You can read about these prophets—most notably, Amos, Hosea, and Jeremiah—in the books of the Bible that are named after them. In their preaching the prophets addressed the religious, political, and social problems of their time. To understand the prophets' messages, we must first examine the kind of people they were. Consider this description:

> The meaning of the word *prophet* is so stretched today that it covers "reformers" and even "statesmen." Strictly speaking, the word denotes a person specially called to be a spokesperson for God. Israel's prophets were charismatic men and women like Miriam (*Exodus 15:20-21*) and Deborah (*Judges 4:4*). They had a deep experience of God, who called them to speak his word in trusting faith. Some report a vision of the heavenly court (*Isaiah 6:1-13; Jeremiah 1:4-19; 1 Kings 22:19-22*). These inspired poets, preachers, and teachers were not microphones. Even though they prefaced their message with expressions such as "The word of the Lord is," they brought to God's message their own personal, historical, and social images and terminology. They were masters of the art of symbolic communication. Their views, like ours, were affected by the conditions and limitations of their time and by the sources of knowledge to which they had access.
>
> Timothy G. McCarthy, *Christianity and Humanism* (Chicago: Loyola Press, 1996), p. 79

Characteristics of the Prophets

Imagine that a group of your friends begins to harshly criticize some people. Your friends become increasingly bold in taunting and teasing these people. Could you stand up to your group and tell them, "No, this isn't what we should be doing. We must stop it!"? Would you have the courage to make such a statement, even if it meant you would be dropped from the group, teased by them, and perhaps have underhanded tricks played on you? Essentially, this describes the dilemma faced by the prophets.

Many of the biblical prophets are among the least likely people we would expect to speak for God. At the time there were official "prophets" employed by the king. The official prophets were known for speaking the "smooth words" that the king and people wanted to hear—nothing that would disrupt their lives. The true prophets, the ones whose words became part of Scripture and have been quoted by Jesus and by Jewish, Christian, and Muslim leaders to this day, often spoke "harsh words" that gave disturbing and unsettling messages. Because of this, the true prophets were reluctant mouthpieces. They often did whatever they could to avoid speaking God's message when they knew it would bring about scornful reactions from their audiences. In spite of the risk of rejection and hardship, however, the prophets spoke. The impact of the prophets lies not in their personal traits or their influence but in the strength of their message.

Prophets of Israel

Amos	Amos was a shepherd from the southern kingdom of Judah who spoke to the people of the northern kingdom of Israel. He was both a member of the peasant class and an alien!
Jeremiah	When called by God to prophesy, Jeremiah responded, "Truly I do not know how to speak, for I am only a boy" (*Jeremiah 1:6*).
Hosea	Chosen as a prophet, Hosea had the dubious distinction of having a wife, Gomer, who was constantly unfaithful to him.
Moses	Moses had difficulty speaking, so much so that he brought along his brother Aaron to speak for him before the pharaoh.

The biblical prophets call people to conversion on both a personal and societal level. They remind people that to do God's will means to love God with all your heart, soul, and mind, and to love your neighbor as yourself. So, doing God's will will always include doing justice. The two can never be separated. Because the prophets speak on behalf of God, they speak on behalf of God's poor—those with no voice in the usual political, social, and economic arrangements of society.

The prophets also speak out about worshiping false gods, and not giving God the prominence in their lives that they promised they would in the covenant. So the message of justice was two-fold: the people were not giving God his rightful due nor giving others the respect, assistance, or acknowledgment that they deserved.

FAITH ACTIVITY

Religion and Politics Form two debate teams. One will defend, the other refute, the following statement: Religion is about spiritual matters. Religious leaders should not address social problems or issues of politics and economics.

Loving God has a social dimension that calls us to meet the needs of God's people who are poor and voiceless. Thus the prophets despised any practice of religion that was not linked to working for justice. Consequently, they condemned religious insincerity when they saw it. Amos, one of the earliest prophets, put the case clearly:

> Even though you offer me your burnt offerings and grain offerings,
>   I will not accept them. . . .
> Take away from me the noise of your songs;
>   I will not listen to the melody of your harps.
> But let justice roll down like waters,
>   and righteousness like an ever-flowing stream.
>
> ✝ Amos 5:22–24

The prophets did not separate religion from politics or from the social conditions of their day. They recognized how easily their countries' leaders made political decisions that contradicted God's laws and his call for justice:

> Because you have trusted in your power
>   and in the multitude of your warriors,
> therefore the tumult of war shall rise against your people,
>   and all your fortresses shall be destroyed. . . .
>
> ✝ Hosea 10:13–14

For the prophets, religion, politics, and social conditions were all matters of justice. Through the prophets, God called for just treatment of all people:

> Thus says the LORD of hosts, the God of Israel: Amend your ways and your doings, and let me dwell with you in this place. . . .
>
> ✝ Jeremiah 7:3

The prophets' view of justice was and is still challenging. They call people to a wholehearted commitment to focusing on their covenant relationship with God, which is very much connected to correcting the mistreatment of the downtrodden members of their society.

A Reason for Hope

Even though the prophets often delivered stinging words, their message also gave people hope for the future. They provided a picture of a redeemed world in which people are motivated by their love of God and work for peace-filled communities built on following God's law, honoring him, and one's neighbor.

> *The LORD will guide you continually,*
> *and satisfy your needs in parched places,*
> *and make your bones strong;*
> *and you shall be like a watered garden,*
> *like a spring of water,*
> *whose waters never fail.*
>
> ✝ **Isaiah 58:11**

The prophets' words of hope often include the promise that in the future God would bring about salvation for all people. In the words of the prophet Isaiah, the Lord says,
"I will give you as a light to the nations, that my salvation may reach to the end of the earth" (*Isaiah 49:6*). We know this light to be Jesus Christ, the Light of the World, Son of God and Messiah. The *Catechism of the Catholic Church* summarizes the promise of the prophets and their work in this way:

> Through the prophets, God forms his people in the hope of salvation, in the expectation of a new and everlasting Covenant intended for all, to be written on their hearts. The prophets proclaim a radical redemption of the People of God, purification from all their infidelities, a salvation, which will include all the nations. Above all, the poor and humble of the Lord will bear this hope (***CCC*** 64).

The prophet Jeremiah brought hope to the people by announcing God's promise of a new covenant:

> *The days are surely coming, says the LORD, when I will make a new covenant with the house of Israel and the house of Judah. . . . But this is the covenant that I will make with the house of Israel after those days, says the LORD: I will put my law within them, and I will write it on their hearts; and I will be their God, and they shall be my people*
>
> ✝ **Jeremiah 31:31,33**

GROUP TALK

Even today politicians and preachers, poets and songwriters, can speak either "smooth words" or "harsh words."

★ Give examples of modern-day people who speak either "smooth words" or "harsh words."

★ What are some of the "harsh words" that people today need to hear in order to live according to God's will?

Jesus Christ

God's active, loving presence in the lives of his people is brought to perfection through the gift of his divine son, Jesus Christ. God's promise of salvation for all was fulfilled through the life, death, and Resurrection of Jesus who established the new covenant.

Who is Jesus, the Christ? Jesus asked his disciples, "Who do people say that I am?" Peter answered, "You are the Messiah." (See *Mark 8:27–29.*) If you had been with them, what would you have said?

Jesus of Nazareth, a Jew born in Bethlehem during the reign of King Herod and crucified under Pontius Pilate in Jerusalem is God made man. "He became truly man while remaining truly God (*CCC* 464). The **Incarnation** (incarnate means "in the flesh") refers to that mystery when "the Son of God assumed human nature and became man in order to "accomplish our salvation." (*CCC Glossary*) Like the prophets before him, Jesus announced the word of God. Unlike the prophets, Jesus has a unique, eternal relationship with the Father and the Holy Spirit.

Jesus not only announced God's word, he is the Word of God, the second Person of the Holy Trinity. He came to earth in human flesh so that we would know the Father's divine love and be reconciled with him. Jesus freely offered his whole life for the sake of our salvation. Jesus fulfills the promise that God made to Abraham. The Father sent him, his own beloved Son, because of his great love for us.

The name *Jesus* in Hebrew means "God saves." This signifies Jesus' mission as the Savior of the world. The name Christ is the Greek equivalent of the Hebrew word *Messiah*. Both words mean "anointed." When we confess that Jesus is the Christ, we signify that God the Father has anointed him with the Holy Spirit for a divine mission. We see this at Jesus' baptism by John and at Jesus' Transfiguration, as we get a

▼ Jerusalem

glimpse into the life of the Trinity. It is with the coming of the Holy Spirit at Pentecost that the Trinity is fully revealed, and we have a better understanding of the distinct but joined roles of each of the Persons.

Each Person of the Holy Trinity is rightly called God. Yet, in our liturgy, prayer, and study, we sometimes refer to the first Person of the Trinity, the Father, simply as God. This does not take away from the other two Persons being fully and eternally God as well, or from the Father having the unique role of Father.

Through his whole life—in both his words and actions—Jesus reveals the way of life to which God the Father calls us. He also makes known to us that he is God our Savior. His entire life was inspired by the Father's loving plan to redeem us. Through his death and Resurrection, Jesus liberates us from sin and opens for us the way to a new life as children of God. Far more than a mere example for living, Jesus is the source of our life.

Though Jesus ascended into heaven, he continues to be present on earth through the Holy Spirit. Jesus Christ, through the Holy Spirit, lives in the hearts of all the faithful. He continues to be present to us through the liturgy, especially the Eucharist, which celebrates our salvation through the Paschal mystery—the mystery of the suffering, death, Resurrection, and Ascension of Jesus Christ. When we participate in the Eucharist, we enter into the mystery of Jesus' dying and rising. The grace of the Holy Spirit unites us to Christ and connects us to the life of the trinity, makes us God's adopted children and prepares us for our vocation and the continuance of Jesus' mission in the world. (See *CCC* 2021.)

FAITH ACTIVITY

Jerusalem in Jesus' Day Research and discuss historical accounts of the political and social climate of Jesus' time. In what way do you think Jesus brought justice and hope to the people? How does he continue to bring justice into the world today?

Jesus' Justice

When we face a choice, it is not always clear which is the way of faith. Even when it is clear, it is not always easy to make the right choice, the choice for what is good and God-like. The rest of this chapter explores some of the things Jesus tells us to help us better understand the life of cooperation to which God calls us—a life that makes it possible for us to grow in our faith and understanding of God's will for us, a life that leads us to be Christ-like and thus helps to increase justice, love, and peace in the lives of those around us. We begin with Jesus' well-known story of the Good Samaritan.

Just then a lawyer stood up to test Jesus. "Teacher," he said, "what must I do to inherit eternal life?" [Jesus] said to him, "What is written in the law? What do you read there?" He answered, "You shall love the Lord your God with all your heart, and with all your soul, and with all your strength, and with all your mind; and your neighbor as yourself." And [Jesus] said to him, "You have given the right answer; do this, and you will live."

But wanting to justify himself, he asked Jesus, "And who is my neighbor?" Jesus replied, "A man was going down from Jerusalem to Jericho, and fell into the hands of robbers, who stripped him, beat him, and went away, leaving him half dead. Now by chance a priest was going down that road; and when he saw him, he passed by on the other side. So likewise a Levite, when he came to the place and saw him, passed by on the other side. But a Samaritan while traveling came near him; and when he saw him, he was moved with pity. He went to him and bandaged his wounds, having poured oil and wine on them. Then he put him on his own animal, brought him to an inn, and took care of him. The next day he took out two denarii, gave them to the innkeeper, and said, 'Take care of him; and when I come back, I will repay you whatever more you spend.' Which of these three, do you think, was a neighbor to the man who fell into the hands of the robbers?" He said, "The one who showed him mercy." Jesus said to him, "Go and do likewise."

✝ Luke 10:25-37

A Just World: A Sacred Place The parable of the Good Samaritan teaches us about love of others, even those considered foreigners or enemies. The parables give us insight into the importance of justice in a broken world. Too many people find themselves bleeding and abandoned by the side of the road, beaten down by poverty or limited opportunities, disabilities, or discrimination. Meanwhile, the rest of the world seems to be moving along the road, oblivious to their plight or deliberately choosing to ignore it.

The story Jesus tells invites us to consider a different world. We know the hero of the story simply as a Samaritan—no one special, and not someone with whom the Jews hearing the story would want to associate.

Samaritans were descendants of Jews who had intermarried with non-Jews. Over the centuries, the relationship between Jews and Samaritans gradually disintegrated. While the Samaritans accepted the Pentateuch, they worshiped on a mountain in Samaria rather than in Jerusalem. Typically, Jews would not have helped an injured Samaritan, and they certainly would not have expected a Samaritan to come to the aid of an injured Jew.

The Samaritan in Jesus' story, however, shows genuine concern for the welfare of the suffering man, who happens to be a Jew. He sees someone in need and responds with compassion, one human helping another. Jesus seems to suggest that the Samaritan is acting in a profoundly human way, while those who pass by without helping put religious laws and human prejudices above the spirit of the law.

A world filled with good Samaritans is the human world at its best. By God's grace and with our cooperation in His plan, it also becomes a more sacred place. To be Christian means many things—believing in God the Father, Son, and Holy Spirit, having faith in Christ and living the life of a baptized follower who participates in the sacraments and continues Jesus' work in the world. This obviously includes participating in fashioning such a sacred world. It means becoming God's co-workers, helping to complete the work of creation and helping to make the world more like the kingdom of God of which Jesus preached. Today, the task looms large. We realize that those in need are both on our own streets and on the other side of the earth. Typically, they lack even the most basic of resources.

Nevertheless, isn't it true that we want a world that would reflect the cooperation of the Good Samaritan with God's kingdom? Its beauty strikes us as too alluring to dismiss. It mirrors the reign that Jesus initiated and that we have prayed for since we were children: "Your kingdom come . . . on earth as it is in heaven" (*Matthew 6:10*).

FAITH ACTIVITY

Jesus' Activity Today The Scripture describes Jesus as being one who repeatedly sought out the 'losers' of his day—lepers, tax collectors, and prostitutes—in order to spend some time with them or even to share a meal with them. With this description in mind, complete the following exercise: Describe in writing one activity that you imagine Jesus would do if he were physically to visit our world today. Write an account of Jesus' activity from the perspective of a newspaper reporter or from the perspective of someone who has been touched by him.

Jesus and the Reign of God

But what is God's kingdom? The reign of God, or **kingdom of God**, has begun on earth but is not yet complete. Jesus brought about God's reign on earth though his preaching, miracles, forgiveness of sins, and ultimately his death and Resurrection. All these signs of the kingdom showed that God's reign was with Jesus because Jesus was the Son of God. It can be likened to a mustard seed—the tiniest of seeds—a seed that will grow into a large tree. (See *Luke 13:18–19*.)

Can you imagine a perfect world? Not just one where all of your needs are met, but one where the relationships between God and his people, and the relationships among people are set right? This is the world that Jesus proclaimed. This is the kingdom of God for which Jesus calls us to repent and believe, to change our ways, to turn to God and to experience forgiveness and wholeness again. The reign, or kingdom, of God was central to Jesus' teaching.

To the best of our knowledge, Jesus was a Jewish peasant who worked as a carpenter until he was about thirty. When he began his brief public life of preaching and healing, he went to his local synagogue and read the following passage from the prophet Isaiah:

> *The Spirit of the Lord is upon me,*
>   *because he has anointed me to bring good news to the poor.*
> *He has sent me to proclaim release to the captives*
>   *and recovery of sight to the blind, to let the oppressed go free. . . .*
>
> ✝ Luke 4:18

This passage, which directly connects Jesus with the tradition of the prophets, also lays out his vision of what God's reign would be like if people truly believed and put their relationship with God first. When this happens, our relationships with others—especially those we may not know but who are in need—are transformed, too. When the love of God is our driving force, love of all God's children must follow, and it requires commitment and action. Jesus proclaimed the basic goodness of groups of people who were frequently overlooked. He expressed concern for their plight and announced that his mission of redemption for all included in a special way the work of transforming the lives of those most alone, forgotten, or mistreated.

Jesus' words and actions proclaim that God's reign is inclusive of all people. He welcomes into God's reign not only people who are poor and outcast but also sinners. Jesus shows that every person has innate worth and dignity. Every person is called to conversion and to believe. Those who accept the call, repent from their sins, and turn to God all have a place in the kingdom.

FAITH ACTIVITY

Gospel Message Choose one of the four Gospels. Note words or deeds of Jesus that you feel have a message related to justice. Select one Gospel passage and write a paragraph describing the justice message that it contains. Create a poster or other work of art that illustrates the message of the passage.

Jesus used parables such as the Good Samaritan to break through misconceptions about the worth of people. Another example is the parable of the day laborers (*Matthew 20:1–16*). Jesus spoke approvingly about a vineyard owner who paid the same wages whether a person worked a full day, a half-day, or just a few hours. The criterion for payment seemed to be "What do these people need?" rather than "What have they earned?"

Jesus also described the reign of God as a wedding banquet to which the invited guests did not come. Instead, unlikely guests were invited. Servants went out into the streets and gathered all whom they found, both "good" and "bad," so the wedding hall was filled with guests (See *Matthew 22:10*). Here again, Jesus presented the inclusive nature (everyone counts and is invited to share in the intimacy of mealtime) of the reign of God, a vision that is as challenging today as it was in his time.

FAITH ACTIVITY

Pleasure and Joy Pleasure and joy are not opposites. Nonetheless, the two experiences can be distinguished. Identify in your own life one event that was pleasant and another one that was joy-filled. Using words or symbols, try to express how the two experiences differed.

GROUP TALK

1. If you were to make a "proclamation of justice" such as Jesus did in his local synagogue, what would you say?

2. Give examples of injustice and describe your vision of justice.

3. Compare your proclamation with those of other class members and synthesize the statements into one proclamation of justice.

A Commitment Required

While it's true that Jesus invited everyone, a response was required. Not everyone who heard the invitation was willing to repent and change their ways in order to enter the kingdom. Jesus expected a commitment from those who heard him and those he healed. He asked them to trust and believe that he could transform their lives. He wanted them to take a different perspective or understanding on how God rules in their own lives, for that's how the kingdom, or reign of God, grows: first in a person's own heart and life, then in the good deeds that flow from that change.

Jesus asks us to evaluate our lives in the same way: what does it mean to say that God rules in our lives? When God's presence is strong in our lives, our priorities shift, our sorrow for sin increases, our treatment of others changes, and our involvement in the people and situations around us does as well. This is the personal conversion that Jesus calls us to, and, the subsequent social conversion that stems from it.

The Christian understanding of justice affirms that, with God's grace, a world of caring and sharing is possible. We help to further this kingdom by overcoming sin and participating with God's grace in making a just world an expanding reality, a gradual building up of a more holy place. Jesus' words challenge us to figure out how we can participate in the life of the Spirit and move the human community toward becoming a more just and sacred place.

God's reign and the Kingdom of Heaven People sometimes equate God's reign with a heaven available to us only after we die. In fact, because of the Jewish reluctance to use the holy name of God, Matthew in his Gospel generally spoke of the "kingdom of heaven" when referring to God's reign. We need to remember that even though the kingdom of God will be fully realized only at the end of time with Jesus' second coming, it was inaugurated with Jesus' first coming So, the kingdom is present now even in an incomplete way. He left his Apostles and disciples to spread the message of the kingdom, and the Holy Spirit has been with the Church since, Thus the signs of the Kingdom's beginnings are within us and among us. Christian hope in the "heavenly city" that awaits us in the next life inspires and frees us for greater involvement in this life.

> [T]he expectation of a new earth should spur us on, for it is here that the body of a new human family grows, foreshadowing in some way the age which is to come. (See Pius XI, Encyclical *Quadragesimo Anno:* AA523 (1931), 207.)
>
> Documents of Vatican II, "The Church in the Modern World," 39

As we pray in the Lord's Prayer, God's reign here and hereafter are intimately intertwined.

Before his Ascension, Jesus said that the time had not yet come for the fulfillment of the kingdom, which would bring justice, love, and peace to all people. According to Jesus, the present is the time for the Spirit and for our witness, for our struggle against evil. It is a time of preparation, a time of waiting, a time of watching. It is also a time for faithful work, the kind of work that helps to foster justice, love, and peace in the world.

This is our challenge. As we face it, God promises that we are not alone. The Holy Spirit is constantly present working to bring about God's plan for the world, a return to the original state of holiness and justice for which he created us: to know him, to become more like him, and to ultimately be united to him as our first parents were.

The Holy Spirit is at work in our lives, especially through the sacraments, to help us grow as God's children cooperating in his plan. Through Baptism original sin was removed and any personal sins were forgiven; we were united with Christ through the Spirit. We renew this life of grace when we participate in the Eucharist. Jesus said, "Those who eat my flesh and drink my blood abide in me, and I in them" (*John 6:56*). The Eucharist unites us as the Body of Christ, and as we are welcomed at the banquet of the Lord, so, too, must we welcome others. Thus the Eucharist commits us to serve those who are poor and in need and strengthens us to do the good that promotes justice.

The Sermon on the Mount, in the Gospel according to Matthew, is a summary of Jesus' key teachings. The beginning section of that sermon contains a list of actions and attitudes that characterize the Christian life. We call these Beatitudes.

The Beatitudes

Blessed are the poor in spirit, for theirs is the kingdom of heaven.

Blessed are those who mourn, for they will be comforted.

Blessed are the meek, for they will inherit the earth.

Blessed are those who hunger and thirst for righteousness, for they will be filled.

Blessed are the merciful, for they will receive mercy.

Blessed are the pure in heart, for they will see God.

Blessed are the peacemakers, for they will be called children of God.

Blessed are those who are persecuted for righteousness' sake, for theirs is the kingdom of heaven.

Blessed are you when people revile you and persecute you and utter all kinds of evil against you falsely on my account. Rejoice and be glad, for your reward is great in heaven.

✝ Matthew 5:3–12

The Beatitudes

The **Beatitudes** can sound so familiar, so taken-for-granted, that the depth of their message can sometimes become lost. The Beatitudes fulfill the promises God made to Abraham by relating them to the kingdom of God rather than to earthly possessions. They are a response to the yearning for happiness that God has placed in the human heart. The Beatitudes give us a glimpse of the end to which God calls us: eternal life and communion with God.

While the Beatitudes guide us in Christian living now, they are also ordered to the eternal life that God offers all of us. They show the relationship between how we act now on earth, and what our life will be like after we die. For Jesus tells us that when he comes again to judge the living and the dead, he will know the inner most aspects of our heart. We will be judged based upon whether we have accepted God's gift of grace and friendship and how we have shown love to others. (*CCC*, 682)

The Beatitudes are a prescription for joy. Sometimes "blessed" is translated "happy," although happy is clearly not a forceful enough word for what Jesus had in mind for the Beatitudes. Think about the pursuit of happiness that occurs in our culture. More specifically, think about the way characters in popular television sitcoms pursue happiness, often with little regard for anyone else. Although amusing, their lives are very shallow. These characters can remind people of their own silly, misguided attempts at pleasure seeking.

The Beatitudes paint a very different picture of what brings true happiness, true joy. They speak about mourning, hungering and thirsting, enduring pain and persecution. Where's the joy in that? The answer lies in the word "passion." As guidelines for Christian living, the Beatitudes encourage us to live life with passion. True passion for life must include compassion—that is, engaging in the struggles and sufferings of those around us. For example, if we have a true passion for music, we probably work very hard to master our instrument or train our voice, and we become excited when we learn a new piece of music. Even if we don't play an instrument or sing well, we might be eager for the latest CD by our favorite musical group or artist.

According to the logic of the Beatitudes, the opposite of a compassionate life is not a life of pleasure but a life of apathy, of not caring, not getting involved, not looking beyond the narrow focus of our own viewpoints. The prescription for seeking justice and peace, then, is to live a life of passion and compassion. Given the state of our world, both often entail suffering.

An event that often brings out the passion/compassion of the Beatitudes is the death of someone close to us. When friends lose someone they love through death, we are naturally drawn to share their suffering. In the words of one author, at such a time we feel compelled: to suffer with those who suffer, to mourn with those who mourn, to walk with those who are weary, to abide with those who are abandoned. Not that we can take their pain away or heal their wounds or bring their loved ones back to life, but rather to remind them by our presence, by our love, by our unspoken words, that they are not alone.

Joseph Nassal, *The Conspiracy of Compassion*
(Easton, KS: Forest of Peace, 1997), 55

GROUP TALK

1 What do you think the reign of God on earth would be like? What is one simple thing that you could do today to help bring about the kingdom of God?

2 What could lead you to become passionate about matters of justice?

3 Do you believe that passion for life must go hand in hand with compassion-feeling intensely for and with others, especially when they are suffering? Explain.

Faith in Action

Young Neighbors in Action

Sponsored by: **The Center for Ministry Development**

Packing paintbrushes, hammers, and volleyballs, more than two thousand teenagers traveled in 2005 from Washington, D.C., to Tijuana, Mexico, to paint and refurbish houses, help out at homeless shelters and soup kitchens, and assist with inner-city tutoring and recreation programs.

> From my experience attending Young Neighbors in Action, I have discovered that it is an awesome opportunity to join together with other people of the same faith in order to serve others.

Jason

As part of Young Neighbors in Action, sponsored by The Center for Ministry Development, these teenagers who work with God's people, help to change their world by changing their perspective.

What is a week of service like? It's about building community one person at a time, connecting to Scripture and Catholic Social Teaching, and having fun while doing it. The Neighbors have opportunities to meet people from many walks of life and experience the culture of the region they serve. They may travel down dirt roads to La Morita, a shanty area in Tijuana, Mexico, to help build a clinic or restore a church. They may serve at Cortland Manor, a housing facility in Chicago, Illinois, for older persons who are poor. There they paint rooms, wash windows, and, on Salon Day, manicure nails and cut and style hair for the residents. But wherever they travel, the Neighbors see the face of Jesus in the face of need, and this changes the way they look at themselves.

Each week-long program involves twenty youths and four adults and is, as one participant puts it, "the Church as Jesus wanted it: a community of believers that serves those less fortunate and 'gathers around the table' in worship."

The Center for Ministry Development has worked with more than 100 Catholic dioceses and organizations in the United States, Canada, Ireland, and Australia and provides ministry to adolescents, youth ministry and adult training, youth leadership and peer ministry training, and ministry to families and young adults. Their mission is expanding to include lifelong, inter-generational faith formation.

◀ **Teens participating in Young Neighbors in Action.**

GO ONLINE

Visit **www.harcourtreligion.com** to learn more about the Center for Ministry Development's program and for a link to its site.

Prayer

Begin by praying the Sign of the Cross.

Leader: Jesus, light of the world,

All: Give us your salvation.

Leader: Jesus, prince of peace,

All: Give us your salvation.

Leader: Jesus, who died to save us,

All: Give us your salvation.

Leader: Jesus, friend to those who are lonely,

All: Give us your salvation.

Leader: Jesus, hope for those who are suffering,

All: Give us your salvation.

Leader: Jesus, healer of those who are sick,

All: Give us your salvation.

Leader: Jesus, friend to the stranger,

All: Give us your salvation.

Leader: Jesus, strength of those who are weak,

All: Give us your salvation.

Leader: Jesus, justice for those who are oppressed,

All: Give us your salvation.

Leader: Jesus, who welcomes outcasts,

All: Give us your salvation.

Leader: Jesus, who suffers with us,

All: Give us your salvation.

Leader: Jesus, who inspires us,

All: Give us your salvation.

Leader: Jesus, who supports us,

All: Give us your salvation.

Leader: Jesus, who forgives us,

All: Give us your salvation.

Leader: Jesus, who brings us joy,

All: Give us your salvation.

Leader: Amen

End by praying the Sign of the Cross.

Review

1. What is a virtue and what types of virtues are there?

2. Describe justice as a virtue.

3. What makes humans distinct from other creatures?

4. Why is the story of creation important for understanding what God's call to justice demands?

5. What is the relationship between sin and injustice?

6. What image of God emerges in the Exodus story?

7. Give an example of a character in Exodus who fought against oppression.

8. What is the Hebrew word for prophet?

9. What did prophets bring to God's message when voicing it?

10. Use an example to illustrate what it means to say that a prophet was an "unlikely mouthpiece."

11. What do the prophets insist is the way to know God?

12. To what does the Incarnation refer?

13. What are the Beatitudes and why are they important to Jesus' message of the coming of the kingdom of God?

14. What does the Christian attitude toward justice affirm?

15. What impact can hope in heaven have on a Christian's attitude toward this world?

Key Words

Beatitudes (p. 32) Jesus' teachings about the meaning and path to true happiness, teachings which depict the attitudes and actions that followers of Christ should have and the way to live in God's kingdom today. They describe the way to attain the eternal holiness or blessedness to which God calls all people.

covenant (p. 12) a solemn promise, or agreement, made between two parties; another word for *testament.*

creation (p. 8) the act by which God began all that exists outside of himself.

Exodus (p. 13) liberation of the Israelites from Egyptian slavery under the leadership of Moses, who was led by God.

Incarnation (p. 24) the singular and unique mystery whereby the Son of God, while not ceasing to be God, assumed a human nature and became man, so that he might accomplish our salvation. (*CCC 464*)

Jesus (p. 24) name that means "God saves"; Jesus of Nazareth is the Savior God sent to redeem people from sin and eternal death.

justice (p. 4) the constant and firm will to give God and other people what is their due. (*CCC 1807*) Justice is a virtue (a dimension of one's character), a process (the work of justice), and a goal (a just world).

kingdom of God (p. 28) God's reign of justice, love, and peace.

Messiah (p. 24) the Anointed One, the Christ. As Messiah, Jesus restored all people to communion and friendship with God through his life, death, and Resurrection.

natural law (p. 6) We find order and design all through creation. The sciences and our human powers manifest a plan that discloses harmony and order. This harmony exists also in humans, where certain laws govern not only our bodies, but what is right and wrong.

original sin (p. 11) the decision by the first humans to disobey God. Thereafter, all people (except Jesus and Mary) began life with a wounded human nature, drawn to selfishness and sin and in need of redemption by Christ.

prophet (p. 19) one who has a close relationship with God and communicates a divinely inspired message.

sin (p. 11) a deliberate thought, word, deed, or omission contrary to the eternal law of God (*CCC Glossary*).

>Our Challenge

God created each of us in his image. Every person has dignity and worth. Justice is violated whenever people are denied a life reflecting their God-given dignity. However, God has also endowed us with a capacity for justice. We can tap into this virtue of justice and dedicate ourselves to working with God in alleviating injustice and bringing about a more just world. Scripture reminds us that people suffer unnecessarily due to attitudes, actions, and social structures of their own making. Through the life, death, and Resurrection of Jesus and the gift of the Holy Spirit, God has made a new way of life possible. This is a life of cooperation with God's plan for the world—a life that fosters justice, love, and peace, and helps to make the world more like the kingdom that God intends it to be.

THE CHURCH
CALLED TO WORK FOR JUSTICE

CHAPTER 2

CHAPTER GOALS

In this chapter you will:

★ discover more about the role of the Holy Spirit in the life of the Church and the ways that the Church continues Jesus' mission in the world.

★ examine more about the roles of conscience and virtue in pursuit of peace.

★ understand that the Church has carried forward God's call to justice throughout history.

★ review major documents of Catholic social teaching and their message for us today.

The Holy Spirit Among Us

what's your opinion?

1. In what ways has your faith influenced you to be more sensitive to the needs of others? How?

2. How can the Holy Spirit help you in being an instrument of justice?

3. Do Christians have a special responsibility to work for justice? Why?

4. Do you connect Catholicism with justice and charity? Why?

Shortly after Jesus ascended to heaven, the Holy Spirit, who had been at work in the world since the beginning of creation, was fully revealed:

When the day of Pentecost had come, they were all together in one place. And suddenly from heaven there came a sound like the rush of a violent wind, and it filled the entire house where they were sitting. Divided tongues, as of fire, appeared among them, and a tongue rested on each of them. All of them were filled with the Holy Spirit and began to speak in other languages, as the Spirit gave them ability.

✝ Acts 2:1–4

▼ The Pentecost, 10th century

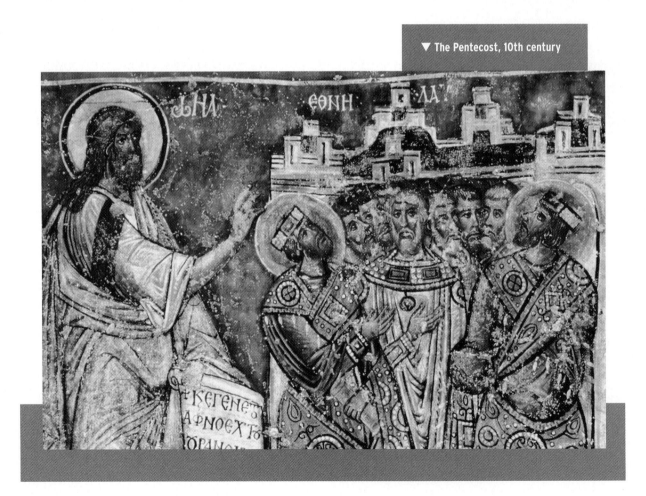

On **Pentecost**, sometimes referred to as the birth of the Church, the Holy Spirit, the advocate whom Jesus had promised, appeared as fire and wind. Through the Holy Spirit the Apostles realized most forcefully that Christ's mission was to be their mission. The Holy Spirit continues to give life to the Church today, which is connected all the way back to the Apostles. By making us holy as he is holy, the Holy Spirit enables us to love and to work for justice. "God's love has been poured into our hearts through the Holy Spirit that has been given to us" (*Romans 5:5*).

Ben looked at the course description:

As a requirement for this course, students are expected to perform twenty hours of volunteer service. Ben first thought, "If it's required, then I'm not really volunteering. Second, my parents are spending money for me to attend this Catholic school. The intention was to get a solid education so that I can get into a good college and succeed at the profession of my choice later in life. I'm taking high-level English, math, and science courses. My goal is to have a financially secure, comfortable life and provide nicely for a family when I grow up. I'm working hard, and I expect it to pay off. Isn't that an honorable goal? Why do I have to go out and 'serve others' as part of a religion course? It's bad enough that we have to take religion classes in the first place."

Ben pictured himself serving franks and beans to disgusting looking people at a soup kitchen for homeless people. Yuk! He then tried to imagine himself helping at the home for the elderly. Ben had been to such a home once when he was in grade school. He didn't care for the moaning sounds some of the old people made as he walked by their rooms, and the smell of urine mixed with heavy-duty cleansers was disgusting. Ben then thought he might join those students who are tutoring the young children at the grade school, but he considered the kids to be bratty. His thoughts drifted to the Special Olympics program for mentally challenged children and adults. He liked the idea that it involved sports and didn't think it would be so bad. Finally he said to himself, "I'll see what my friends are doing. There has to be a way to make this as painless as possible."

GROUP TALK

1. What do you think about Ben's attitude toward Catholic education and his religion course requirement?

2. Do you believe that Catholic schools should include a requirement for students to do service projects? Why?

3. Do you believe that, to a greater extent than other schools, Catholic schools should be noted for community service? Why?

4. What are some ways teenagers can bring about more justice and peace in the world?

The origin of the word *spirit* sheds light on how the Holy Spirit works. *Spirit* comes from the Hebrew *rûah*, meaning wind, breath, or air. Jesus said to Nicodemus, "The wind blows where it chooses, and you hear the sound of it, but you do not know where it comes from or where it goes. So it is with everyone who is born of the Spirit" (*John 3:8*).

A People Called by God

A Visible and Spiritual Reality Christ is present and at work in the world today through his Church. The word *church* means an assembly or convocation of people who have been called together, usually for a religious purpose. The **Church** refers to all of the people called together by God in all ages and throughout the whole world. Through Baptism people become members of the Church and share in its mission. Therefore, the Church is a visible organization of people spreading the Good News of salvation and new life and continuing Jesus' work of calling people to conversion and faith. Through the celebration of the sacraments, prayer, and their everyday choices, Church members help one another live according to God's will, and grow as brothers and sisters of Christ.

The Church is also a spiritual reality. The spiritual reality is the communion that exists between God and his people in Christ. Images such as the Body of Christ, the Temple of the Holy Spirit, the People of God, and the Bride of Christ describe the Church's divine nature. In Baptism we are united to Christ, and to all others who have been baptized. Through the action of the Holy Spirit, we are all united as a community of believers as the one Body of Christ. In the Eucharist, we receive Christ's Body and Blood and though his presence in us, we grow as his Body. Christ is the head of the Body. We live in and for him, and he lives in us. So, by his presence in the Church, and by the Holy Spirit's action that which gives us life and makes us holy, the Church is a spiritual reality.

For this reason, the Church can never be reduced to any one place or time period, any one person or group of people. The good work that the Church and her members do now to help create a more just world mirrors the world that is to come since the Church is both the means and the goal of God's plan. The Church on earth working for justice is inseparable from her spiritual reality where justice and peace already reign.

The *Catechism of the Catholic Church* explains: "The Church is in history, but at the same time she transcends it. It is only 'with the eyes of faith' [*Roman Catechism*] that one can see her in her visible reality and at the same time in her spiritual reality as bearer of divine life" *(CCC 770)*. In every age, the Church passes down to each generation all that she believes through doctrines, liturgy, and life. The ongoing transmission of the teachings of Jesus in the Church is called Tradition. Tradition and Sacred Scripture together make up God's revelation to us.

A Eucharistic Community As both a visible and a spiritual reality, the Church connects the moral life (the way we live) with the spiritual life (the way we pray and worship). The two are intertwined and connected; one feeds the other, making the other possible. The Church is a sign and instrument of the unity of all people with God and with one another. This unity is manifest most fully on earth in the celebration of the Eucharist—the heart and summit of the Church's life. Through the Eucharist we partake of the grace achieved through Christ's sacrifice on the cross. Participating in the Eucharist increases our union with Christ and his Church.

When we celebrate the Eucharist, we do so joined with all the angels and saints who are already taking part in the heavenly banquet. Our hope is that one day all will be at that table with God the Father, Son, and Holy Spirit, when God's plan of salvation has come to completion.

Participating in the Eucharist is not just a foretaste of heaven. It is a constant reminder of how we should live our daily lives. The sacrament forgives venial sins and preserves us from graver ones. A Eucharistic community is the Body of Christ in the world. It welcomes all people to hear the Good News and see it at work in their lives. It shares food with people who are hungry and works to eliminate social structures that contribute to people being hungry in the world. Through the Eucharist, and works that reflect the spirit of the Eucharist, the Church manifests herself as "the sacrament of the *unity of the human race*" *(CCC 775).* Saint John Chrysostom warned, "You have tasted the Blood of the Lord, yet you do not recognize your brother" *(CCC 1397).* It becomes a justice issue because not sharing food with those in need is dishonoring the table of the Eucharist.

A Community Modeled on the Trinity The Holy Trinity provides a model for how people should relate to one another. God is a communion of three Persons—Father, Son, and Holy Spirit—united in love. The universal Church is "a people brought into unity from the unity of the Father, the Son, and the Holy Spirit." We are called to establish human relationships that resemble the unity of the three divine Persons. In the words of the U.S. Catholic bishops, "God reveals himself to us as one who is not alone, but rather as one who is relational, one who is Trinity. Therefore, we who are made in God's image share this communal, social nature. We are called to reach out and to build relationships of love and justice" (*Sharing Catholic Social Teaching*).

> ## FAITH ACTIVITY
>
> **Marks of the Church.** The Church has four identifying marks. It is *one, holy, catholic, and apostolic.* It has one Lord and one faith. It is one body given life by one Spirit and sharing one hope. Although made up of sinners, the Church is holy through the sacrifice of Christ. We can see signs of her holiness in Mary and in the saints. As catholic, meaning "universal," the Church has the fullness of truth meant for all people of all times and places. The Church is also directly connected to Christ through the Apostles and their successors, the pope and bishops. For each of the four marks of the Church, write down one practical implication it has for the Church's mission of justice.

Catholic Moral Teaching and Justice

FAITH ACTIVITY

Christian Martyrs Today Many Catholics live out their responsibility to pursue good and eliminate evil. Even in recent times there have been Christian martyrs for justice. Search the Internet or recent newspapers and magazines for examples. Share your findings with the class.

We find in Catholicism a great legacy of moral guidance. The Church's Tradition—its Precepts, its teachings about conscience, the Commandments, responsibility, and freedom—are meant to be applied to concerns of justice. So, it's important to get a sense of how these elements guide us in our moral decision making. Then we can make connections on how to use them in our response to social justice issues.

Freedom and Conscience: Our Moral Compass

God has created us with both intellect—the ability to reason and think—and free will—the ability and freedom to make choices. With these gifts we are created for eternal happiness with God and are called to work toward that perfection by searching out and loving what is good and true. This includes what is good and true in society and what promotes the life and dignity of each person, the centerpiece of every society. Because we can understand our options and because we are free to decide how to act, we have the responsibility of making right choices. We are responsible for our freely chosen actions. It's not always easy to know what's good and then have the courage, strength, or desire to choose it. That's where our conscience, and the Holy Spirit, come into play.

Our **conscience** is the ability we have to recognize whether an action is morally right or wrong. It's like an inner voice that lets us know the quality of something we have done, are going to do, or are in the process of doing. Sometimes it's like a nagging voice, making us feel guilty for what we innately know is wrong. Our conscience calls us to follow the natural law God has written in our hearts, to do what is good and just and loving.

Because of conscience, the moral compass within us, we have the responsibility to pursue the good and avoid what is evil. But it's more than staying away from evil, it's eliminating or transforming evil.

We must always follow the certain judgment of our conscience. Our conscience must be well formed and we must do what we can to make sure that we don't make decisions of conscience in isolation. We form our conscience as we do everything, with the help of the Holy Spirit and other members of the Church. We are continually forming our conscience by reflecting on Scripture and Jesus' teachings and example, by studying Church teachings, by seeking the advice of wise people of faith, and by calling on the Holy Spirit in prayer. When we make the effort to do these things, we can gain the proper perspective and counter negative influences of society.

Justice constantly invokes our conscience since conscience means applying thoughtful discernment to concrete situations to determine a moral course of action. (*CCC* 1796) For instance, a shabbily-dressed man stands at an entrance to a mall holding a sign reading, "will work for food." What do we do? In the mall, a store is selling sneakers we know are made by child workers operating under sweatshop conditions. What do we do? An older person walks unsteadily toward us while we and our companions sit on a bench. What do we do? How does conscience guide our choices in these situations?

Responsibility Certain factors can diminish our responsibility, but nonetheless part of our dignity as human beings is the freedom that makes us responsible for our actions. If we remain in ignorance or make wrong judgments even when following our conscience, that doesn't mean that we are necessarily free from guilt. That's why it's so important to educate our conscience. When we turn to God's word in Scripture and make connections with the decisions we face in our lives, we are acting conscientiously.

While we are free to choose, it does not mean we are free to do whatever we want. We are bound by God's laws and the laws of our nation. And, there are certain actions that are always wrong despite our being free to choose them. We must recognize that some actions are always wrong (*CCC* 1761). To say, "Let us do evil so that good may come," is to incur just condemnation. Furthermore, to knowingly and willingly choose something gravely contrary to divine law is to commit mortal sin and break our relationship with God. Unrepented, mortal sins will lead to being separated from God forever. Less serious sins, called venial sins, weaken our friendship with God, but do not remove his life from us. His love remains within us, but continuing to repeat venial sin results in attitudes and vices that lead to more sin. (CCC 1874–1876). The grace of the Sacrament of Penance can help strengthen us to avoid venial sin and the situations that might present the opportunity to sin.

GROUP TALK

Discuss the following situation in light of responsibility and conscience:

★ An organization wants to transform a house in your neighborhood into a home for mentally disabled adults.

God's Law and Justice

We know from Scripture "the Law" is God's fatherly instruction that helps us know the ways of love leading to happiness forever with him and the ways of evil leading us away from him. We know from the previous chapter that human beings have an innate sense of the natural law because we are made in God's image and thus have knowledge of what is good and right. Natural law describes the basic rights and duties that stem from our inherent dignity. It remains the same throughout history and in all societies.

The Law revealed in Scripture and demonstrated in the workings of nature is not the same as the specific laws that govern a nation, a local community, or a school. However, all specific laws are valid insofar as they reflect the divine and natural law. An example of specific laws that reflect divine law are the precepts of the Church, which require keeping holy the holy days of obligation, observing days of fast and abstinence, and providing for the Church's material needs.

The first stage of divine law, also called "revealed law" since it is revealed in Scripture, is found in the Old Testament. The Ten Commandments summarize God's covenant with his people and all of the Old Law, which serves as preparation for the Gospel, or New Law. Since natural law is timeless, it applies to current situations as well. For instance, as we will discover in the chapters addressing poverty, the commandment "Do not steal" holds direct implications for economic, political, and social life today.

The New Law is the Gospel itself or "the grace of the Holy Spirit received by faith in Christ" (*CCC* 1983). We find the New Law characterized by the Beatitudes and the ministry of healing, forgiveness, feeding, and giving of life that Christ instituted and the Church continues in the celebration of the sacraments. To find a lengthy expression of the New Law, read the Sermon on the Mount in the Gospel according to Matthew. This collection or compilation of teachings by Jesus contains many challenging implications for justice.

Through Christ, his Church, and the sacraments we receive the grace to follow Jesus' new commandment to love one another as he loves us as well as all of God's commands.

Political Authority The Fourth Commandment reminds us that civil and political authority comes from God's authority and his care for all people. Governing others is an awesome responsibility and a service meant for the good of all. Those in charge of governments must uphold the rights and dignity of all citizens and should also promote justice and peace. In other words, public authority overseeing the common good represents a natural order of things. The term **common good** refers to a long-standing Christian concept advocating that society should be organized so that, as much as possible, all people, either in groups or as individuals, are given the opportunities to reach their fulfillment more fully and easily. The common good in a society requires respect and advancement of the rights of people, prosperity or success society-wide, and peace and security among its people. All aspects of society and forms of government must reflect a proper vision of humanity and its destiny. Without the perspective that Scripture provides about relationships, injustices can prevail and societies can even become totalitarian.

For society to promote the common good through its laws and practices, it must consider the human person as the center of human society. Organizations and structures of society and government need to have the well-being of all people as their goal. A government which is committed to the common good and utilizing morally acceptable methods most clearly reflects the natural law.

Society should promote virtue and good values. The Church is concerned with social matters when fundamental rights or salvation of souls requires it. The Church is concerned with the common good of people because they are ordered to the sovereign Good, their ultimate end. Certainly society should not obstruct the practice of virtue. For this reason we need to be involved in the political arena. Political authorities must maintain moral order and create an atmosphere conducive to the exercise of freedom and justice.

GROUP TALK

★ What fundamental principles should guide all exercise of public authority within a society?

The Church Through The Ages

Where Do I Fit? Where do you situate yourself in relation to the Church? For instance, since the Church is an instrument of justice, are you a participant, a recipient, or a bystander in the Church's work of justice? Give examples.

History provides a context for understanding the Church's work for justice today. The historical snapshots included in this chapter demonstrate the variety of circumstances in which the Church has found herself over time and describe some ways Christians have responded to the call to justice. As you learn about these historical events, remember that the Church is a mystery with both divine and human elements. Her history is the story of human actions as well as the working of the Holy Spirit in and through human actions. Every age has been characterized by a need for justice. We discover that in every age the love of Christ urges his people to carry out his mission. Our faith assures us that in the end God's kingdom will prevail in heaven and on earth. Meanwhile we look for signs of the Holy Spirit at work so that we can join in the mission of the Church to bring all people into the communion present in the Trinity.

The Early Church: A Revolutionary View of Justice

Christianity came into being during the Roman Empire. The Roman world valued justice, which it equated with law and protection of rights. The word *justice* is derived from the Latin word *ius*, meaning "law." Within Roman society,

authority, rights, and duties were clearly defined based on where one fell in the social order. Being born in Rome, for instance, did not make one a citizen. Actually, most people living in Rome at the time were slaves. Male property owners possessed the greatest power, followed by free men who did not own land, such as artisans. Next in descending order, there were freed slaves, slaves, and people who were not considered to be civilized—such as the people of the groups surrounding the empire. Women and children generally held secondary status to adult men. Justice referred to living by the system of laws that maintained this order.

On the positive side of the Roman understanding of justice. Laws clearly spelled out rights and duties that were important for maintaining what was understood as the common good. In time, the Church would adopt elements of Roman justice into her own Christian view of justice. However, the earliest accounts we have of a Christian community indicate a radically different model of social organization:

> *All who believed were together and had all things in common; they would sell their possessions and goods and distribute the proceeds to all, as any had need. Day by day, as they spent much time together in the temple, they broke bread at home and ate their food with glad and generous hearts, praising God and having the goodwill of all the people. And day by day the Lord added to their number those who were being saved.*
>
> ✝ Acts 2:44-47

At the time simply sharing a meal with people from a lower level of society was unheard of. The Christian community, made up of people from the various levels of society, not only shared meals but also took steps to meet the other material needs of its members. This new sense of oneness in Christ, celebrated in the Eucharist that was at the heart of the early Church's life, contributed to the growth of the Church. The vision of equality and common concern that characterized the new life in the Holy Spirit stood in stark contrast to the divisions and inequality of wealth and power that marked the dominant culture.

> *[I]n Christ Jesus you are all children of God through faith. As many of you as were baptized into Christ have clothed yourselves with Christ. There is no longer Jew or Greek, there is no longer slave or free, there is no longer male and female; for all of you are one in Christ Jesus.*
>
> ✝ Galatians 3:26-28

FAITH ACTIVITY

Role of Power Imagine that you will be debating the topic "Power corrupts." Prepare a statement on the topic from each point of view: pro and con. Then consider the characteristics of the power we are talking about when we profess belief that the Church is empowered by the Holy Spirit to work for justice in the world.

We Are All United

Choose one food you have eaten today. Find out as much as possible about the probable origins of this item and about the people who were involved in making it available. Based on this information, how would you describe the mutual well being among the people who make, distribute, and consume these goods?

FAITH ACTIVITY

The First Christians Read the Apostle Paul's words to the Church at Corinth for more insight into some of the struggles of the first Christians. (See 1 Corinthians.) Write a brief essay exploring one of those struggles.

Communities of Compassion The early Christian communities, though not free from disagreements and disputes, strived to show compassion for one another and those in need. Early Christians understood themselves to be members of the Body of Christ—united with Christ and with one another—sharing in each other's joys and sorrows. For example, Saint John Chrysostom, a famous preacher as well as the archbishop of Constantinople around A.D. 400, was particularly concerned with the attitude of rich people toward people who were poor. He felt that poor people—servants, beggars, and circus performers, for instance—were viewed as non-persons and therefore abused.

Chrysostom received his nickname—"Golden Mouth"—because he kept his congregations spellbound with his preaching. He spoke up for the dignity of all people, and twice he was sent into exile for his strong words. He warned his congregation against not caring for those who were poor; "Don't you realize that, as the poor man withdraws silently, sighing and in tears, you actually thrust a sword into yourself, that it is you who receive the more serious wound?"

People from all parts of society—poor, outcast, rich, powerful—responded to God's call to be part of the Church and to continue the mission of Jesus in the world. Their lives were rooted in a vision of social relations characterized by mutual care and concern—by love. Of course, their actual lives did not always live up to this ideal. Paul, for example, criticizes the Corinthians for the divisions that were apparent among them when they gathered for the Eucharist.

GROUP TALK

Is there evidence today that people who are poor and people who perform certain tasks in our society are viewed as non-persons? Explain.

Saint Francis of Assisi

The Middle Ages in Europe conjures up images of nobles, knights, and peasants—each group assigned its particular role in society. In time, opportunities for prosperity opened up for commoners through trade, artisanship, and business. Many people seized the opportunity and grew in wealth and material possessions. Meanwhile, those at the bottom of society had poverty, hunger, and powerlessness as constant companions. Into this changing medieval world, an exceptional person was born—a man who challenged the prevailing world view. One historian has called Francis of Assisi (1181-1226) the greatest spiritual figure that Europe has ever produced.

Since his father was a wealthy Italian cloth merchant, Francis had the opportunity to enjoy the "good life" and, during his youth, he did. When he was a young man Francis went off to war with a neighboring city, outfitted with the finest knightly attire. Imprisoned in his first battle, Francis had time to think about his life and his values. He recognized that money, possessions, and power too often lead to corruption. To free himself, Francis did more than show compassion for people who were sick and poor. He shared his wealth with them. While still in his early twenties, Francis rejected his father's wealth and married "Lady Poverty." From that time on, he kept no possessions and urged his followers to do likewise. And so, in a radical manner, Francis went against the popular emphasis on gaining wealth and material comforts.

Yet Francis' embrace of poverty was not joyless. Indeed, he sang with joy as he extended himself in compassion to all creatures and all people. He thought of himself and his followers as clowns of God, humbly celebrating the simple joys of life that can be overlooked when one's focus is solely on accumulating wealth. Francis's unconventional decision to move from "riches to rags" actually reflects two surprising decisions at the very core of Christian faith: the decision of God to send his Son into the world of poverty and the decision of Jesus to die stripped of everything in order to show us the way to a new and glorious life.

Francis was particularly concerned about the connection between possessions and warfare: "If we have possessions, we must have weapons to defend them, from which come quarrels and battles." He also saw that greed had a stranglehold on many people, diminishing their capacity to enjoy the simple things of life and preventing them from seeing the people suffering around them.

Francis challenged the people of his era by calling them back to the purity and simplicity of Christ's message. In a society in which budding cities offered new opportunities for wealth, Francis preached voluntary poverty. Francis refused priesthood for himself because he considered himself unworthy of ordination—once again demonstrating his commitment to "littleness."

Perhaps the most universally popular saint of all time, Francis continues to inspire people today to work for justice, peace, and protection of all creatures and of the environment.

In many ways the culture of Francis's day resembles our own. The decision by Francis to reject wealth and to delight in simple things was at first viewed as foolhardy. Yet Francis and his early followers, by their own choice "little brothers and sisters" or "clowns of God," spread such joy that they transformed both the Church and the Europe of their day.

▼ St. Francis,
painting by Francesco Raibolini, circa 1500.

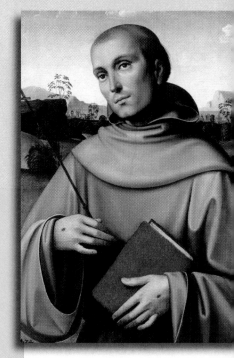

1. What sort of wisdom do you see masked behind clowning?

2. Are you or do you know a "class clown"? If so, do you or does this person serve an unusual but beneficial function in your group? Explain.

3. What is the appeal of Saint Francis? Is his message important for us today? Explain.

4. Name someone who you believe parallels one or more characteristics of Saint Francis today. In want sense?

New Worlds and New Challenges

Toward the end of the Middle Ages the feudal system was breaking down. While some people discovered new ways to make money, many people were left out. During the age of discovery European countries vied with one another to conquer territory either newly discovered by them or newly opened to their control. This led to **colonialism**, the conquering of territory to benefit the conquering nation. Typically, the people in the conquered lands suffered great hardships.

New Responses to New Social Problems While political and social changes brought new forms of human suffering, there also emerged members of the Church who boldly and effectively addressed these problems. The seventeenth to the nineteenth centuries were peopled with many saintly men and women who felt deeply the pain of those around them and who took steps to lighten their sufferings. Examples abound, demonstrating how Christians creatively applied the Gospel message of service to address emerging needs.

- In the 1600s in France, Vincent de Paul and Louise de Marillac founded orders for men and for women that addressed the needs of the people who were hungry and sick and who crowded into the cities of their time.

- John Baptist de la Salle (1651—1719) organized men to teach homeless boys and prisoners in Paris.

- In the 1800s, Elizabeth Ann Seton and other women began orders of women to teach the increasing Catholic population in the United States. Typically, Catholic immigrants to the United States were poor and not well educated. Frequently, the Catholic schools established by Seton and other religious sisters protected and nurtured immigrant children as they adapted to their new country.

- Katharine Drexel, a wealthy Philadelphia Catholic, saw a particular need to serve Native American and African American populations. She founded a religious order to work with these groups who were often overlooked.

- As Europeans conquered other lands, Christian missionaries were among the first to travel to these lands in order to introduce native people to the Gospel. Sometimes missionaries were also exploiters of these groups. More frequently, missionaries were the only voices demanding that these native Asians, Africans, and Americans be treated with respect and compassion.

FAITH ACTIVITY

Colonization In small groups, research a country that has a history of being colonized. Explore the effects that colonization has had on the country. Compare your results.

▼ Elizabeth Ann Seton

The legacy of these efforts is seen in today's Catholic hospitals and schools, convalescent homes, hospitality centers for the hungry and homeless, and various other social service organizations. Even community hospitals are by products of works initiated by these and other people who believed that everyone has a right to education, health care, and basic community services. Christianity emerged from this period split into Catholics and Protestants. Individual groups of Christians in both traditions kept alive the Church's response to justice.

" In the end people are saints for the way they love. "

Mary Reed Newland

FAITH ACTIVITY

Justice Saints List specific ways that church groups in your area assist people in need. Discuss what kind of "justice saints" we are most in need of today.

Saint Peter Claver–Missionary to Slaves One of the developments that accompanied colonial expansion was the enslavement of people from Africa who were shipped in chains to foreign lands against their will. Conditions under which they were transported were atrocious; their conditions under slavery continued to be horrible. In 1602 a Spaniard named Peter Claver entered a relatively new religious order called the Society of Jesus, or Jesuits. Following his studies he went to Cartagena, in modern Colombia, where many slaves entered the Spanish colonies to work the mines there.

▼ Saint Peter Claver

Claver made attempts to end the slave trade but failing that, for forty years he managed to visit the slave ships docked in Cartagena harbor. He would bring food and water to the slaves, treating their wounds and offering whatever comfort he could. He would also remind them of their dignity as persons, telling them that they were precious in the eyes of God. This message was completely contrary to the message these people were receiving from the slave traders and owners, who treated them as non-persons.

It is estimated that Claver baptized over 300,000 slaves during the time he dedicated his life to them. Baptism proclaims a person a child of God. How great a gift this must have been to the people who were stripped completely of their dignity through slavery. Claver applied the first principle of Christian social teaching to the people of his time who were most exploited—recognizing and helping them recognize that they possessed God-given worth and dignity.

The Modern Era

Sometimes the Holy Spirit works in strange and fascinating ways. In the early 1800s a French girl name Marie-Eugénie Milleret was raised in a family that had no interest in religion. Her father held political office and her family was passionate about the cry for liberty and justice that accompanied the fall of Napoleon and the rise of industrialization. However, Marie-Eugénie was never introduced to a possible connection between these concerns of the age and the Catholicism that at least in name dominated French religious life. Marie-Eugénie's parents separated. She moved to Paris with her mother, away from her father and her brother who had been her constant companions. Shortly thereafter her mother died suddenly, and still a teenager, she went to live with her aunt and uncle.

▼ Marie Eugenie Milleret

Marie-Eugénie never lost her fervor for current social and political concerns that she had received from her parents and their friends. She was distraught about the many people in need of help around her and the plight of industrial workers. Near the end of her teenage years her father hoped to introduce her to society with the intention that she would marry well. However, a priest who knew her recognized that Marie-Eugénie had gifts and passions that could make a difference to society. He convinced her that education held the key to changing society and helping people, especially the education of girls who were often neglected in this regard. Marie-Eugénie gathered together some women to begin this work and thus began a new order of sisters known as the Religious of the Assumption. They established many schools, and engaged in works of charity.

Marie-Eugénie remained active for much of the nineteenth century. She believed strongly that the life of faith impels us to get involved in contemporary social issues. She also believed that the desire to work for justice is sorely lacking if it does not include the faith, love, and hope that only the Gospel can provide. She believed that "God willed to establish a social order where no man would have to suffer from the oppression of others" (*A Woman of Faith, A Woman of Action*, booklet published by the Religious of the Assumption, p. 8). The love of liberty instilled in her as a child remained with her throughout her life and she came to see a critical link between Christ as liberator and the transformation of society. She was one of many Catholics who, inspired by the Holy Spirit, paved the way for this emphasis in modern Catholic thought.

Another thinker of the time, Karl Marx (1818–1883), the father of modern Communism, was also deeply concerned about factory workers. He believed that religion stood in the way of workers taking action against their oppression. Marie-Eugénie, on the other hand, believed that Christian faith was essential for anyone to find true liberation from oppression.

" We are pioneers. We must plough our furrow and feel the weight of the earth "

Marie-Eugénie Milleret

In 1891, when the people of Europe were struggling with what liberty and justice meant, Pope Leo XIII wrote an **encyclical** that began a great series of written statements from the popes about justice and Christian faith that continues to the present day. He addressed the rights of workers in light of the troubling conditions produced by industrialization. His encyclical, *On the Condition of Workers* (in Latin, *Rerum Novarum*), is considered a landmark because it is the first official Church teaching that sought to rectify social problems in the modern era. It marks the beginning of modern **Catholic Social Teaching**. The writings related to this social teaching express the interpretation by church leaders of historical events in light of what has been revealed to us through Jesus and the Holy Spirit. These teachings include principles for reflection, criteria for making judgments, and guidelines for future action.

The Church Challenges Socialism and Capitalism

On the Condition of Workers criticized the **socialism** preached by Karl Marx, in which the government owned and administered the means of production and distribution of goods. The encyclical condemned socialism because it gave to the state the rights belonging to the individual and the family. For this reason, socialism can jeopardize the dignity of the individual. Pope Leo's fear was borne out by the loss of personal liberties in the communist countries that were established after 1917.

Although Pope Leo condemned socialism, he also strongly criticized aspects of **capitalism**. This shocked many political leaders and owners of industries of the time. In a capitalist system, people who invest money (capital) in industry or farmland determine what is produced and the conditions under which it is produced. Today, because of the existence of trade unions and the right to strike, we take for granted that workers also have a say in determining working conditions. However, in the late 1800s, such practices of laborer groups were considered disruptive to the established order. Yet *On the Condition of Workers* supported the right of workers to form unions and to strike. It also advocated fair wages and decent working conditions.

Later popes felt strongly enough about Pope Leo's call for economic justice that they wrote their own social encyclicals on various subsequent anniversaries of his 1891 letter. A reading of these encyclicals and other related Church documents makes it clear that, since the late nineteenth century, the Catholic Church has expressed significant concern about human suffering due to social and economic conditions. In giving shape to modern Catholic Social Teaching, popes and other Church leaders have not shied away from taking strong positions on controversial issues. The Church takes a stand on economic and social matters when the fundamental rights of the person are not being respected or protected because how this life is lived should be ordered to what is good and right. As a result the Church has become one of the most consistent voices in the world speaking on behalf of those who are suffering the consequences of injustice.

Catholic Social Teaching did not stay on the level of theory. It had an impact on Catholics faced with addressing issues related to industry and commerce. For instance, in Europe many political parties that embraced the Church's social teachings sprang up. Also, workers' unions and other labor organizations based on Christian principles became popular.

Dorothy Day and the Catholic Workers Movement

The story of Dorothy Day and the Catholic Worker Movement presents an enlightening saga about the power and appeal of Catholic Social Teaching. In her autobiography, *The Long Loneliness*, Day recounts her journey toward faith. In her teenage years, she was drawn to involvement with those who were poor, but she dismissed religion as a potential instrument for such involvement:

Children look at things very directly and simply. I did not see anyone taking off his coat and giving it to the poor. I didn't see anyone having a banquet and calling in the lame, the halt and the blind. And those who were doing it, like the Salvation Army, did not appeal to me. I wanted, though I did not know it then, a synthesis. I wanted a life and I wanted the abundant life. I wanted it for others too. I did not want just the few, the missionary-minded people like the Salvation Army, to be kind to the poor. I wanted everyone to be kind. I wanted every home to be open to the lame, the halt and the blind, the way it had been after the San Francisco earthquake. Only then did people really live, really love their brothers. In such love was the abundant life and I did not have the slightest idea how to find it.

The picture Day had of religious people was very different from what she thought it should be: "I knew the rich were smiled at and fawned upon by churchgoers. This is all that I could see" (39). In college, this negative impression of religion deepened.

At the time, Marxists seemed to demonstrate the concern for the poor for which Day was looking. Thus, she became a socialist. Day was drawn to the masses of poor people living simple lives as best they could in run-down sections of big cities. However, she also noted that great numbers of those who were poor were not attending socialist meetings. Rather, in every city she visited, they were pouring out of churches on Sunday mornings. She was coming to realize that the Catholic Church was where people who were poor went—the people whom she claimed to want to help.

Day became a Catholic and kept up her radical identification with street people and laborers. With Peter Maurin, she began The Catholic Worker newspaper to offer an alternative to both socialism and capitalism and to emphasize that Catholicism can serve as inspiration and instigation for involvement with those who were poor. Maurin and Day opened up a house of hospitality for people who were homeless in New York. In a haphazard but steady progression, others, combining Catholicism and compassion, opened similar houses in major cities throughout the United States. Even though Day died in 1980, The Catholic Worker newspaper and movement continue to be an active presence where Catholics are committed to helping people who are the poorest of the poor.

▼ **Dorothy Day,** *The Long Loneliness*
(Harper San Francisco, 1952), 39

GROUP TALK

1. What changes do you see in society from the time of Dorothy Day to now?

2. What changes do you see in the Catholic Church from that time to now?

3. Do you believe that faith in Christ is necessary for oppression to be overcome?

FAITH ACTIVITY

Times of Crisis Dorothy Day noticed that after the San Francisco earthquake, people were helpful to those in need. The terrorist attacks in 2001 brought forth an even greater response. In your experience, have you found that people are more helpful in times of crisis? Research a recent national or local disaster. What groups, organizations, and individuals pitched in to help? What kind of help did they offer? Report on your findings.

Catholic Social Teaching Today

Since the publication of *On the Condition of Workers*, the modern Church has continued to give attention to justice-related concerns across the world. During this time, the geographical center of Christianity in general, and of Catholicism in particular, has been changing. For example, Latin America contains the largest concentration of Catholics in the world today. Africa now far outnumbers North America in numbers of Catholics. And the breakdown of the former communist bloc nations in the early 1990s led to increased religious freedom where it formerly had been suppressed.

Catholicism's shift from being predominantly a European religion to being one of truly global dimensions has created new questions regarding justice. Because the Church's presence is worldwide, extending beyond the interests of one country or one continent, the Church is uniquely suited to speak on global justice-related issues. The documents ratified by Catholic bishops during the Second Vatican Council (1962–1965) signaled the Church's desire to make justice and concern for human suffering keys to her stance toward the world: "The joys and hopes, the grief and anguish of the people of our age, especially of those who are poor or afflicted, are the joys and hopes, the grief and anguish of the followers of Christ as well. Nothing that is genuinely human fails to find an echo in their hearts" (*Documents of Vatican II*, "The Church in the Modern World," 1).

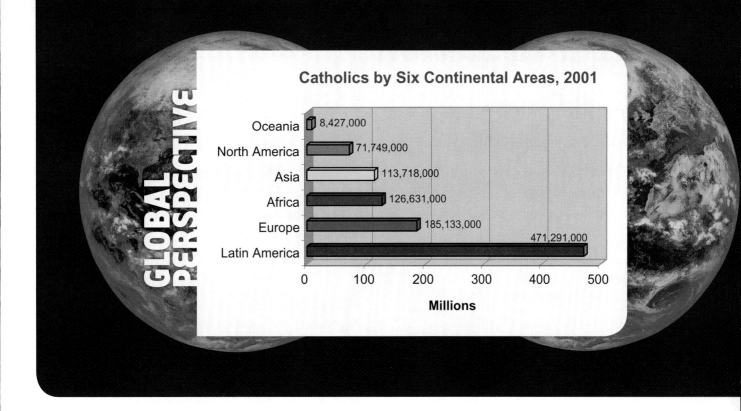

Catholics by Six Continental Areas, 2001

	Millions
Oceania	8,427,000
North America	71,749,000
Asia	113,718,000
Africa	126,631,000
Europe	185,133,000
Latin America	471,291,000

In other words, as Dorothy Day and other Catholics committed to justice have affirmed, the Church proclaims that she has been called by the Father in Jesus Christ and through the Holy Spirit to identify herself with those in most need. The Church does not offer a brand of religion that numbs people to present injustices with the promise of salvation after death. On the contrary, the salvation after death that Jesus promises cannot be separated from people's liberation from injustice now.

GROUP TALK

1. Do you identify at all with the teenage Dorothy Day's desire to associate herself with "the masses"? How would following her example change your life?

2. How strongly are Catholicism and compassion linked in the perception of most people today? How are they linked in your perception?

Faith in Action

Crossing Borders

Sponsored by: **Maryknoll Missionaries and the Scalabrini Missionaries**

A view of the "real world" often starts at the U.S.-Mexico border for youth group members and high school students in the Archdiocese of Los Angeles.

> " Seeing the culture and poverty of so many people in Mexico left a lasting impression on my heart. As a result, I have a deeper faith, and a longing to help others. "
>
> Stephanie Boerger

Crossing Borders, an immersion program sponsored by the Maryknoll Missionaries working in collaboration with the Scalabrini Migrant Center in Tijuana, offers teenagers a first-hand look at a culture stuck in a cycle of poverty. By entering the lives and struggles of the people there, participants come away with a better understanding of the root causes of the problems facing these people of another country and another culture.

The students' weekend trip to Mexico starts with a dinner with migrants at the Scalabrini Migrant Center, which is run by the Scalabrini Missionaries and houses migrant men who are en route from the United States to their homes.

In the following two days, the teenagers tour a Tijuana memorial of crosses stretching a mile, each cross in memory of one person who lost his or her life crossing the border. Participants are asked to choose one person to think of while in Mexico. Another memorial stretches along a beach fence where the border runs into the Gulf, also a memorial to those who died trying to cross the border. Participants visit homes for migrant men, women, and children, a pre-school, and a dining facility operated by the Missionaries of Charity; and facilities run by the Franciscans and the Oblates of the Immaculate Heart. The group experiences a typical lunch with a local family from one of the poor neighborhoods (colonias), usually thin soup and tortillas

The weekends also offer time for discussions on the history of the U.S.-Mexico border, its culture and social-economic problems, as well as time for prayer and reflection.

Crossing Borders is about life lessons, learning to see life through the eyes of a homeless migrant.

◀ **Teens doing volunteer work for Crossing Borders.**

GO ONLINE Visit www.harcourtreligion.com to learn more about the Maryknoll Missionaries and the Scalabrini Missionaries and for a link to its site.

Prayer

Begin by praying the Sign of the Cross.

Leader: It is truly right to give you thanks, it is fitting that we offer you praise, Father of mercy, faithful God. You sent Jesus Christ your Son among us as redeemer and Lord. He was moved with compassion for the poor and the powerless, for the sick and the sinner; he made himself neighbor to the oppressed. By his words and actions he proclaimed to the world that you care for us as a father cares for his children.

Reader 1: Keep your Church alert in faith to the signs of the times and eager to accept the challenge of the Gospel.

Reader 2: Open our hearts to the needs of all humanity, so that sharing their grief and anguish, their joy and hope, we may faithfully bring them the good news of salvation and advance together on the way to your kingdom.

Reader 1: Open our eyes to the needs of all; inspire us with words and deeds to comfort those who labor and are burdened; keep our service of others faithful to the example and command of Christ.

Reader 2: Let your Church be a living witness to truth and freedom, to justice and peace, that all people may be lifted up by the hope of a world made new.

All Amen

Selections from "Masses for Various Needs and Occasions"

End by praying the Sign of the Cross.

>Review

1. Why can Pentecost be considered "the birthday of the Church"?

2. Define Church. What does it mean to say that the Church is both visible and spiritual?

3. What are the four marks of the Church?

4. How does the Holy Trinity serve as a model for our relationships with one another?

5. What is the relationship between conscience and justice? Where do freedom and responsibility fit into this connection?

6. How do you form your conscience and how can your conscience lead you in your choices?

7. What is the common good and how does it relate to civil and divine law?

8. How do we receive the grace to follow God's commands?

9. Describe the difference between a pre-Christian

Roman understanding of justice and that of the early church.

10. Who was Saint John Chrysostom? What message did he have for people in his congregation who were rich?

11. In what way did Saint Francis of Assisi go against the prevailing spirit of his day? What did Francis say about the connection between possessions and warfare?

12. What did Christian missionaries do as Europeans conquered other lands?

13. Describe Pope Leo XIII's contribution to Catholic Social Teaching.

14. What led to Dorothy Day's journey from socialism to Catholicism?

15. What insight did Marie-Eugenie Milleret have regarding her era's cry for liberty and justice?

>Key Words

capitalism (p. 56) Individual ownership and administration of the production and distribution of goods.

Catholic Social Teaching (p. 55) The body of official Church documents written by Church leaders in response to various social, political, and economic issues.

Church (p. 42) The community of the faithful who through holy Baptism are nourished by and become the Body of Christ (See *CCC 777*.)

colonialism (p. 52) The political and economic system by which one country controls and exploits another, holding it in a subservient role.

common good (p. 47) A long-standing Christian concept advocating that society should be organized so that, as much as possible, all people, either in groups or as individuals, are given the opportunities to reach their fulfillment more fully and easily.

conscience (p. 44) The capacity to make good judgments involving a process of discernment about right and wrong as well as judgment itself.

encyclical (p. 55) An official letter to the whole Church written by a pope.

Pentecost (p. 41) The event, fifty days after Easter, when the Holy Spirit appeared as fire and wind to Christ's Apostles. As a result, the Apostles began actively to proclaim the Gospel. The feast is celebrated each year to mark the ongoing presence of the Holy Spirit in the Church.

socialism (p. 55) Government ownership and administration of the production and distribution of goods.

›Our Challenge

The Church is the Body of Christ empowered by the Holy Spirit and called to continue Jesus' mission in the world. Throughout history the Church has carried forward God's call to justice and the Good News proclaimed by Jesus. The Church addressed the sins of each age using the guidance provided it through Christ and the Holy Spirit. For instance, over the course of the modern era Church leaders have created a body of work called Catholic Social Teaching, in which they have addressed particular social problems in light of God's revelation. In chapter 3, we turn our attention to a more in-depth discussion of Catholic Social Teaching.

A JUST WORLD

THE CATHOLIC VISION

CHAPTER GOALS

In this chapter you will:

★ explore the central themes of Catholic Social Teaching and their implications for living.

★ examine how societies should meet the needs of their people.

★ evaluate social institutions in light of how they affect people's life and dignity.

★ look at characteristics of contemporary U.S. culture to discover how that culture can influence the work for justice.

Catholic Social Teaching

The Church's social teaching is articulated in a number of documents addressed to the whole world—universal documents—such as papal encyclicals and conciliar documents. Social teaching has also been articulated by the U. S. Conference of Catholic Bishops and other regional groupings of bishops throughout the world. These different documents have varying authority within the Church's teaching. In order to understand the various types of writings and statements put forth by the Church, we need to look at the role of the magisterium in the Church's life.

The **magisterium** is "the living teaching office of the Church, whose task it is to give authentic interpretation to the word of God, whether in its written form (Sacred Scripture), or in the form of Tradition: (*Catechism*, Glossary). The college of bishops in union with the pope (the bishop of Rome) form the magisterium, who guarantee that the Church remains faithful to the teachings of Jesus and the Apostles in matters of faith and morals. They are authentic teachers of the moral life, and it is their responsibility to preach how natural law and reason are to be applied in our world. (CCC 2050)

Christ, who is the Truth, conferred on the Church a share in his own infallibility in matters of faith and morals. This charism is exercised by the pope when, in virtue of his office as bishop of Rome and pastor of the whole Church, he proclaims a doctrine pertaining to faith or morals. Infallibility is also present in the body of bishops when, together with the pope, they propose a doctrine for belief as being both divinely revealed and as the teaching of Christ. The People of God, under the guidance of the pope and the bishops, are called to unfailingly adhere to the faith that has been handed on by the Apostles with the obedience of faith. Conciliar documents (those that result from ecumenical councils such as Vatican II are typically decrees or constitutions. The Code of Canon Law (1983) and the *Catechism of the Catholic Church*, which was presented to the Church in 1992 with an apostolic constitution, carry the same authority as the Vatican II documents issued by the pope and bishops.

Papal teachings in encyclicals, apostolic letters, or exhortations typically expound upon or explain existing teaching or law. Other explanatory documents, such as instructions, also give information on how to implement Church teaching and or law found in the authoritative universal documents.

Catholic Social Teachings: The Vatican

1891 *On the Condition of Workers (Rerum Novarum),*
Pope Leo XIII

- strongly affirms the belief that the human person has basic rights, especially the rights to food, clothing, shelter, and a living wage
- declares that the rights of those who are poor must be "specially cared for and protected by the government"
- addresses the plight of industrial workers following the Industrial Revolution
- calls for protection of those who are suffering in light of industrialization
- rejects socialism and the "class struggle" approach to solutions
- affirms the right to private property
- affirms the right of workers to form and join professional organizations

1961 *Christianity and Social Progress*
(Mater et Magistra), **Pope John XXIII**

- affirms the role of the Church as teacher and guardian of those who are poor and oppressed
- calls for greater awareness of the need for all people to work
- voices concern for workers, women, and newly independent nations
- gives special attention to the plight of farmers and farmworkers
- warns that spending on nuclear weapons and the widening gap between rich and poor nations threaten society

1963 *Peace on Earth (Pacem in Terris),*
Pope John XXIII

- emphasizes that all people are "the children and friends of God"
- identifies respect for people and a just social order as the basis for peace
- spells out rights that all people possess:
  - the right to civil, political, social, and economic services
  - the right to respect
  - the freedom to search for truth, express opinions, and worship
  - the right to choose one's state in life, to marry and have a family
  - the right to work for a just wage in a safe environment
  - the right to hold private property
  - the right to work freely for the common good
  - the right to move within one's own country and to emigrate to other countries

1965 *"The Church in the Modern World"*
(Gaudium et Spes), **Documents of Vatican II**

- notes the growing interdependence of the international human family and the importance of safeguarding every human's basic rights
- affirms that the Church should work with other elements in society to improve conditions for all people
- addresses many specific issues facing people living in the modern age and lays out a Christian response to them

1967 *On the Development of Peoples*
(Populorum Progressio), **Pope Paul VI**

- focuses on the economic rights and the economic well-being of all persons
- notes that we are all responsible for each other and that the economic development of those who are poor and the moral development of those with means are interlinked
- decries the worsening marginalization of those who are poor
- presents various dimensions of a wholistic program for genuine human development

1991 *Hundredth Year (Centesimus Annus),*
Pope John Paul II

- marked the hundredth anniversary of Pope Leo XIII's *Rerum Novarum*
- called for relief of nations' debts, for living wages, and for just human ecology beginning at the family level while reaffirming the rights of profit and private property

1995 *The Gospel of Life (Evangelium Vitae),*
Pope John Paul II

- examines expressions of a "culture of death" in the world including abortion, capital punishment, and euthanasia
- proposes ways to promote a culture of life–a world of care

2005 *God is Love (Deus Caritas Est),*
Pope Benedict XVI

- describes love, emphasizing God's command and his enablement through his love for us
- informs the debate on social justice by the Church's faith-purified reason which always has love as its goal

FAITH ACTIVITY

Catholic Social Teaching To deepen your appreciation of the documents listed in the charts on Catholic Social Teaching, log on to www.harcourtreligion.com to access the USCCB or Vatican Web site and locate one document from each chart. Read at least two pages of each document and, for each, prepare a summary of what you have read.

A national conference of bishops, such as the U.S. Conference of Catholic Bishops, explains how universal Church teaching applies to their country or how it is to be followed in their country. Pastoral letters are among this type of document, and to be effective or binding, the Holy See typically needs to recognize or confirm them. In the chart that follows, *Brothers and Sisters Are Us, The Challenge of Peace, and Economic Justice for All* fall within this category.

Within the conference of bishops, various committees and subcommittees issue statements, some of which are not approved by the full body of bishops. These statements do not carry any binding authority for they do not represent the thinking of all the bishops of the country.

Individual bishops can issue documents or guidelines that have authority in his local diocese, as long as they do not contradict the universal teachings of the Church or those put forth by the national conference of bishops. Regions of bishops can do the same, which is the case with the document *This Land Is Home to Me.*

GROUP TALK

1. What topics surprised you in the documents from the Vatican? Why did they surprise you?

2. What topics surprised you in the statements by the U.S. bishops? Why did they surprise you?

3. Describe specific ways that these proposals are still relevant today.

Catholic Social Teachings: U.S. Bishops' Statements

1974

This Land Is Home to Me, Catholic Bishops of Appalachia
- describes in poetic form conditions calling for justice in the Appalachian region of the United States

1976

Society and the Aged
- affirms the human rights of people who are elderly
- explores the role of the Church regarding people who are elderly and their families

1979

Brothers and Sisters to Us
- examines racism, declaring it to be a sin

1983

The Challenge of Peace
- provides a comprehensive examination of principles regarding war and peace
- addresses major issues related to war in light of Christian principles
- calls for an end to the arms race, the reduction of weapons, and a ban on nuclear testing, noting that money used for weapons should go to those who are poor

1986

Economic Justice for All
- proposes that the U. S. economy must be judged in terms of what it does for people, especially people on the margins of society
- reaffirms that the Universal Declaration of Human Rights and internally accepted human-rights standards "are strongly" supported by Catholic teaching; they are "moral issues" because they are "all essential to human dignity and to the integral development of both individuals and society."

Major Themes of Catholic Social Teaching

" Action on behalf of justice and participation in the transformation of the world fully appear to us as a constitutive dimension of the preaching of the Gospel, or, in other words, of the Church's mission for the redemption of the human race and its liberation from every oppressive situation. "

World Synod of Catholic Bishops, *Justice in the World*, 6

Jesus began his public ministry by announcing the coming of the kingdom and calling people to repent and believe. He proclaimed his divinely-anointed mission as one to "bring good news to the poor . . . release to the captives . . . recovery of sight to the blind" (*Luke 4:18*). Not only do we preach a message of conversion and new life in Christ but we also seek to give flesh to the love and justice that Jesus proclaimed. The message of Jesus and the Church over the past centuries is reflected in seven themes that have been identified as underlying Catholic Social Teaching. These themes run through the many Church statements on justice extending back more than a century. The U.S. Catholic bishops articulated these seven themes in a *Sharing Catholic Social Teaching: Challenges and Directions, A Reflection of the U.S. Bishops* issued in 1998 after the release of findings by a task force on Catholic social teaching spearheaded by several U.S. Bishops' Committees. The goal of the task force and the reflection was to increase awareness of Catholic social teaching as integral to the faith and to educate Catholics of all ages on the rich heritage of social teaching and action.

Approved by the full body of bishops, this document relies heavily on Scripture and the major papal and conciliar documents of the past century. As a reflection and explanation of existing teaching, the document reminds us that Catholic social teaching needs to be understood within the context of the entirety of our faith, as part of the Gospel message and the call to conversion in all its dimensions. These themes or principles in the United States guide the Church and her members in her mission to be a beacon of justice in the world. As we will see, certain words are constantly repeated in these themes—dignity, rights, responsibilities, participation, community, solidarity. That's because all the themes are an aspect of one theme, justice. For now we will name and briefly describe each theme. The remainder of our text is an application of these themes to specific issues of justice.

The Principles

1. Life and Dignity of the Human Person

"The Catholic Church proclaims that human life is sacred and that the dignity of the human person is the foundation of a moral vision for society. Our belief in the sanctity of human life and the inherent dignity of the human person is the foundation of all the principles of our social teaching."

U. S. Conference of Catholic Bishops, *Sharing Catholic Social Teaching*

This theme is first because it is the foundation for all the other principles or themes. Every single person has enormous value, and no one's value is greater than anyone else's. Elderly people nearing the end of life, unborn children, the wealthy, the poor, people on both sides of disputes and wars, criminals, victims of crimes, sinners, business owners, workers, people with AIDS, healthy people, the uneducated, and the educated are all equal in **dignity**. We sometimes call this dignity *inherent* or *intrinsic*; this means that it is a part of being human. It comes from God, and no one can take it away. The Catholic Church's defense of all human life, from conception to natural death, is rooted in this principle and reflected in the fifth commandment, "You shall not kill."

▼ East Nepal, group of children during Dasain Festivaly

> Whatever is opposed to life itself, such as any type of murder, genocide, abortion, euthanasia or willful self-destruction, whatever violates the integrity of the human person . . . whatever insults human dignity, such as subhuman living conditions, arbitrary imprisonment, deportation, slavery, prostitution, the selling of women and children, as well as disgraceful working conditions where [workers] are treated as mere tools for profit, rather than as free and responsible persons; all these things and others of their like are infamies indeed. They poison human society . . . they are a supreme dishonor to the Creator.

Documents of Vatican II, "The Church in the Modern World," #27

FAITH ACTIVITY

Community Service Describe an occasion when you were part of a group project whose goal was helping others or improving your community. Write about how working together was an important part of the success of the project.

2. Call to Family, Community, and Participation

> [O]ur tradition proclaims that the person is not only sacred but also social. How we organize our society . . . directly affects human dignity and the capacity of individuals to grow in community. The family is the central social institution that must be supported and strengthened, not undermined. While our society often exalts individualism, the Catholic tradition teaches that human beings grow and achieve fulfillment in community. We believe people have a right and a duty to participate in society, seeking together the common good and well-being of all, especially the poor and vulnerable.

U. S. Conference of Catholic Bishops, *Sharing Catholic Social Teaching*

Humans are by nature social. We thrive only in community. The good of each person is tied to the common good. By common good, we mean the totality of conditions in society that allow people to reach fulfillment and live the life of dignity that God intends.

The Common Good requires three elements:

- respect for the rights of all people
- the social well-being and development of the group
- peace, which includes security

When people who are poor talk about their experiences, they seldom mention their inadequate food, shelter, or income. Instead they use words like "hopelessness," "helplessness," and "being stuck." They encounter multiple problems that set them on a downward spiral into increasing desperation—poor education and job training, transportation systems that don't get them to the better job sites, debilitated health due to poor diet and medical care, a poor credit rating that makes purchasing a house out of the question, and so on. They feel cut off from the mainstream. The dignity of the human person requires opportunities for participation and pursuit of the common good by everyone. The state is responsible for assuring that its structures promote and defend the common good. Since the human community doesn't end at a nation's borders, concern for the common good calls for participation and organization on the international level as well.

FAITH ACTIVITY

Human Dignity Research the world's population. What implications do the Catholic Social Teaching that all people are entitled to dignity have? Write what steps you and society could take to help extend dignity to everyone.

> It is necessary that all participate . . . in promoting the common good. This obligation is inherent in the dignity of the human person. Participation is achieved first of all by taking charge of the areas for which one assumes *personal responsibility*. . . . As far as possible citizens should take an active part in *public life*. . . . Much care should be taken to promote institutions that improve the conditions of human life.
>
> *CCC, 1913-1916*

3. Rights and Responsibilities

> The Catholic tradition teaches that human dignity can be protected and a healthy community can be achieved only if human rights are protected and responsibilities are met. Therefore, every person has a fundamental right to life and a right to those things required for human decency. Corresponding to these rights are duties and responsibilities—to one another, to our families, and to the larger society.
>
> U.S. Conference of Catholic Bishops, *Sharing Catholic Social Teaching*

The Church teaches that every person has a right to certain things. Every person has the right to life, which includes having one's basic needs for food, shelter, rest, and health care met; economic rights, which includes employment, education, and equal opportunity; and political and cultural rights, which includes various freedoms, among them privacy and religious expression. It is not enough to say that society owes us these things. We owe them to one another. Therefore, rights come with responsibilities. For instance, the *right* to adequate food creates the *responsibility* for a society and its members to see to it that no one starves . In other words, when-ever we list rights we also need to list responsibilities that make those rights a reality.

> When the state does not place its power at the service of the rights of each citizen, and in particular of the more vulnerable, the very foundations of a state based on law are undermined.
>
> *CCC 2273*

4. Option for the Poor and Vulnerable

> In a world characterized by growing prosperity for some and pervasive poverty for others, Catholic teaching proclaims that a basic moral test is how our most vulnerable members are faring. In a society marred by deepening divisions between rich and poor, our tradition recalls the story of the Last Judgment (Mt 25:31-46) and instructs us to put the needs of the poor and the vulnerable first.
>
> U.S. Conference of Catholic Bishops, *Sharing Catholic Social Teaching*

The passage from Matthew cited by the bishops likens Christ's judgment to a king who gives eternal life to those who have cared for the hungry, the thirsty, the stranger, the naked, the sick, and the imprisoned. The king said to them "just as you did it to one of the least of these who are members of my family, you did it to me" (*Matthew 25:40*). The king gives eternal punishment to those who failed to care for them. This is a strong, clear message about the urgent need to care for the poor and vulnerable. The goods of creation should reach everyone. The right to private property does not negate this. People who do not care for those who are poor and vulnerable in society violate the seventh commandment, "You shall not steal." When we fail to practice justice and charity in the way we handle the goods of the earth and the fruits of human work, we participate in a type of theft. God's call to work for justice is a call to work on eliminating sinful inequalities that prevent people who are poor from meeting their basic needs and realizing their God-given dignity.

▲ Poverty in Juarez, Mexico

These concerns go beyond merely providing for the basics necessary to stay alive.

> The 'option for the poor' . . . is not an adversarial slogan that pits one group or class against another. Rather it states that the deprivation and powerlessness of the poor wounds the whole community. The extent of their suffering is a measure of how far we are from being a true community of persons. These wounds will be healed only by greater solidarity with the poor and among the poor themselves.
>
> U.S. Conference of Catholic Bishops, *Economic Justice for All*, #88

FAITH ACTIVITY

Greater Equality From the perspective of either a CEO of a leading company on the New York Stock Exchange or a member of a union of peasant farmworkers in a poor country, prepare a presentation for the class on the following statement: *The wide gap that exists between the richest and poorest members of society is both sinful and unjust. We should take steps to ensure greater equality both of wealth and of opportunity for all.*

Fair Trade

A typical farmer in Nicaragua receives only about a penny from the $1.50 spent on a cup of coffee. Research fair trade products by visiting **www.harcourtreligion.com** to link to the Catholic Relief Services Web. Find out ways to identify fair trade symbols on coffee labels and support small farmers.

You pay: $1.50   The farmer gets: < 1¢

5. The Dignity of Work and the Rights of Workers

In a marketplace where too often the quarterly bottom line takes precedence over the rights of workers, we believe that the economy must serve people, not the other way around. Work is more than a way to make a living; it is a form of continuing participation in God's creation. If the dignity of work is to be protected, then the basic rights of workers must be respected. . . Respecting these rights promotes an economy that protects human life, defends human rights, and advances the well-being of all.

U.S. Conference of Catholic Bishops, *Sharing Catholic Social Teaching*

Economic activity in society is meant to provide for the needs of its members and the entire human community, not increase the profit, power, and position of a few. Individuals have the right to contribute to the common good through work and fair wages. Work is more than a means to meet one's needs. It expresses one's cooperation with God in his plan for creation. Work and economic activity are carried out for the sake of the common good. The seventh commandment clearly underlies these teachings, providing the proper perspective in which to consider the purpose and fruits of work. In fact, many of the social teachings and doctrine of the Church are situated within the framework of the seventh commandment as a response to the respect for the integrity of creation, most especially humans, and the fruits of creation.

Pope John Paul II was a particularly strong voice for the dignity of work, giving priority to labor over capital. He pointed out, for instance, that workers produce many wonderful things that enhance human life, such as cars, computers, refrigerators, and musical instruments. On the other hand, capital (the money required to run a business) is an instrument at the service of their production. The pope warned that treating workers as mere instruments in the production of goods and services dehumanizes them and diminishes the dignity of work. At its best, the creativity of work is a way human beings image God the Creator. For Pope John Paul II, this spirit of creativity and contribution should apply to any and all jobs.

6. Solidarity

> Our culture is tempted to turn inward, becoming indifferent and sometimes isolationist in the face of international responsibilities. Catholic social teaching proclaims that we are our brothers' and sisters' keepers, wherever they live. We are one family, whatever our national, racial, ethnic, economic, and ideological differences. Learning to practice the virtue of solidarity means learning that 'loving our neighbor' has global dimensions in an interdependent world.

U.S. Conference of Catholic Bishops, *Sharing Catholic Social Teaching*

FAITH ACTIVITY

Changes in Society In a small group, brainstorm ways that society must change if it is to better live out the demands of Catholic Social Teaching. Prepare a presentation for the class using a medium of your choice to present the ideas your group generated.

The call to **solidarity** means that working for justice involves working with, not just working for, other people. Those striving to help people in need do not simply cry, "We must feed the poor." Instead, they also say: "We must learn from people who are poor how they can help us, as well as how we can help them help themselves. We need to give those who are voiceless a voice. We need to share important decisions among those who are rich and those who are poor." Solidarity is that quality of justice that breaks down barriers between people: the powerful and the powerless, rich and poor, men and women, black and white, Eastern and Western, Hispanic and Anglo-American, young and old, those in prison and those who are free. Solidarity goes beyond the sharing of material goods to include spiritual goods so that every person has a chance to fulfill his or her God-given dignity.

> *Solidarity* helps us to see the 'other'—whether a *person, people,* or *nation*—not just as some kind of instrument, with a work capacity and physical strength to be exploited at low cost and then discarded when no longer useful, but as our 'neighbor,' a 'helper' (cf. Gen. 2:18-20) to be made a sharer, on a par with ourselves, in the banquet of life to which all are equally invited by God.

Pope John Paul II, *On Social Concern,* 39

The call to solidarity challenges us to search for ways to work with people to solve problems. With a partner or small group, role-play how you might address the following problems, first using a working-for approach, then using a working-with approach.

- A classmate is receiving failing grades.
- A friend develops a drinking problem.

- A neighborhood near you is in serious disrepair.
- Your parish would like to help those leaving prison who have no place to go.
- Your grandmother is alone and homebound.

GROUP TALK

In what ways are your working-with scenarios a better application of the principles of Catholic Social Teaching?

FAITH ACTIVITY

Concern for Environment Research to find a statement of concern for the environment. Evaluate the proposals contained in the statement in light of Catholic Social Teaching, as well as in terms of their practicality and benefit. Report to the class on your findings.

7. Care for God's Creation

On a planet conflicted over environmental issues, the Catholic tradition insists that we show our respect for the Creator by our stewardship of creation. Care for the earth is not just an Earth Day slogan, it is a requirement of our faith. We are called to protect people and the planet, living our faith in relationship with all of God's creation.

U.S. Conference of Catholic Bishops, *Sharing Catholic Social Teaching*

An eighty-five-year-old man works painstakingly in his garden. He plants trees and flowering bushes that will show their true beauty only ten years from now. He knows he may never enjoy the gift of their full beauty. Nonetheless, he views his accomplishment with great joy. His garden is not for himself but is a blessing for God, a way for him to share God's blessing of creation with others in this one small way.

In Genesis, God created everything for us, and we are to be stewards and caretakers of all his creation. It is not at our disposal for whatever we wish but for us to make it an offering to him.

At its core, the environmental crisis is a moral challenge. It calls us to examine how we use and share the goods of the earth, what we pass on to the future generations, and how we live in harmony with God's creation.

U.S. Conference of Catholic Bishops, *Renewing the Earth*

Applying the Principles

Gifts for the Poor A service club in a suburban Catholic high school decided to collect toys and clothing for children living in an urban parish. Club members planned on dressing up in Santa Claus outfits and personally distributing the gifts on Christmas Eve.

The pastor of the urban parish visited their club to speak to the students. "I appreciate your work on behalf of our children," he told them, "but I can't have you delivering toys to the children themselves. Parents should be Santa Claus for their children, not wealthy young people from the suburbs. It would diminish the self-esteem of our parents if you brought the gifts to their children. Instead, I suggest that you bring the toys and presents to the church hall the week before Christmas. Then our parents can come and choose the things that they feel would be best for their children. In that way, the children will receive gifts at Christmas, and the parents will also participate in the giving."

GROUP TALK

1 Why were the pastor's concerns justified?

2 Explain how each theme of Catholic Social Teaching is reflected in the pastor's decision about how to handle the gift giving.

A Just World In a song, painting, poem, story, collage, mime, or other art form, create an image of a just world. To help you design your image, reflect on the themes named in this chapter.

Examining Social Institutions The first theme of Catholic social teaching points out that "the measure of every institution is whether it threatens or enhances the life and dignity of the human person." The *Catechism* further states, "The human person . . . is and ought to be the principle, the subject, and the object of every social organization" (*CCC* 1892). What are the institutions of a society to which they refer? We will look more closely at social institutions, or the structures of a society, in the next chapter. It's also important to recognize the institutional impact on the various specifics of justice we will examine later in the course.

All societies establish certain ways of meeting the needs of their people. Social institutions include production and distribution of food and products, education, business and finance, health care, the criminal justice systems, the media and entertainment industries and marriage and family life.

▼ White House, Washington D.C.

In the case of the media, society has a right to information but it should be grounded in truth, freedom, and justice. Moderation and discipline should be practiced when using social communications media.

People create and shape these institutions; people are also shaped by the institutions in which they live. For instance, in one society, food may be produced on a small scale and distributed at local levels, such as at village markets. In another society, food production and distribution may take place primarily through large-scale farming. In some cases, the people harvesting crops make barely enough to keep themselves sufficiently fed! The U.S. Catholic bishops insist that all institutions must be evaluated in light of their effect on people's life and dignity.

GROUP TALK

1. For each of the seven themes of Catholic social teaching, name one problem in your immediate society or environment that needs to be addressed. How could the problem be solved or lessened?

2. For each theme, name one way one of your communities has addressed a related problem and helped solve or lessen it.

3. Give an example of how the way a society's institutions are structured can have an effect on the common good.

Examining Our Culture in Light of Justice

E very culture is multi-faceted, and U.S. culture is no exception. However, every culture also exhibits some dominant values and viewpoints. If we want to create a just world, we need to develop our awareness of the current directions and values in our culture.

Individualism Versus Interdependence

Early European colonies in America emphasized community spirit more than "rugged individualism." However, in time **individualism** became a value associated with the United States. On the positive side, individualism led to an emphasis on self-reliance. But, *excessive* individualism can lead to losing sight of the interdependence and concern for the common good that are important for any society. "I've got to be me" and "Every man for himself" are themes that can have dangerous implications because our choices constantly affect others.

A classic study of American values, described in the book *Habits of the Heart*, identifies individualism as a long-standing core theme in American life. The study describes moral individualism in these terms: "The ultimate ethical rule is simply that individuals should be able to pursue whatever they find rewarding, constrained only by the requirement that they not interfere with the 'value systems' of others" (6). The authors, Robert Bellah and his team, interviewed people from across the country to demonstrate this theme. A young man had this to say:

> One of the things that I use to characterize life in California, one of the things that makes California such a pleasant place to live, is people by and large aren't bothered by other people's value systems as long as they don't infringe upon your own. By and large, the rule of thumb out here is that if you've got the money, honey, you can do your thing as long as your thing doesn't destroy someone else's property, or interrupt their sleep, or bother their privacy, then that's fine.

Robert Bellah, et al., *Habits of the Heart* (New York: Harper & Row, 1985), 6-7

FAITH ACTIVITY

A More Just World Research a project, organization, or group of people that strives to create a more just world. Write a report indicating how they put one or more of the principles of Catholic social teaching into practice.

The Catholic concern for solidarity and the common good reminds us that our world is a "global village" and that either we learn to live and work together or we perish together. In that sense, a realistic description of our world acknowledges that we are neither totally independent nor dependent. Rather, we are **interdependent**.

Interdependence can sound so abstract. One way to picture the concept more concretely is to think about the reality that your great-great-grandchildren will be direct descendants of fifteen people in your generation besides yourself who are living today. If you care about your own great-great-grandchildren and their children, shouldn't you also be concerned about the people around you today who may end up being their great-grandparents or great-great-grandparents?

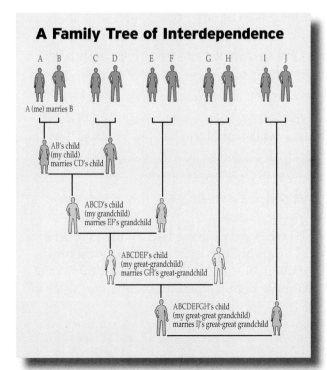

A Family Tree of Interdependence

FAITH ACTIVITY

Culture Wars Part of the "culture wars" going on in the United States is between those who emphasize the value of individualism and those who emphasize interdependence. Debate the pros and cons of each position.

When a new strain of a disease emerges in a small village somewhere, the entire world's population is soon under threat.

An accident at a nuclear power plant anywhere on earth affects levels of radioactivity everywhere.

Instability in one oil producing country affects the entire world's economy. When oil prices go up, the cost of all consumer goods goes up.

The U.S. heartland serves as the breadbasket of the world because it provides a large portion of the earth's grain. Drought in the United States leads to hungry people on the other side of the globe

Brazil's enormous jungles act as the earth's oxygen tank, producing much of the oxygen we breathe. Destruction of rainforests damages the entire earth's air supply.

Clearly, stressing individual initiative and responsibility is valuable. Individualism has helped make our country great. However, it is important that we acknowledge how much we are interdependent. A spirit of cooperation is needed for our mutual survival.

GROUP TALK

Do you believe that the young man describing life in California on page 80, speaks for most people in the United States? In what sense does his attitude reflect your own? In what sense does it not reflect your attitude? What characteristics would reflect a Catholic perspective?

Consumerism Versus Conscientious Consumption

> Christian faith and the norms of justice impose distinct limits on what we consume and how we view material goods. The great wealth of the United States can easily blind us to the poverty that exists in this nation and the destitution of hundreds of millions of people in other parts of the world. Americans are challenged today as never before to develop the inner freedom to resist the temptation to constantly seek more. Only in this way will the nation avoid what Paul VI called 'the most evident form of moral underdevelopment,' [Pope Paul VI, On the Development of Peoples (1967), 19] namely greed.
>
> U.S. Conference of Catholic Bishops, *Economic Justice for All*, 75

The people of North America have had a long love affair with the frontier. Throughout most of our history, there was always more land available "out West." If one locality could no longer support more people, then it was always possible

for some of the people to move on. North America seemed to offer limitless land, limitless resources, and limitless opportunities. Even when the land was parceled out and some resources showed signs of running out, we put our faith in space as "the final frontier."

Consumerism is a key problem contributing to the **crisis of limits**. Think of TV commercials or magazine ads you have seen recently. Chances are they tried to convince you how much better your life would be if you possessed whatever it is they were selling. Ads allure us into believing that our lives will be more comfortable, more interesting, more fun, or more rewarding if we possess this year's hot toy for children or adults. In the face of this allurement, three things can be associated with consumerism: blindness, lack of freedom, and moral underdevelopment.

All of us *consume* things; otherwise, we would be dead. **Consumerism** means allowing a passion for possessions to control us to the point that possessions become an end in themselves. Consumerism preaches that "we can buy happiness." It blinds us to what is really important and to how our consuming affects other people around the world.

The tenth commandment, "You shall not covet your neighbor's goods," forbids the greed that arises when we have a passion for wealth and the power it can give us. Being envious of other people's possessions and having an excessive desire for them is wrong. Envy is the kind of sin, sometimes referred to as a *capital sin*, that easily gives rise to more sins.

FAITH ACTIVITY

Interdependence List examples of how we are interdependent on personal, community, national, and global levels. Then answer the following questions. In what ways does your school foster more a spirit of interdependence than individualism? Does success in life depend more on individual achievement or on cooperation?

GROUP TALK

1 What are some ways that consumerism manifests itself in your life?

2 What are some ways that you attempt to counteract consumerism?

FAITH ACTIVITY

What's Right for the Economy?

List purchases you have made over the past three months. Identify items on your list (1) that are frequently advertised, (2) that could be considered fads, (3) that you could easily do without, (4) that are a necessity. Interview someone familiar with the business world. Discuss whether buying and consuming or reducing consumerism is better for the economy and report to the class.

The Dangers of Consumerism For one thing, excessive consumption takes resources away from people most in need of them. That is, money spent on a new car when our existing one runs fine or the latest CD when we already have many could be spent in ways that benefit people in greater need. Second, consumerism affects consumers as well. That is, it equates happiness with having rather than with being. When we do buy the new car, the CD burner, or the latest laptop computer, we eventually find that we have more possessions but not necessarily more happiness. Affluent persons sometimes commit suicide, and impoverished persons can struggle heroically to hang on to life in any way they can. Finally, consumerism can change people into commodities. Just as we may feel that we need to own a particular make of car, we may also feel compelled to wear a certain hairstyle or certain clothes, or to be seen with certain people. In this way, consumerism makes commodities—consumer goods—of us and of the people around us. We package ourselves like any other consumer good. This is how Pope John Paul II explained the problem:

Side-by-side with the miseries of underdevelopment, themselves unacceptable, we find ourselves up against a form of *superdevelopment*, equally inadmissible, because like the former it is contrary to what is good and to true happiness. This superdevelopment, which consists in an *excessive* availability of every kind of material goods for the benefit of certain social groups, easily makes people slaves of 'possession' and of immediate gratification, with no other horizon than the multiplication or continual replacement of the things already owned with others still better. This is the so-called civilization of 'consumption' or 'consumerism,' which involves so much 'throwing-away' and 'waste.' An object already owned but now superseded by something better is discarded, with no thought of its possible lasting value in itself, nor of some other human being who is poorer.

On Social Concern, 28

FAITH ACTIVITY

Consumerism Advertising reflects consumerism. Watch the ads on a typical evening of commercial television and list the possessions that the ads suggest lead to happiness. Then describe the "benefits"—such as being "cool," achieving status, or satisfying a manufactured need—that are used to sell these products. Make a video presentation or some other kind of report to illustrate your conclusions.

GROUP TALK

1. What does it mean to say that "consumerism makes commodities of us and of the people around us"? What evidence do you see of this?

2. Think of the last purchase you made. Was the product a *need* or a *want* on your part? If it was a *want*, how could you have used the money to benefit another? Was the happiness from the product short or long term?

3. What attitude did Jesus have toward possessions? What example did he set for his followers, and what did he say about being preoccupied with things?

▼ Rusted metal cans and other debris cover the ground at a trash dump in the Monument Valley Navajo Tribal Park.

Simple Living: An Antidote to Consumerism We might conclude that in a consumer society people value material things. In fact, this is seldom the case. Instead, we may have so many things, and crave possessing other things, that we do not take time to value what we do have. As a result, a consumer society is often a **throwaway society**. The things craved yesterday become the junk of today. Usable materials and products are squandered. Our world can become overburdened with junk. If we apply the attitude of a throwaway society to the treatment of people, then we find in a consumer society that those who appear to be noncontributing members may be relegated to human junkyards. That is, if the primary value is only "beautiful people" or people useful to us, then "out of sight, out of mind" threatens to become the response of our society toward people confined to jails and mental wards or trapped in pockets of poverty.

An antidote to consumerism is responsible use of what we have, conscientious consumption. One expression of conscientious consumption is cultivating an appreciation for **simple living**. Simple living does not imply devaluing things. Rather, it means cultivating a spirit of reverence for both things and people. Simple living means buying and using only what is needed in our daily living, out of respect for people and resources. It includes reducing the amount of energy and resources that we use. It also suggests discovering how to enjoy the many goods of the earth, including manufactured goods and the wonders of modern technology, in ways that are truly appreciative and not possessive.

FAITH ACTIVITY

Decrease Waste Study the throwaway evidence in your school. In small groups, plan an all-school campaign to decrease unnecessary waste of some resource—water, paper, food, heat, and so on. Include at least one quote from or based on a Church document.

Attributes of Simple Living

It is an act of *solidarity* with all those who have little, not by choice but by circumstance.

It is an act of *self-defense* against the dangers of over-consumption.

It is a *celebration* of the true God-given worth of persons and things.

It is a statement of *faith* in being, not having.

It is an act of *resistance* against sin and a high-pressure, achievement-oriented culture.

It leads to greater *sharing* of public space and common goods.

It *redirects our energy* away from satisfying artificially created wants toward an appreciation of truly valuable goods and services.

It *responds to God's call* to be a steward of creation.

Reading the Gospels, we discover that more than any other social issue, Jesus speaks about the dangers of wealth and the lure of possessions. In the Gospel according to Mark, Jesus tells the rich man that if he truly seeks eternal life, in addition to keeping the Commandments, he must give all that he has to those who are poor. When his followers are shocked at this teaching, Jesus repeats it—twice! If Jesus felt the need to stress the dangers of riches in his comparatively simple society, then how much more in our highly affluent society do we need to remain vigilant to the dangers of consumerism?

GROUP TALK

1. Which reasons for choosing a simple lifestyle appeal to you most? In light of these reasons, identify ways that you and your family already practice simple living. Name other activities that you might do that would reflect the spirit of simple living

2. Name ways that consumerism and simple living could have an impact on your spiritual life.

Fatalism Versus Hope

We can easily allow the many problems facing us to create a spirit of defeat. We may sense that the world and its problems are too big for us, that we can do little against the overwhelm-

ing powers of darkness filling our world. When we hear about a new crisis or trouble spot, what can we do? Where do we start? How do we counteract **fatalism**?

The Catholic response to fatalism is **hope**. Too often we use the word *hope* only when things are out of our hands. For example, we might say, "My teacher just saw me walk into the classroom late again. I sure hope she doesn't give me a detention." Genuine hope is more than wishful thinking and involves more than things of this world. While "wishing" is passive, hope is a virtue, which means that it leads to action.

Human beings have a built-in longing for happiness, and Christian faith proclaims that true happiness does await us and can be found by growing closer to God. Hope is a theological virtue. It is a gift from God that moves us to trust in the eternal life and happiness that he offers us. We don't have to rely on our own strength. If we are people of hope, the Holy Spirit infuses us with his life to sanctify us and heal us of sin. This new life in us leads to constant, ongoing conversion, which is a social dimension that inspires us to work for justice. We are called upon to be faithful to the Spirit. Any good works we do are really an expression of the grace of Christ. Hope, therefore, is a virtue that sustains us on our journey now and leads us to eternal life.

The Beatitudes are a particularly powerful statement since they offer hope to people experiencing great tribulations and "trace the path that leads through the trials that await the disciples of Jesus" (*CCC 1820*). Expressions of injustice today still cry out for Christ's message of hope. If we get involved in the struggles of people experiencing injustice, we will find that only hope in Christ prevents discouragement, anchors us, and keeps us focused on our ultimate goal. In the words of Scripture, "We have this hope, a sure and steadfast anchor of the soul, a hope that enters the inner shrine behind the curtain, where Jesus, a forerunner on our behalf, has entered. . . ." (*Hebrews 6:19-20*).

It would . . . be to give a one-sided picture, which could lead to sterile discouragement, if the condemnation of the threats to life were not accompanied by the presentation of the *positive signs* at work in humanity's present situation.

Unfortunately, it is often hard to see and recognize these positive signs, perhaps also because they do not receive sufficient attention in the communications media. Yet, how many initiatives of help and support for people who are weak and defenseless have sprung up and continue to spring up in the Christian community and in civil society, at the local, national and international level, through the efforts of individuals, groups, movements and organizations of various kinds!

Pope John Paul II, *The Gospel of Life*, 26

GROUP TALK

1 What problems would you encounter in trying to live more simply?

2 Do you see signs that the world could become more of a community of justice? Give examples to support your position.

›Faith in Action

Fair Trade Coffee Program

Sponsored by: **Catholic Relief Services**

Sitting in a gourmet coffee shop with friends sipping a foamy latte is a nice way to relax, but who thinks about where the coffee comes from? Who worries how or what the coffee farmer is getting paid? Catholic Relief Services (CRS) does.

> "Pura Vida customers vote their values with their dollars by purchasing our specialty coffees from all over the world which benefit the at-risk children in those coffee-growing communities. With our unique business model, we see customers buy $20 worth of coffee, and then tack on a $50 direct donation"
>
> **Scott James, Pura Vida Coffee**

CRS works overseas to help low-income coffee farmers enter the Fair Trade market, a clear and just alternative to the conventional coffee trade. When CRS began working intensively with coffee farmers in Nicaragua in 2003, some of them earned only nineteen cents per pound for their coffee. That works out to less than one penny per cup of coffee. Fair Trade guarantees the farmers a fair price for their coffee, no less than $1.26 per pound. This extra money helps them cover their costs of production and gives them more money to provide their families with a

decent standard of living. But just as important as a fair price is the commitment that Fair Trade companies make to the farmers who grow their coffee. These companies build direct, long-term relationships with their coffee-farmer partners rooted in mutual respect and understanding.

Fourteen Fair Trade coffee companies in the United States participate in the CRS Fair Trade Coffee Program and contribute a percentage of their coffee sales to CRS to support its work with low-income farmers overseas.

One of these companies is Pura Vida Coffee, based in Seattle, Washington. Pura Vida has sold Fair Trade coffee exclusively ever since a passionate employee pointed out that the company's mission to eradicate poverty in coffee-growing countries by providing hope to at-risk children really needed to start at the beginning of the "coffee cycle," with the coffee farmers. The company uses coffee from eleven countries around the world including some grown by CRS-supported coffee farmers in Guatemala and Nicaragua. Pura Vida Coffee is one hundred percent charitably-owned, and all of its resources go to help at-risk children in coffee-growing countries from Central America to Africa.

Yet the CRS Fair Trade Program involves much more than coffee. CRS has promoted Fair Trade handcrafts since 1995 through its Work of Human Hands Program, a partnership with another non-profit called A Greater Gift. CRS also introduced a Fair Trade Chocolate Program in 2005 featuring Divine Chocolate, whose chocolate is made exclusively with 100 percent Fair Trade cocoa from a single cooperative in Ghana.

Holy Family Parish in Newark, Delaware, serves Fair Trade coffee at all parish meetings and sells it and offers taste tests at monthly parish coffee socials. Parish youth group members sell Fair Trade coffee and handcrafts from the Work of Human Hands Program at diocesan middle and high school rallies. The parish also sells handcrafts for the Work of Human Hands program each year during the holiday season. By doing so they offer high-quality, one-of-a-kind handcrafts and the people who created them get hope for a better future for themselves and their families.

CRS is the official relief and development agency of the Catholic community in the United States.

Visit www.harcourtreligion.com to learn more about CRS and for a link to its site.

Prayer

Begin by praying the Sign of the Cross.

Leader: God of justice and compassion, help us know you and know our sisters and brothers with your mind and heart. May we remain attentive to these words of Saint Teresa of Ávila:

Reader 1: Christ has no body now but yours; no hands, no feet on earth but yours.

Reader 2: Yours are the eyes through which he looks with compassion on this world; yours are the feet with which he walks to do good; yours are the hands with which he blesses all the world.

Reader 3: Christ has no body now on earth but yours.

All Amen.

End by praying the Sign of the Cross.

›Review

1. Name five topics related to justice that have been addressed in documents from the Vatican.

2. Name five topics of Catholic social teaching that have been addressed in statements by the U.S. bishops.

3. Name the seven major themes of Catholic social teaching.

4. Which theme is the foundation for all other principles or themes?

5. What happens as a result of failure to practice justice and charity in handling the earth's goods?

6. List three rights of workers. Why does Pope John Paul II give priority to work over capital?

7. What is solidarity? Why is it important?

8. What role do humans have in relation to the rest of nature?

9. What are social institutions? According to the U.S. Catholic bishops, upon what basis should a society's institutions be evaluated?

10. Define consumerism.

11. What three dangers does the text identify with consumerism?

12. Define the term throwaway society and give an example.

13. Describe an action and an attitude associated with simple living.

14. Define fatalism.

15. What does it mean to say that hope is a virtue?

›Key Words

Basic rights (p. 67) Rights that all people possess because of their very nature as humans; inalienable rights.

Consumerism (p. 83) The distorted desire to possess things out of proportion to our needs or normal wants.

Crisis of limits (p. 83) The finite and irreplaceable nature of essential resources, such as oil and rainforests.

Fatalism (p. 88) The belief that the world is out of the control of humans and in the hands of blind fate.

Dignity (p. 70) The respect owed to all humans because they are made in God's image.

Hope (p. 88) The theological virtue by which we desire and expect from God eternal life and the grace necessary to attain it. Hope envisions a better world and affirms that, with God's help, a better world is possible.

Individualism (p. 80) A way of being and acting that emphasizes personal independence and the rights of individuals over interdependence and concern for the common good.

Interdependent (p. 81) Reliance on one another for survival and well being.

magisterium (p. 66) The living, teaching office of the Church by which it gives authentic interpretation of the world of God. (CCC Glossary)

Simple living (p. 86) A way of life in which a person buys and uses only what is needed, out of respect for people and resources.

Solidarity (p. 75) A spirit of unity and mutual concern; the quality of justice that breaks down barriers between people.

Throwaway society (p. 86) A social group in which it is acceptable to squander usable materials and products.

A commitment to justice is at the heart of what it means to be Catholic. The Church's social teaching provides us with principles that help us figure out what the Gospel demands of us in response to the challenges that face us today. This social teaching can guide us as we dedicate ourselves to making the world a more just place. This chapter introduced the principle themes of Catholic Social Teaching and explored some of the characteristics of contemporary culture. As we move along in this course, we will examine in greater detail what justice involves. The themes described in this chapter will shed light on the difficult issues that our world faces. Always looking to Christ, we will discover that working for justice and peace is challenging but always hopeful. Through the power of the Holy Spirit, justice will prevail.

GUIDELINES FOR CHARITY

CHAPTER 4

DOING JUSTICE, LIVING JUSTLY

CHAPTER GOALS

In this chapter you will:

★ examine the relationship between charity and justice.

★ discover mercy and social action as ways of addressing problems in today's world.

★ analyze the effects that social structures have on society in promoting or hindering justice.

★ learn how compassion is the attitude that mirrors Jesus in working for charity and justice.

Charity and Justice

what's your opinion?

1. Name three ways that people are hurting in our world today.

2. What causes these hurts? Divide the causes into those related to individual decisions and those that exist because of the way society and its institutions are structured.

3. List three organizations that are involved in trying to help people who are hurting in some way. Describe the work the organizations do. Is their work geared more to directly helping people in need (direct aid) or to changing social structures so that they better serve people in need?

4. Give three examples that illustrate the relationship between justice and charity.

FAITH ACTIVITY

What Can I Do? Reflect on a situation in which people are hurting. Identify one type of charitable activity that you would find meaningful. Identify one social change that you would be willing to work for. Describe one response that you could realistically make. Compare your answers with the class.

The theological virtues of faith, hope, and charity inform all moral virtues. Without charity, the greatest of these, justice is soulless and dead. In other words, justice requires that we give to God and our neighbor what is their due, the most important, first thing being love. Charity, also called love, moves us to imitate Christ in our response to the Father and to one another. Charity gives life to and prompts all the virtues, including justice.

There are many ways to illustrate how charity gives life and force to justice. Some of the most important ways that we give God the love, time, and focus he deserves is by following the first three commandments. When we honor him above all else, put our faith and trust in him, and try to live by his will for us, it follows that we won't make things or people "idols" that take our focus away from God. We learned in the previous chapter that preoccupation with things or people is a source of unjust attitudes and leads to unjust action and structures. By taking part in the Sunday celebration of the Eucharist, we make God a priority in our lives. We worship the Father for all the gifts he has given us, most especially his Son, and call on the Holy Spirit to open our hearts as we listen to God's word and receive the Body and Blood of Christ. The Gospel proclaimed at Mass calls us to consider the reign of God in our lives and in the world. So while we are giving God what is rightly his, we are reminded and strengthened to give others what is rightly theirs.

By following the first three commandments in our lives, we are honoring the first part of the Great Commandment to love God with all our hearts, souls, minds, and bodies. And, we are given the grace to follow the fourth through seventh commandments and thus the second part of the Great Commandment to love our neighbors as ourselves. Catholic action on behalf of social justice is rooted in those commandments, especially the fifth and seventh commandments. So love gives life and meaning to the virtue of justice.

For instance, we may hear about a program that provides food, clothing, and shelter for people who lack these basic necessities. We could conclude that in justice people have a right to have these services provided. However, what would lead us to get involved and take action on their behalf? Charity elicits a response on our part, since by loving one another we imitate the love Christ showed toward us. Justice without charity is a burden; charitable justice is participating in God's work. "The practice of the moral life animated by charity gives to the Christian the spiritual freedom of the children of God". Saint Paul goes so far as to say that without charity we are nothing.

If I speak in the tongues of mortals and of angels, but do not have love, I am a noisy gong or a clanging cymbal. And if I have prophetic powers, and understand all mysteries and all knowledge, and if I have all faith, so as to remove mountains, but do not have love, I am nothing. If I give away all my possessions, and if I hand over my body so that I may boast, but do not have love, I gain nothing.

✞ 1 Corinthians 13:1-3

Two Ways to Help—A Fable

Once upon a time, there was a small village on the edge of a river. The people there were good, and life in the village was good. Then one day a villager noticed a baby floating down the river. The villager quickly jumped into the water and swam out to save the baby from drowning.

The next day this same villager was walking along the riverbank and noticed two babies in the river. He called for help, and both babies were rescued from the currents. The following day, four babies were seen caught in the turbulent waters. And then eight, then more, and still more.

The villagers organized themselves quickly, setting up watchtowers and training teams of swimmers who could resist the swift waters and rescue babies. Rescue squads were soon working twenty-four hours a day. But each day the number of babies floating down the river increased.

The villagers organized themselves efficiently. The rescue squads were now snatching many children each day out of the water. Groups were trained to give mouth-to-mouth resuscitation. Others prepared formula and provided clothing for the chilled babies. Many people were involved in making clothing and knitting blankets. Still others provided foster homes and placement.

While not all the babies could be saved, the villagers felt that they were doing well to save as many as they could. Indeed, their priest blessed them in their good work. And life in the village continued on this basis.

One day, however, one villager raised the question, "But where are all these babies coming from? How are they ending up in the river? Why? Let's organize a team to go upstream and discover the source of the problem." The seeming logic of the elders countered: "And if we go upstream, who will operate the rescue operations? We need every concerned person here."

"But don't you see," cried the one lone voice, "if we find out why they are in the river in the first place, then we might be able to stop the problem and no babies will drown. By going upstream, we could eliminate the cause of the problem."

"Our job is saving babies," decided the elders, "not expeditions upstream. We must continue our good work."

And so the number of babies in the river increases daily. Those saved increase, but those who drown increase even more.

Adapted from Inter-Religious Task Force
for Social Analysis, *Must We Choose Sides?*

GROUP TALK

Identify ways that this story could be applied to contemporary problems.

1. Are organizations that are addressing problems in society today doing so more in the style of the village elders or in that of the lone voice? Explain.

2. What circumstances would make one or the other approach more effective?

3. The fable implies that people often overlook "going upstream" to find root causes of problems. Do you believe that this is true in your community and in the world today?

In the first half of this chapter, we will look at two ways we can apply charity to the work of justice. In the second half, we will explore how we can manifest charity in our personal lives.

Direct Aid

A starting point for doing justice is asking the question: How are people hurting? The answer to that question varies. Likewise, the way we help people can vary. The introductory story uses a shocking image—drowning babies—to make a case for expanding our vision of how we normally view people's problems.

No one escapes pain and suffering. Some hurts are related to **personal causes**. Other pain is brought about by **underlying causes**. Catholic tradition is filled with stories demonstrating two approaches to easing people's suffering: works of mercy to meet the immediate physical and spiritual needs of others, and social action to change society's structures where needed. Understanding each approach gives us a better sense of how we can help people who are hurting in our own communities, in our nation, and around the world.

Works of Mercy When we see people hurting, our hearts cry out to help. The starving child holding the empty bowl begs to be fed, to be cared about. The sudden illness of a classmate motivates us to visit or to show some other sign of care. When a natural catastrophe strikes a neighboring community, we pool our resources to help. By doing charitable actions directly to help people in need, we are performing **works of mercy**. Mercy is charity on a person-to-person level—caring for others, sharing their hurts, taking care of their needs as best we can.

Such works have been espoused by Jesus and his Church since the beginning. ". . . and whoever gives even a cup of cold water to one of these little ones in the name of a disciple—truly I tell you, none of these will lose their reward" (*Matthew 10:42*). Jesus sent the disciples out to proclaim the kingdom of God and to heal. (See *Luke 9:2*.) Jesus actually identified what became the Works of Mercy when he told the story of the Judgment of Nations to describe his Second Coming and the Last Judgment of the living and the dead (See *Matthew 25:31–46*). We briefly discussed this in the previous chapter's treatment on the Option for the Poor and Vulnerable. In his story, Jesus equates himself with the least of those in society, telling us that when we help those in need, we help him. "Truly I tell you, just as you did not do it to one of the least of these, you did not do it to me" (*Matthew 25:45*). He teaches us that we will all be held accountable for our actions, or lack of action, in this life, and this will impact on our eternal life with him, the Father, and his Spirit. This is because God's reign is here, if only partially, and it is the same reign that will come at the end of time.

Works of Mercy
Corporal Works
Feed the hungry.
Give drink to the thirsty.
Clothe the naked.
Visit the sick.
Shelter the homeless.
Visit the imprisoned.
Bury the dead.
Spiritual Works
Counsel the doubtful.
Instruct the ignorant
Admonish the sinner.
Comfort the sorrowful.
Forgive injuries.
Bear wrongs patiently.
Pray for the living and the dead.

As God's children, we cannot separate who we are now with who we will be in the future: we are always God's children called to live in union with him.

Caring for widows and orphans, sharing bread with those incapable of meeting their own needs, and other acts of mercy set the early Christian communities apart from their neighbors. Today, through organizations such as hospitals and Catholic Charities, and through the acts of individuals, the Church continues to relieve suffering and to help people in need. Catholic schools, too, are charitable institutions, aimed at helping young people in need of education and formation in their faith.

> "Hence, those who are oppressed by poverty are the object of a *preferential love* on the part of the Church which . . . has not ceased to work for their relief, defense, and liberation through numerous works of charity which remain indispensable always and everywhere"
>
> **(Congregation for the Doctrine of the Faith, instruction,** *Libertatis conscientia*, **68).**
>
> *CCC*, 2448

Often Christians do works of mercy only after their eyes have been opened to the needs of others. A young woman from Farmington Hills, Michigan, whose sports career is interrupted by an accident, fills her time by getting involved in school service projects. A boy from suburban Philadelphia begins tutoring children at an inner-city center because his high school requires service hours. When his requirement is completed, he still continues to help out. Sometimes, involvement in service accompanies preparation for the Sacrament of Confirmation. At Thanksgiving or Christmas time, school clubs or organizations often run drives aimed at feeding hungry people or giving financial support to people who are poor. Whatever the motivation or circumstance, it is hard not to associate works of mercy with being Christian.

GROUP TALK

Have you ever participated in a service project that involved a work of mercy?

1 Describe the experience. How did it feel?

2 What motivated you to participate in this work?

3 Did you feel as though you were helping another person or group?

Religious Life and Social Action

The religious lives of monks and nuns can be traced to the fourth century. Most early monastic communities focused on contemplative prayer and work for the redemption of the world. In the early fifth century, Saint Patrick, patron saint of Ireland, was the first to emphasize evangelization in the monastic lifestyle. It is this mindset that has inspired countless people to reach out to others in need of spiritual and physical aid. Blessed Mother Teresa of Calcutta is a recent—and visible—example who was spiritually fed through prayer and the Eucharist to work tirelessly to establish social justice among the poorest of the poor in Calcutta and worldwide.

Mother Teresa: A Model of Mercy

Mother Teresa of Calcutta (1910-1997) won the Nobel Peace Prize in 1979. Her careworn face framed by a simple Indian veil became a universal symbol of mercy. In India, she was known simply as "Mother." Her speeches were so often punctuated with the word *love* that she would have sounded naively sentimental if her actions had not proclaimed love so strongly. Whether working among starving and homeless people in Calcutta, garbage pickers in Mexico City, oppressed aborigines in Australia, or lepers in Africa, Mother Teresa's followers embody mercy in its clearest form.

Appropriately, Mother Teresa's order of sisters is called the *Missionaries of Charity*. Works of mercy perfect the Christian virtue of charity. Missionaries of Charity take a vow of "wholehearted, free service to the poorest of the poor." They take Jesus at his word when he said, "Truly I tell you, just as you did it to one of the least of these who are members of my family, you did it to me" (*Matthew 25:40*). Mother Teresa saw the face of Christ in the face of every poor person she met. The work of her order bears witness to the dignity and worth of every human person.

Mother Teresa cared little about political action and changing social structures. She cared about people—helping those who are poor and encouraging others to love in whatever capacity they are capable. She drew upon her intense love of the Blessed Sacrament and her deep prayer as sources for her self-giving. She viewed her calling as working among the numberless people who fall between the cracks of social structures.

Through her untiring work of mercy, Mother Teresa symbolized the spirit of compassion that must characterize all Christian service. If questioned about how to help those in need, she would simply say: "What you can do, I can't do, and what I can do, you can't do, but together we can do something beautiful for God."

"What we need is to love without getting tired. How does a lamp burn? Through the continuous input of small drops of oil. What are these drops of oil in our lamps? They are the small things of daily life: faithfulness, small words of kindness, a thought for others, our way of being silent, of looking, of speaking, and of acting. Do not look for Jesus away from yourselves. He is not out there; He is in you. Keep your lamp burning, and you will recognize Him."

Mother Teresa, *No Greater Love* (Novato, CA: New World Library, 2001), p. 22

In 2003 Mother Teresa was named *Blessed;* the Church recognizes her holiness and holds her up as a model for all those who call themselves Christian.

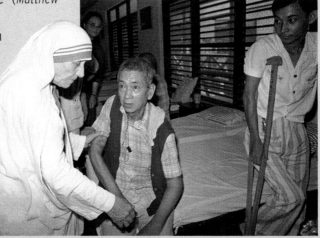

▲ *Nobel Peace Prize Winner Mother Teresa of Calcutta comforts a patient at a Home for the Destitute.*

GROUP TALK

Mother Teresa's Missionaries of Charity have grown in great numbers worldwide since their humble beginnings a few decades ago.

1 Describe the type of work her religious order performs.

2 How do you account for the appeal of her order?

3 Why do you think members of her order seem so joy-filled?

Changing Social Structures

The story about the townspeople helping the drowning victims demonstrates mercy in action, and it also raises important questions about other ways of helping people who are hurting. In addition to showing mercy to individuals in need of help, are there other things we can do? Would it be helpful to identify underlying causes to immediate problems and seek **long-term solutions** to them? Are certain people hurting because of attitudes, values, and structures deeply embedded within a particular society? Babies are relatively powerless, but what about other people who are hurting? Is it possible to engage them actively in their own care and cure?

Social Action

As the *Two Ways to Help* fable suggests, seeking to alleviate *causes* of a problem is an appropriate way to help people who are hurting. In this approach to justice, social structures are examined for possible changes to those structures. In the fable, if the villagers had investigated the situation upstream, they might have discovered that the babies were victims of injustice. Perhaps food shortages in another village led to this drastic measure, or discrimination against an oppressed group resulted in their babies being disposed of so heartlessly. Perhaps extreme overpopulation instigated a bizarre social policy of disposing of all infants. Identifying the causes of the problem would lead to dealing with social structures, societal values, and perhaps government policies.

Examining underlying causes and social structures, along with seeking long-term solutions and shared involvement of people, is a **social action** approach to justice. Like works of mercy, social action is a work of justice and an expression of charity. Although it tends to be more indirect in helping people, social action is just as concerned with meeting people's needs as works of mercy are. It also recognizes that providing only immediate relief for people who are mired in long-term problems does not address the real causes of their suffering. Also, when people are always on the receiving end of a relationship, they can develop a diminished sense of personal dignity. As a result, they might feel powerless to help themselves. By addressing the impact of social structures on people's suffering, long-term solutions to problems might be uncovered.

> Respect for the human person proceeds by way of respect for the principle that "everyone should look upon his neighbor (without any exception) as 'another self,' above all bearing in mind his life and the means necessary for living it with dignity" (Gaudium et spes 27 § 1).

CCC, 1931

GROUP TALK

1 Do you believe that performing works of mercy leads to social action? Explain.

2 Describe one way in which social action could improve conditions in your school or community.

What Are Social Structures? Peter Maurin, co-founder of the Catholic Worker Movement, once said, "society should be so structured that it is easy for people to be good." Social structures are commonly accepted ways of doing things that characterize social relationships. The structures of a society reflect written and unwritten rules. They include customs, such as a father dancing with his daughter at her wedding. They also include laws and social policies, such as a father being financially responsible for his children, whether or not he is married to their mother. A social structure can be as simple as telephone etiquette or as complex as a nation's educational system or its method of providing health care.

The structures present in society can promote justice or hinder justice. Society promotes justice when it provides the conditions in which everyone can obtain what he or she is due.

Here's an example to illustrate the importance of social structures in terms of meeting or failing to meet people's needs: Requiring a wheelchair for transportation creates special problems. Yes, if we don't need a wheelchair ourselves, we might offer to help those who do by shopping for them or transporting them places. But what happens when we can't be with them? What about those who require wheelchairs and have no one to assist them?

What changes could occur in a society that would help all people who use wheelchairs? With this question, we address the issue of social structures. For instance, many communities build sidewalks with ramps at intersections so that people in wheelchairs can better travel by themselves. Special parking places and ramps to public buildings also help those in wheelchairs become more self-reliant. Such societal changes can do as much as many hours of volunteer help. These changes also free people to have access to those things they need to be fully human. Attending to social structures is an essential part of respecting the God-given dignity of all people.

Social structures are created and affected by decisions people make. However, these structures can take on a life of their own. We can even come to believe that "the way things are now" is the only way a society can be organized, even though people may be hurting unnecessarily under the current organization.

A former director of Catholic Charities for the United States points out that there can be either graced social structures or sinful social structures. **Graced social structures** are "those which promote life, enhance human dignity, encourage the development of community, and reinforce caring behavior." **Sinful social structures** "destroy life, violate human dignity, facilitate selfishness and greed, perpetuate inequality, and fragment the human community" (Fred Kammer SJ. *Doing Faith Justice*. Mahwah, NJ. Paulist Press, 1991), 174). It's important to keep in mind that Father Kammer is not denouncing social structures themselves. Rather, he is reminding us that we may be living under "structures of sin," which we should not accept. The Catechism calls socially-constructed situations and institutions contrary to God's plan for human well-being **social sin**.

For instance, a country's economic system can function more or less competitively and more or less directed toward the common good. The way we conduct business and deal with money matters is not carved in stone, and it can be more sinful or more an expression of grace.

FAITH ACTIVITY

Who Benefits? Some examples of social structures include healthcare systems, the criminal justice system, systems of education, your family, and government systems. Choose one and answer the following questions: What is its primary goal? Who benefits from the way this system is structured? Do some groups benefit more that others? Would you recommend any changes in this social structure? If yes, what changes?

Taxation is one expression of a social structure. Taxes can be structured in ways that either promote care for those with fewer resources or benefit those with greater wealth. While no politician would claim to advocate a tax plan that harms any group within society, justice and charity ask us to examine how it affects those with the greatest need—as Jesus required of his followers: ". . . just as you did it to one of the least of these who are members of my family, you did it to me" (*Matthew 25:40*).

GROUP TALK

1. Taxes are a necessary aspect of any society. What would you say is the American attitude toward taxes?

2. If you believed strongly that an increase in taxes would benefit people at the lowest rung of the economic ladder, would you support the tax increase? Why or why not? Do you believe that you would have an obligation in justice to support such a tax increase?

3. How are people who are poor affected by the creation, sales, and advertising of goods and services in the world?

"Power Over" Versus "Power With"

People engaged in works of mercy can "give till it hurts" and even put themselves totally at the service of those in need. However, people on the receiving end of acts of mercy have little or no say in whether or not they get what they need. Some members of society, such as people with Alzheimer's disease, are in constant need of direct care. (This does not mean that they do not give in return. In a sense, their need is their gift to others.) However, for other people their need for assistance is temporary. Social action seeks to assist these people to be active participants in making decisions that affect them. In that sense, social action addresses directly the issue of power and seeks to create circumstances in which all people have **decision-making power**, as much as they can.

A person who is homeless and begging for money on a street corner seeks help from people passing by who may or may not respond favorably. The homeless person may try different approaches to get people to give money: "It's not for

Illiteracy

★ Over 855 million people in the world are illiterate, or one sixth of all people.

★ Two thirds of the illiterate are women.

★ What social structures contribute to illiteracy? What social action could be taken to aid people who are illiterate?

me; it's for my children." "My car broke down. Could you spare some change for bus fare?" Ultimately, passersby with money have the power to give or to refuse to give. A social action approach to justice seeks ways to increase the power of people who find that they have little recourse other than to beg on street corners—for instance, by instituting policies making inexpensive housing available in the neighborhood or by providing job assistance programs for unskilled or illiterate workers. A social action approach also includes trying to restore people's dignity by helping people who feel powerless to become contributing members of society.

Here is an illustration of changing the distribution of power to address a situation where people might be in need: A multinational corporation is a business that operates in more than one country. Having international operations offers a corporation increased power over its employees and over its competition. If workers in one country do not approve of the corporation's wage scale, then the business can threaten to move its plant to a country where workers will settle for lower wages. The corporation's workers, therefore, are rendered essentially powerless, lacking control over wage scales and working conditions while living under the threat of unemployment.

Steps could be taken to increase the power of employees of such a corporation. For one thing, workers might organize on an international level, in which case the workers of different countries would not be in competition with one another. Obviously, in this era of global economy such a movement is proving to be extremely difficult. Second, workers might gain some say in the actual running of the corporation. Or workers might organize to seek passage of laws that would forbid the import of goods from companies that fail to meet certain standards.

Equal Access Choose an aspect of an institution of society (such as education, housing, business opportunities, or health care). Apply the following questions to that institution. Who has greater or lesser access to the benefits of this institution? What "fences" (real or symbolic obstacles) need to be torn down in order to make benefits of the institution equally available to all? Report your findings to the class.

Since social action aims to change the relationship between "haves" and "have-nots," it can be threatening to people who possess greater power in a society. Social action doesn't simply advocate the maxim, "Give people a fish, you feed them for a day. Teach people to fish, you feed them for a lifetime." Social action includes an additional step. It asks, "Who has access to the pond where there are fish? Who claims ownership of the pond? Is it necessary to know the right people to have access to the best fishing spots? Can we tear down the fence that allows only a select few to fish and prevents others from fishing?" Questions such as these suggest that changes in power arrangements may be called for if justice is to be achieved. Ideally, positive social change is a "win-win" situation in which everyone is better off. However, even positive social changes can appear to be a "win-lose" experience to people who feel their own power or privilege threatened by proposed changes.

A Model of Social Action

What immediately comes to mind when you think of Montgomery, Alabama? Chances are that in grade school you learned about the Montgomery bus boycott begun by the late Rosa Parks near the end of the era of the segregated South. This African American woman refused to give her seat on the bus to white passengers, sparking a protest that transformed the United States. It is interesting and appropriate that almost one hundred years before it became the site of the beginnings of the civil rights movement, Montgomery served as capital of the Confederacy.

In the mid-1950s, across the square from the Confederate government building, sat Dexter Avenue Baptist Church, whose pastor first gained fame by leading a boycott of the segregated public bus system. In 1964, that same pastor, Dr. Martin Luther King Jr., received the Nobel Peace Prize for his work benefiting African Americans and people of the United States who were poor.

▶ *Rosa Parks smiling at a medal ceremony on Capitol Hill.*

Were Rosa Parks and other black women and men who rode the buses hurting? When asked why she didn't get out of her seat on this particular day, Mrs. Parks replied simply, "My feet hurt." But no doubt the psychological and emotional hurt of giving up a seat simply because of the color of her skin was the greater hurt. How did Dr. King set out to help ease the hurting that existed in the black community of Montgomery? Along with other African American leaders, he called for a boycott of the buses. That is, he urged local citizens to walk places rather than taking a bus. Then he realized that he had to rouse the people to remain steadfast in their boycott. In a sense, he was inviting them to greater suffering, walking to work instead of riding a bus—even the back of a bus. But the suffering he was offering people this time was their choice, a way for them to take greater control over their lives. This suffering was aimed at changing a long-standing social structure of the South—forced segregation. In the end, changing the way that society was structured would lead to better living conditions for *all* people hurting under this unjust system.

In other words, the civil rights movement, which we today associate with Dr. King, was a social action movement. Like works of mercy, its aim was to relieve suffering. And yet clearly it differs greatly from mercy in how it seeks to achieve the same goal. Dr. King didn't give gifts to the people he wanted to help; he challenged them to use their combined strength to change a social system. He realized that a true response to the message of Jesus required more than works of mercy; it required changes in unjust social structures. Together, works of mercy and social action can be called "the two feet of Christian justice."

You know, my friends, there comes a time when people get tired of being trampled over by the iron feet of oppression. There comes a time, my friends, when people get tired of being flung across the abyss of humiliation where they experience the bleakness of nagging despair. There comes a time when people get tired of being pushed out of the glittering sunlight of life's July and left standing amidst the piercing chill of an Alpine November.

Martin Luther King Jr. in Richard Lischer, *The Preacher King* (New York: Oxford University Press, 1995), p. 87

GROUP TALK

1 What was Dr. King's message in this passage?

2 What groups in our society today might be "tired" of being oppressed?

The Two Feet of Christian Justice

Here are some key differences between works of mercy and works of social action.

Works of Mercy	Works of Social Action
concern with the present symptoms of injustice	concern with the underlying *causes* of injustice
focus on individual needs	focus on changing social structures
look for immediate solutions	look for long-term solutions
provide a direct service with temporary results	provide indirect help aimed at permanent change
involve "haves" sharing with "have-nots"	involve "haves" and "have-nots" working together and sharing power
require no change in social structures	require working toward changes in social structures

The Two Feet of Christian Justice The works of mercy and the works of social action are often called *the two feet of Christian justice*; to walk in justice requires that we walk with both feet. For instance, some organizations collect funds to help children in need who live in underdeveloped countries—an act of mercy. Other organizations publicize when companies exploit poor children in their manufacture of athletic shoes, soccer balls, or other items. They use this information to mount a boycott of these companies—a social action. Both "feet" of justice seek to help children who are poor. Children who are poor, like all children, like all people, have the right to live with dignity, because that dignity is God-given and must be honored if we call ourselves Christian.

GROUP TALK

1. Describe a situation in which you or someone you know possessed power or lacked power. Was there evidence of "power with" or "power over" at work? Explain.

2. What appeals to you about Dr. Martin Luther King Jr.'s approach to lessening hurtful conditions? What "power" did he possess? How did he use it?

Compassion, Charity, and Justice

Our liberation and salvation is bound up with those in our midst who are suffering, who feel separated, who hunger for food and thirst for justice. Our liberation begins when we recognize in the routine of our lives that there are people who live in poverty and pain every day of their lives. Our liberation begins when we allow their look to seep through the cracks of our own broken hearts and move us to compassion.

Joseph Nassal, *The Conspiracy of Compassion* (Easton, KS: Forest of Peace, 1997), 82

In the story of Jesus healing two blind men, we read: "Moved with compassion, Jesus touched their eyes. Immediately they regained their sight and followed him" (*Matthew 20:34*). The words "moved with compassion" imply that he was moved "in his gut." Being moved with compassion, in the depth of our being, for people who are hurting is the starting point for getting involved in works of justice. Compassion leads to action, as it did for Jesus. Compassion for others leading to works of mercy and concern for justice represent the dual dynamics of Christian charity. All charity flows from God becoming human in Christ out of compassion and for our salvation.

Another scene in the Gospels shows Jesus overcome with sorrow when he hears that his friend Lazarus has died:

▼ **Sculpture Relief Depicting Christ Healing the Blind Man, 18th century**

When Mary came where Jesus was and saw him, she knelt at his feet and said to him, "Lord, if you had been here, my brother would not have died." When Jesus saw her weeping, and the Jews who came with her also weeping, he was greatly disturbed in spirit and deeply moved. He said, "Where have you laid him?" They said to him, "Lord, come and see." Jesus began to weep. So the Jews said, "See how he loved him!"

✝ John 11:32–36

GROUP TALK

Have you ever been "moved with compassion"?

1. What were the circumstances?

2. Did it lead to any action or to your getting involved with others? Explain.

3. Did the event relate to justice in any way? If so, how?

4. Describe the relationship between compassion and justice.

5. Explain why compassion is an important component of Christian charity.

Living with Compassion

Most of us feel compassion from time to time. We see a news story on TV or hear about a friend undergoing difficulties. But often, the feeling passes and we go about our business. We are called to live everyday with compassion—in our actions, our conversations, and our prayers. How do we live out this calling on a day-to-day basis?

Compassion and Action We are not often moved by people at a distance. More typically, we get involved in struggles to overcome injustices, and, in the midst of these struggles, we come to feel the pain of others and take it on as our own. In other words, action does not necessarily follow compassion. Instead, action and compassion go hand in hand. Works of mercy often start people off on the journey of doing justice. From there they might move to involvement in social action as well.

True charity is anything but wimpy; it breaks down barriers between people. Isn't it true that there are plenty of people from whom we would like to be separated by large barriers? Charity often pushes us beyond our usual comfort level toward involvement with people with whom we may not initially feel comfortable. The call to charity can lead us to look at people, problems, or parts of a city we might prefer not to look at. We might end up meeting with people spending time in prison, serving meals to people who haven't changed their clothes in weeks, or wiping the mouth of an incapacitated old woman. Charitable action is just, courageous, heroic action.

Read the following descriptions of various actions. Identify each of them as an example of a *work of mercy* or *social action*. Be prepared to explain your choices. If you decide that an action fulfills both functions write "both." When you have categorized this list, think of your own examples of works of mercy and social action.

Which situation below is an example of a work of mercy, and which is an example of social action? Explain the reasons for your choice.

1. Before Thanksgiving a high school student government holds a canned-food drive for families with low incomes.

2. A high school pro-life club participates in a march held on the anniversary of the U.S. Supreme Court's decision that legalized abortion.

3. A group of parents monitors TV programs for children and publishes ratings based on the amount of violence shown.

4. A group of students visits a care center for an hour a week to fulfill a requirement for their religion course.

5. A student tutors a student from another country in the English language.

6. A student writes a letter to her local newspaper protesting the building of a nuclear power plant on a nearby river.

7. An environmental organization lobbies members of Congress to pass legislation promoting clean air and water.

8. A restaurant donates its surplus food to a local soup kitchen.

9. The American Cancer Society raises funds to support research into the causes of cancer.

10. A parish group holds protest demonstrations outside a local video rental store that carries pornographic movies.

11. A parish converts its former convent into a drug rehabilitation center for teenagers.

12. A group of citizens organize into a watch program to patrol neighborhood streets at night.

Speaking with Charity   When we see injustice, the compassionate response is to let others know about it. Through our speech, we can promote justice or support injustice. Charitable speech accompanies compassionate listening. Compassion results when we listen to others and treat their stories with great reverence. To do that, we must also hold our own stories in great reverence. Our experiences of hurting, then, are not an obstacle to charity; but rather they serve as the very engine that propels us toward charitable action. In other words, in working for justice we are all "wounded healers." If we approach others with great reverence, then we will be very careful in how we speak about them.

FAITH ACTIVITY

Prayers of Compassion In small groups, in words or a work of art, compose prayers of compassion.

Compassionate Prayer Most teenagers in the United States say that they pray and that they value prayer. However, our current culture works against prayer, as we live in what is often aptly called a "rat race." Keeping busy is now a key characteristic of our lifestyle. Even when we slow down, seldom are we without the noise of TV or radio. "Taking a break" means playing solitaire on a computer.

Prayer is a different kind of living, a different way of being. Through prayer we seek to keep company with God. We respond to God's invitation to know him and learn from him, allowing God into our inmost being and ask him to help us see ourselves and our world with his eyes. In that sense, all praying is a prayer of compassion.

One aspect of prayer is acceptance of ourselves as we are. Compassionate prayer directed toward ourselves is self-affirming, not guilt-inducing—unless, of course, a healthy dose of guilt nags at us to act justly in ways we have been trying to avoid. However, compassionate prayer is not simply a pat on the back. Jesus urged his disciples to love others as they loved themselves, and he assured them of his love. He also challenged them to take steps that must have overwhelmed them. If we actually take time to settle into prayer, listening for his guidance, searching for God's will, we are likely to be surprised at what he has in store for us.

Moreover, compassionate prayer for just action is not a despairing plea for God to make things better. Rather, it asks God to fill us with the hope, strength, and courage to know compassion and to act charitably and justly. Since we need both inwardness and outwardness to experience God's presence, compassionate prayer includes both solitary, or individual, and communal forms of prayer. When we gather together in Christ's name, he is in our midst. He hears our prayer and the Holy Spirit helps us to know Christ's presence and become more the Body of Christ in the world. The perfect prayer to inspire us toward charity is the Eucharist. We need to make conscious choices to make time for prayer the weekly participation in the Mass. We need to cherish and honor those times faithfully.

Choosing to Live Charitably The term *life choices* refers to the choices we make that affect the way we live. For example, we may choose to spend a great deal of money on cars and clothes. But then, what happens when we need to buy textbooks or ponder whether or not to donate to an important cause? Our lives are influenced by the choices we make. Choosing to live charitably leads us to live in ways that are considerate of people who are poor and that keep us in touch with those who are hurting. For most Christians, charitable life choices do not mean living like the poorest of the poor, although some heroic Christians throughout history and in our present time have chosen to do so. It does mean that we question things like the materialistic style of life and individualism promoted and idealized by our culture. Are our choices selfish? Are they wise? Are they compassionate? Are they an expression of Christian charity?

GROUP TALK

Explain in your own words the following statements. Do you agree or disagree with them? Use concrete examples to illustrate your position.

1. The least compassionate response is not speaking up.
2. Our own experiences of hurting help us be charitable.
3. The way we speak about people is a matter of justice.
4. Our liberation and salvation are bound up with those in our midst who are suffering.
5. We are all "wounded healers."

Building Communities of Compassion and Charity

The film *Weapons of the Spirit* tells the little-known story of Le Chambon, a village in the south of France, whose residents sheltered refugees fleeing the Nazis. The citizens of this small town, comprised mostly of poor farmers, hid, fed, and housed five thousand Jews seeking to escape Hitler's holocaust.

The film documents how the townspeople helped those on their way to freedom from the Nazis. It contains interviews with many who were given sanctuary in Le Chambon and with villagers who opened their doors to them. "There were scattered individuals who did this sort of thing everywhere in Europe, of course," one woman said, "but this was an entire community effort . . . by people so poor they had almost nothing to share, but shared it anyway—and risked everything to do so. I never heard of that happening anywhere else."

"They risked their lives," one of the people who found refuge in Le Chambon said. "It was an unimaginable outburst of solidarity."

One of those who opened her doors to the Jewish refugees said, "It happened quite naturally. We can't understand the fuss. I helped simply because they needed help." (See Joseph Nassal, *The Conspiracy of Compassion*, pp. 106–107.)

Le Chambon was a compassionate community of people who lived out their compassion doing charity for desperately needy people, at great risk to themselves. As one villager pointed out, the action they performed seemed natural.

When people are hurting, charity seems to be the natural response—a human response and certainly a Christian one. When an entire community is built on charity, it reflects Christ's call to love one another.

However, it is important to remember that communities of compassion and charity might also be **communities of resistance**. Such communities resist movements, trends, and cultural practices and values that are harmful to people's well-being. The citizens of Le Chambon most certainly mounted a campaign of resistance to Nazism. Here again, it is important to recall that charity in the form of resistance takes courage. It demands a price of individuals and of communities. What price does a community pay for dedicating itself to charity? What price does a community pay when it refuses to make charitable responses to people in need? What price would your school community pay if it ignored the demands of charity? As you can see, charity by individuals and communities responds to hard questions.

Avoiding "Compassion Fatigue" In the late 1980s, a strange illness began striking a number of North Americans, many of them women. Symptoms varied; therefore, it was labeled a *syndrome* rather than a specific disease. A characteristic common to all sufferers was extreme fatigue, and thus *chronic fatigue syndrome* achieved its name.

We may feel drawn to getting involved in justice projects, but an initial spark of enthusiasm can easily fizzle into "compassion fatigue syndrome." Compassion fatigue refers to the combination of feelings that drains our energy and lessens our dedication, keeping us from giving ourselves to works of justice in any form. Fortunately, we have many sources of grace to strengthen us to respond to Jesus' Gospel call. First, we need to take into consideration that action prompted by compassion is one dimension of the total faith response to which we are called. When the various dimensions of our faith life are being nurtured—reflection on the life and teaching of Jesus in Scripture and Tradition though faith formation, participation in the sacraments and the life of our parish community and the wider Church, making connections between faith and every day life—then we are on the whole strengthened to live out the social dimension of the Good News.

The grace we receive through the sacraments motivates us to respond to those in need. Holy Communion strengthens the bond of love between Christ and us, and among all believers who form the Body of Christ. This increased unity makes it possible for us to act together in the world, to be Christ's witness, and his hand, feet, and voice for others. In the Sacrament of Confirmation, we are sealed with the Gift of the Holy Spirit first received at Baptism. We receive in a special way the seven gifts of the Holy Spirit—wisdom, knowledge, reverence, courage, understanding, right judgment, and wonder or awe (fear of the Lord)—and are united more closely to Christ, his Church, and her mission. We are anointed to take an active role in the Church, and these gifts prepare us to respond to the needs of others. When we fail to follow God's commands or participate in actions that take away or disregard the dignity of others and we are truly sorry, we are offered God's forgiveness in the Sacrament of Reconciliation. Examining our conscience and seriously reflecting on the ways we have and have not followed Jesus is an important part of conversion and preparation for the Sacrament of Reconciliation. When we evaluate our life and seek forgiveness for the times we have fallen short, we receive God's grace to make better choices for what is good and right. Having our relationship with God healed gives us new life and hope, and prompts us to follow Jesus, who himself was moved to compassion.

The ART of Catholic Social Teaching

The ART material was drawn from Leader's Guide to Sharing Catholic Social Teaching (USCC, 1998), pp. 13, 14, and 36

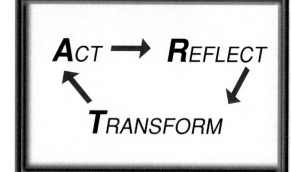

How do we decide what actions to take in the face of injustice? The situations we face in our communities and beyond can be very complex, leaving us unsure how best to respond. Here's a three-step framework that can help with this decision making:

1. ACT—Do something that helps to alleviate an immediate need. Give food to someone who is hungry. Shelter someone who is homeless. Visit a person who is sick. Help with the resettlement of a refugee family. Recycle your garbage. Collect Christmas gifts for children living in poverty. Make a monetary donation. Collect medical supplies to send to war-torn areas. Initiate a special collection of canned goods, clothing, or other supplies at Sunday Mass, and have the youth group deliver the materials. Work with members of your class to plan a school day of prayer to raise awareness of a specific group in need.

These actions of direct service bring us face to face with people in need. They help us begin to understand the nature of the problems faced by far too many people.

These actions also can lead to frustration. We realize, for example, that in giving food to the hungry we have only temporarily met a need. We strive to do more than solve the problem one meal at a time. This leads us to the next step—reflection.

2. REFLECT—Explore the underlying causes of injustice. Ask questions. Why are people hungry and homeless? Why is the environment in crisis? Why do we have discrimination? Who benefits from the current situation? Who will lose if the problem is solved? What are the reasons behind unfair labor practices?

Gather information from the social sciences and listen to the victims of injustice themselves for insights into the situation. Look to Scripture and Catholic Social Teaching to find out what the Church says about the social issues and their causes. Listen attentively to the proclamation of the Word at Sunday Mass and see what God might be saying to you about the issue. Pray about the underlying causes, being open to the silence of your heart. This reflection prepares us for the third step, transformation.

3. TRANSFORM—Take action aimed at changing or transforming the social structures responsible for bringing about suffering and injustice. This work involves actions that aim to eliminate the causes of injustice, actions that go beyond meeting immediate needs. Here are some examples: advocate for changes in law and public policy, live simply, boycott companies that exploit workers, invest in businesses that are socially responsible, and promote the building of low-income housing.

FAITH ACTIVITY

ART Process Select an unjust situation affecting people in your local community. As a class, make a list of things that can be done at each step of the ART process.

GROUP TALK

1 What do you do to counteract the rat-race pace of modern society?

2 What people or groups do you like to keep at a distance? Why?

3 How do you think citizens of Le Chambon felt after World War II about the choice they had made to help so many Jews?

›Faith in Action

Youth Ministries for Peace and Justice

Sponsored by: **The Catholic Campaign for Human Development**

When a Catholic church in the South Bronx, New York, was torched in 1992 in response to an anti-drug rally organized by a parish community action group, the neighborhood responded by creating a youth center which would be open to all young people in the area.

> " We are the people . . . reclaiming our community piece by piece as our original village . . . I am the change I want to see in the world . . . I love my land and will not part with it."
>
> Anthony Thomas

Youth Ministries for Peace and Justice (YMPJ), established in 1994 as a faith-based Catholic ministry, pursues peace and justice through community organizing and development. Young people are taught how to look at their surroundings with a critical eye and how to organize campaigns to improve what they don't like.

The RIVER Team, a YMPJ project funded by the Catholic Campaign for Human Development (CCHD), is reclaiming the area around the Bronx River which runs through the Bronx River/Soundview Community. Prior to the Team's involvement, the three miles of river had not seen restoration since 1924. Hazardous waste, illegal dumping, and sewage outfalls jeopardized not only the health and land, but the morale of the residents.

Team members, after two years of research, started working alongside adult-led local and state groups to formalize a six-point campaign called Project R.O.W. (Reclaiming Our Waterfront).

In 2005, after helping to raise millions of dollars, the Team broke ground for a neighborhood park on the site

of the abandoned, ten-acre Edgewater Road Cement Plant. City officials had 10,000 dumped tires removed and are working to clean up contaminants from the site. The park is set to open in 2007.

So far, $33 million of public funds have been set aside to launch the East Coast Greenway along the riverfront. This would link communities along the river. The Team envisions a youth hostel and young adult residence along the greenway. The Team is also campaigning the state to decommission the under-utilized Sheridan Expressway. They are working with community residents and groups to develop a plan for usage of the twenty-eight-acre parcel of land for affordable housing, parks, and small businesses.

Restoration of the river is an ongoing project, including river festivals, canoe trips and tours for residents, salt marsh restoration, and cleanup. Monthly monitoring for water quality provides data for local and state environmental agencies.

The Team was successful in helping to raise $6 million to improve the abandoned sixty-year-old Starlight Park. When the team learned that it is the site of a buried manufactured gas plant, they began a campaign to ensure that Con Edison does a full cleanup of the location. Once completed, the park will have new ball fields and a river house to store canoes.

As the waterfront improves and the community around it becomes a more appealing place to live, the Team is addressing the possible displacement of local residents due to higher property taxes.

How do they do all this? They pressure elected officials and government agencies to do what is needed for environmental justice through letter writing campaigns, protests, and presentations at public hearings. As one participant put it, they get to the root cause and don't just "put a Band-Aid over it."

For thirty-five years CCHD has been building solidarity and offering a preferential option for and with the poor. CCHD does this by funding organizations that help poor and low income people help themselves. CCHD believes that the best way to end poverty is to involve the poor in creating long-term solutions.

GO ONLINE Visit www.harcourtreligion.com to learn more about the Catholic Campaign for Human Development and Youth Ministries for Peace and Justice and for links to their sites.

Silently reflect on the words of Saint Ignatius.

Lord Jesus, teach me to be generous;
teach me to serve you as you deserve,
to give and not to count the cost,
to fight and not to heed the wounds,
to toil and not to seek for rest,
to labor and not to seek reward,
except that of knowing that I do your will. Amen

Saint Ignatius of Loyola

Review

1. What is the relationship between charity and justice?

2. What are the two ways of helping people in need described in the text?

3. List the Corporal and Spiritual Works of Mercy.

4. Define *social structures*.

5. What are the two categories of social structures?.

6. Define *social sin*.

7. How does social action go beyond giving people aid and teaching people skills?

8. List the "two feet of Christian justice" and explain how they differ.

9. What does the Gospel term for compassion literally mean?

10. Why is charitable action challenging?

11. To what does choosing to live charitably lead?

12. What are the two forms of compassionate prayer named in the text?

13. Give an example of how life choices affect the way we live.

14. What does it mean to say that communities of compassion and charity must also be communities of resistance?

15. To what experience does the term compassion fatigue syndrome refer? How can this be countered?

Key Words

communities of resistance (p. 115) Groups that take a unified stand against an area of injustice.

decision-making power (p. 104) Ability to make choices regarding an institution or one's life.

graced social structures (p. 103) Structures of society that encourage and strengthen life, dignity, and the development of community.

life choices (p. 113) Decisions about living made by an individual or group.

long-term solutions (p. 101) Changes that provide ongoing resolutions to problems.

personal causes (p. 98) Individual actions that lead to problems.

sinful social structures (p. 103) Structures of society that discourage and weaken life, dignity, and the development of community.

social action (p. 102) Steps taken to change society's structures.

social sin (p. 103) A term referring to sinful social structures resulting from the effects of personal sin and leading to social conditions and institutions that do not embody God's goodness; "structures of sin" (John Paul II, Reconciliatio et paenitentia 16). (CCC 1869.)

underlying causes (p. 98) Ways society is structured that affect people.

works of mercy (p. 98) Charitable actions aimed at meeting the physical and spiritual needs of others.

❯Our Challenge

When people are hurting and unable to fully live out their God-given dignity, change is necessary. Change might be immediate, one-to-one, and short-term—a work of mercy. Or change might be long-term—social action directed toward identifying deep-seated causes of problems and aimed at changing social structures. Whichever path we choose to become involved in, when we are guided by the Spirit and our passion for life blends with compassion for others, we are living the great Christian virtue of charity.

A CONSISTENT ETHIC OF LIFE

CHAPTER 5

JUSTICE ACROSS THE LIFE CYCLE

CHAPTER GOALS

In this chapter you will:

★ learn that human life is sacred, and must be protected from the moment of conception to natural death, and that the Church has a special responsibility to protect life.

★ discover how ageism influences what growing old is like for most people and how the Church's teaching on the value of life calls us to respond.

★ come to understand the innate value and worth of persons with disabilities and the challenges they face.

★ explore the relationship between social justice and criminal justice as a particular life issue in the United States.

A Seamless Garment

what's your opinion?

Answer **agree, disagree, or uncertain** to the following statements. Explain your answers.

1. The dominant values in our society inspire us to protect and cherish life in all of its stages.

2. I have a clear sense of Church teaching regarding abortion and concern for the unborn.

3. Dignity is not based on being productive, but on being human.

4. If I were older and in good health, I would live in a community exclusively for older people.

5. Our society has taken adequate steps to provide for persons with disabilities.

6. If I were a person with a disability, I would feel welcomed in my school.

7. The threat of prison helps prevent crimes.

8. Generally speaking, the criminal justice system in the United States is fair and treats everyone equally.

In our society one group stands out as being particularly defenseless—children taking shape in their mothers' wombs, making their way toward birth. The Church, Church-related organizations, and many individual Catholics have been leaders in trying to give a voice to these voiceless ones, many of whom are discarded or experimented upon as if they were a property to be dealt with as we wish. A culture of life does everything it can to protect and cherish human life in every form.

Any discussion of the justice issues surrounding the unborn needs to take place within the bigger picture of the Church's teaching on the Fifth Commandment, "You shall not kill." The basis of this law is the sacredness of all human life as a gift from God. Each and every person shares in God's image. What is sacred and holy in a person doesn't begin arbitrarily at some point when an unborn child can survive outside his or her mother's womb. The sacredness and dignity does not end when an adult is no longer a "productive" part of society. This sacredness and dignity does not skip those who are born with disabilities. Human life in its essence is a sacred gift from the point of conception to death. (*CCC*, 2319).

Obviously the Fifth Commandment forbids murder, but some people don't consider abortion or **euthanasia** murder. That's why it's so important to teach people about the dignity and worth of life at all its stages. Some Church leaders have labeled this "a consistent ethic of life," such as late Joseph Cardinal Bernardin (*CCC*, 2324).

"When the soldiers had crucified Jesus, they took his clothes and divided them into four parts, one for each soldier. They also took his tunic; now the tunic was seamless, woven in one piece from the top. So they said to one another, 'Let us not tear it, but cast lots for it to see who will get it'" (*John 19:23-24*).

In reflecting on this Gospel story, we can see that the fabric of God's creation is threatened when we tear it, gamble over pieces of it, or claim ownership of any part of it. That's the Catholic belief we have toward human life. No life should be torn, ruined, destroyed.

From the idea of the dignity of all human lives, the late Joseph Cardinal Bernardin, Archbishop of Chicago, described the Church's teaching as a "consistent ethic of life." This meant that Catholics should honor, respect, and defend all life. Bernardin taught that Catholics must be consistent, or seamless, in opposing abortion, the death penalty, war, the nuclear arms race, and anything that threatens life. Being seamless in our approach to the sacredness of human life makes the human family, and the Church, stronger.

The Value of Unborn Children

The two stories on the next page are a study in contrasts. In both cases a human person six months along in development encountered modern technology and medical science, doctors, nurses, and early separation from the life-sustaining environment of a mother's womb. One journey led to life, the other to death. How can some of the best that the modern world has to offer serve such drastically different purposes? How can one life be so cherished and receive such care and attention while the other is discarded?

Two Fates

The baby girl was born three months prematurely in a hospital in Minneapolis. She weighed only three pounds. The doctors told her parents that she was not expected to live, but promised to do everything possible to save her life. As scores of people around the country prayed for this little girl, the most sophisticated medical technology available was employed to aid her fight for survival.

During the first six weeks of her life, which she spent enclosed in an incubator, she began to develop serious complications. Her weight began to drop. Her lungs had not had time to fully develop within the safety of her mother's womb, so she struggled with hyaline membrane disease and other pulmonary infections. Each day was a life-and-death battle.

She was kept on oxygen and monitored by machines and nurses twenty-four hours a day. Later, she was placed on a respirator and administered a powerful drug that temporarily paralyzed her entire body. At this point, one of the doctors took the father aside and told him, "You should begin to prepare your wife for the worst. We think your baby probably won't live much longer."

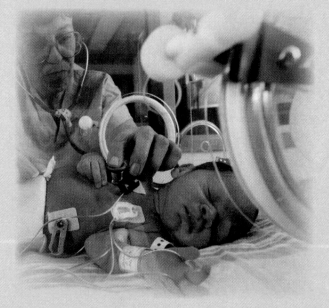

But the baby did live, and within a few more weeks the battle appeared to be won. She began to gain weight and strength, and was finally released to go home with her parents. Today, she is a completely normal, happy, healthy woman, full of life. The pediatric radiologist who cared for her has shown the X-rays of her lungs at medical conferences around the country, demonstrating to other physicians that it is indeed possible for a baby so premature and critically ill to survive.

Less than two years earlier, in a Boston hospital in late 1973, another child, a boy, snuggled in the womb of his mother, growing within her for about six months. But this little boy would never be born. He was scheduled to be aborted.

The doctor prepared to inject a saline solution into the amniotic fluid that surrounded the child. Normally this is a simple procedure. The concentrated salt solution causes the child to convulse and die within the womb, after which the mother goes into labor and expels the dead child.

After repeatedly attempting to make the injection the doctor proceeded to perform a hysterotomy, that is, he surgically opened the mother's womb through an incision in her abdomen. If the objective is a live birth, this procedure is called a cesarean section; if the objective is abortion, it is merely called a hysterotomy.

The doctor completed the incision, then waited several minutes. The child's struggles ceased.

The doctor then removed the child and placed his hand on the child's chest for only three to five seconds to check for life signs. Since the doctor clearly did not want to find any life signs (the object of this procedure, after all, is a dead child), he failed to make even a minimal effort—such as taking just one minute to listen for heartbeat and breathing with a stethoscope—to determine whether or not the baby was truly alive or dead. He then placed the child in a steel basin held by a nurse and instructed her to dispose of it.

Adapted from Dr. Ron Lee Davis with James D. Denney, *A Time for Compassion* (Old Tappan, NJ: Fleming H. Revell Company, 1986), 11-14

GROUP TALK

1 What justification might each doctor use for doing what he did?

2 What would be the Catholic response to each doctor's reply?

A Culture of Death The late Pope John Paul II observed that all of us today find ourselves in the midst of a clash of cultures—one a **culture of death** and the other a **culture of life**. His insights, presented most forcefully in his 1995 encyclical, *The Gospel of Life*, are worth pondering. They are a meditation on Church teaching regarding the unborn as expressed in the Catechism:

> From its conception, the child has the right to life. Direct abortion, that is, abortion willed as an end or as a means, is a 'criminal' practice (Gaudium et spes 27:3), gravely contrary to the moral law. The Church imposes the canonical penalty of excommunication for this crime against human life (*CCC* 2322).
>
> Because it should be treated as a person from conception, the embryo must be defended in its integrity, cared for, and healed like every other human being (*CCC* 2323).

Pope John Paul II linked dismissal of the value of unborn children with other signs of a culture of death: reliance on warfare to solve international conflicts, the use of capital punishment as a means of addressing crime and social ills, overlooking the problems of starving children in the world, and supporting euthanasia as a solution to problems associated with sickness and old age.

In a culture of death, the "values of *being* are replaced by those of *having*" (*The Gospel of Life* 23). This distortion of values represents a whole different viewpoint on both persons and things. Emphasizing *being* means treating people and things as precious in themselves. On the other hand an emphasis on *having* leads to the belief that the "only goal which counts is the pursuit of one's own material well-being" (23). No doubt, in the previous story the parents and medical staff intended to guide the prematurely born girl through to a full and wholesome life. They did not see her as a means to their own material well-being but as a person of inner beauty and worth, precious in herself.

Modern technology makes it possible to identify many characteristics of children before they are born. By contrasting attitudes of *being* versus *having*, Pope John Paul II reminded parents that their goal is not to fashion "designer children," who meet their desires, but to be caretakers of the gift of life given them.

FAITH ACTIVITY

Life and Death Bring to class an example of a culture of life and an example of a culture of death. Sources may include contemporary music, advertising, movies, or some other product. Explain your examples.

God, "Defender of the Innocent"

In old stories of life-threatening crises the cry would go up, "Women and children first!" The idea was that the most vulnerable members of society deserved special care and attention. Those who possessed the ability to protect the less powerful were to use their strength not for themselves alone but for those most in need. A scene from the movie *Titanic* has an unscrupulous man using this principle for his own selfish advantage. He grabs a baby girl from her mother's arms in order to gain a spot for himself on one of the few remaining lifeboats.

When people give of themselves to those most in need of help, they are acting in God-like fashion. Scripture reveals that God defends the innocent. He cares for human beings at every stage of existence and in every form. Pope John Paul II paraphrased Psalm 139 to describe this attitude of God toward human life:

> Human life is sacred and inviolable at every moment of existence, including the initial phase which precedes birth. All human beings, from their mother's womb, belong to God who searches them and knows them, who forms them and knits them together with his own hands, who gazes on them when they are tiny shapeless embryos and already sees in them the adults of tomorrow whose days are numbered and whose vocation is even now written in the *"book of life"* (Cf. Ps 139:1, 13-16).

The Gospel of Life, 61

Call Things by their Proper Name On this point, Pope John Paul II described how we can attempt to mask the culture of death in deliberately deceptive language. During warfare, language used to report on military operations and their casualties has often shrouded the real horrors of war. For example, a civilian hospital hit by a stray missile is referred to as "collateral damage." He noted a similar tendency toward a widespread use of deliberately unclear wording to deceive people about the true nature of abortion. For instance, abortion is referred to as an *interruption of pregnancy*, those who favor abortion refer to themselves as *pro-choice*, the unborn child is *pregnancy tissue* or the *product of pregnancy* or *an unwanted pregnancy*. Even the word *fetus* can be used as a way to imply that an aborted or unborn child is something other than a human person. To counteract the temptation of self-deception, he called for courage "to look the truth in the eye and to call things by their proper name" (*The Gospel of Life 58*).

A Contemplative Outlook Our society doesn't help us to stop and think. If anything, it favors those who are good at "multi-tasking." To counteract the culture of death and the deception that accompanies it, Pope John Paul II urged developing "a contemplative outlook." Contemplation is being attentive to life and approaching life filled with a sense of wonder. Contemplation requires slowing down, taking notice, thinking and praying. Essential to living life filled with wonder is accepting the gift of life itself. *The Gospel of Life* describes a contemplative outlook in this way:

> It is the outlook of those who see life in its deeper meaning, who grasp its utter gratuitousness, its beauty and its invitation to freedom and responsibility. It is the outlook of those who do not presume to take possession of reality but instead accept it as a gift, discovering in all things the reflection of the Creator and seeing in every person his living image (Cf. Gen 1: 27; Ps 8:5) (83).

God Has Made Us Responsible

Initially, contemplation may appear to be a passive gesture—sitting back basking in the wonder of life. However, Pope John Paul II connected contemplation with action. Specifically, if we truly see others as gift, then "we must care for the other as a person for whom God has made us responsible" (*The Gospel of Life 87*). Being responsible for one another is not an add-on to what it means to be human; we are always people-in-relationship. We are by nature caretakers of life in all its manifestations. As with our concern for other people, seeking justice for the unborn means examining values and practices on a personal as well as on a societal level. For that reason, working for justice includes being involved in political activity and helping to shape laws that reflect "Christian doctrine and life."

Social and political involvement addressing the concerns of the unborn is particularly important since they are incapable of speaking for themselves. At the same time, to transform our society into one that protects unborn children it is important to examine how our cultural priorities and attitudes support or devalue all human life. For instance, there is a connection between concern for unborn life and concern for the lives of children living in poverty, people in prison, and potential loss of life through war.

The pope's words on responsibility once again link care for unborn children with care for all those groups crying out for justice in our world.

> As disciples of Jesus, we are called to become neighbors to everyone (Cf. Lk 10: 29-37), and to show special favor to those who are poorest, most alone and most in need. In helping the hungry, the thirsty, the foreigner, the naked, the sick, the imprisoned—as well as the child in the womb and the old person who is suffering or near death—we have the opportunity to serve Jesus.

The Gospel of Life, 87

FAITH ACTIVITY

Supporting Life Find out about a local Catholic organization whose goal is combating abortion by helping pregnant women who have a limited support system. What type of work does the organization do? Report on your findings to your class.

Pope John Paul II's Prescription for a Culture of Life

One: Value being itself over having

Two: Defend the innocent

Three: Call things by their proper name

Four: Be attentive to the wonder of all life

Five: Act responsibly

Attitudes That Influence The Fifth Commandment calls us to respect and protect life. We've considered protecting the unborn. In the following sections of the chapter we will address the aged and the Church's response to euthanasia, those who have been marginalized because of disability, and the right to protect ourselves and society but still respect those who perpetuate crimes against both. In later chapters we will address the concepts of safeguarding peace, avoiding war, and just war principles. All of these life issues fall under the umbrella of the Fifth Commandment and have clear justice implications.

While some might not think of respect for self as a justice issue, it is. How we respect and care for our selves and value our own lives has a tremendous impact on how we respect and value the life and dignity of others.

Suicide Sometimes life is so difficult that people don't feel valued or respected; or they may be totally overwhelmed, feeling helpless and unsure. They may be marginalized or treated as outcasts for many different reasons. Their pain is real, and they may lose sight of the fact that their life is a gift from God. God wants us to stick with this precious gift. Suicide is never an option, and the Fifth Commandment forbids it. Taking one's own life isn't something a person has the right to do because God alone gives life.

Suicide disregards love of self, love of neighbor (for families, friends, and community are so greatly affected by the loss), and love of God (for not trusting and hoping in him and his ability to help in a time of need). As with all grave sin, a person is responsible for his actions when he or she has freely and knowingly chosen the act. Sometimes serious psychological factors can decrease a person's responsibility for taking his or her own life.

The Church reaches out to people who are in such pain that suicide seems the only option. Many dioceses and schools have suicide prevention and intervention programs, sometimes as part of their family outreach or ministry division.

GROUP TALK

1. Identify and discuss ways that modern society seems to be a culture of death. Identify and discuss ways that modern society seems to be a culture of life.

2. Give examples of how the use of language can deceive or soften what is really happening in life and death situations, especially situations related to abortion and unborn children.

3. Are there specific ways that you might practice responsibility toward unborn life? Describe the possibilities.

Valuing Life to Its End

A consistent ethic of life requires us to respect and treasure life at all its stages, not only during the "prime" of one's life. The shift from judging worth based on productivity to acknowledging worth that comes from God-given dignity isn't always an easy one. However, by taking a stand and by modeling respect for life, Catholics can help transform society from a culture of death to a culture of life. We can also make the challenges older persons face less difficult by influencing attitudes, values, and policies.

The Graying of the United States

In an earlier chapter, one of the characteristics mentioned concerning underdeveloped countries was their growing populations. That means that there are large numbers of children and a smaller percentage of older people. By contrast, in the United States, women and men over the age of sixty-five are the fastest-growing age group. One hundred years ago, the average person in the United States lived to be only forty-seven years old. Today the average is in the mid- to late seventies. Reaching the age of one hundred, although still noted with fanfare, is becoming more and more commonplace. According to best estimates, soon one in six people in the United States will be what is now considered an older person.

This graying of the country is a relatively recent event. As a result, not only are problems associated with old age growing ones, they are also comparatively new ones.

GLOBAL PERSPECTIVE

Worldwide Aging

★ About **419 million people** are 65 years of age or older worldwide.

★ About **35 million people** are 65 years of age or older in the United States.

★ What are the advantages and disadvantages of an increased number of elderly in society? Which of those is applicable to the U.S., and what are the unique effects of an aging population the U.S.?

Snapshots of Old Age

★ Betty never seemed to recover from her husband's death. With some relief, a great deal of fear, and a deep sense of despair, Betty accepted the moves from her own home to her daughter's home and now to a care center. She feels continually anxious over the most basic concerns: When will she eat? Who will help her to the bathroom? Will her medication ease her aches and pains? Since she never seems to get beyond thinking about these elementary needs, family members visit her less and less. Whether she suffers from the strokes that damaged her mind and body or simply from a broken heart, Betty is a shell of the vital, energetic person she used to be.

★ Mr. and Mrs. Boyle are preparing for a trip to Italy—their third such vacation since retirement. Both are physically healthy and mentally alert. Although a number of their friends have died in recent years, the Boyles never lack for companions or activities. Their lives are full and rich. They look forward to many active years together.

★ Helen spent three years caring for her husband as he sank further into Alzheimer's disease. Helen would bring her husband to family affairs, even though he spent most of his time asking his children and grandchildren what their names were. Helen finally agreed with her children that a managed-care facility was best for her husband, even though it would deplete the savings they had collected through years of thrifty financial management and uninterrupted work. Nonetheless, she spent most of her time by her husband's side and even helped other residents on her husband's floor of the nursing home. Helen, whose life was already marked by years of service to her children and her community, continued to serve even into her old age.

GROUP TALK

Based on experiences you have had with older people, write a description in story, essay, song, or poetry of what it might be like to be old. Consider the needs and fears of older people, as well as the joys and pleasures.

Aging Versus Ageism Biological aging refers simply to the amount of time a person lives. Biological aging brings on problems associated with health, relationships, and vulnerability. Societal aging refers to how attitudes, values, policies, and practices in a society affect people as they age. For example: How does society feel about its older members? How are they treated? Do they have a place in the society? How do older people feel about themselves? All of us will grow old, God willing, within a society. Some societies have little use for older people. Some societies promote negative and discriminatory attitudes and, therefore, unjust policies and practices regarding older people. That is **ageism**, a term first coined in 1968. Ageism parallels two concepts addressed earlier—sexism and racism. As you read through the following problems associated with old age, consider how ageism influences what growing old is like for most people.

Problems of Growing Older

America . . . is an aging nation which worships the culture, values, and appearance of youth. Instead of viewing old age as an achievement and a natural stage of life with its own merits, wisdom, and beauty, American society all too often ignores, rejects, and isolates the elderly.

Catholic Bishops of the United States, *Society and the Aged*, no. 1

Physical Health Physical problems are an important concern for older people. Being sick is frightening. Being old and sick is doubly frightening since every illness or health problem is a reminder of overall physical decline. However, it is important to remember that "being old" and "being sickly" are not the same thing. Ben Franklin helped write the Constitution of the United States while in his seventies. Ronald Reagan was elected president for the first of two terms at age sixty-nine. W.E.B. Du Bois, a civil rights leader for over half a century, continued working on his monumental *Encyclopedia Africana* into his nineties. Mother Teresa of India received the Nobel Peace Prize at age sixty-nine and remained active for many years thereafter.

The list of active, energetic contributors to world culture whom we would label as "old" could go on. We can also cite studies indicating that older workers, people in their fifties and sixties, often have better records than younger workers: less absenteeism, greater stability, a steadier rate of production, and a higher quality of work.

Mental Health Have you ever forgotten someone's name, someone whom you had been introduced to several times? Have you ever begun to tell someone a story, only to have your listener say, "You told me that yesterday"? Has someone ever asked you to do something for him or her, and it totally slipped your mind? If so, perhaps you are growing senile.

Actually, when we are younger, we can laugh off occasional forgetfulness. But for an older person, it's not funny. Forgetfulness is not occasional; for many older people, it is ever present. It can be caused by senility or the beginning stages of Alzheimer's disease. With **senility**, there is no real physical problem that can be seen. Unfortunately, senility can be used simply to support the belief that older people are incapable of being productive members of society. **Alzheimer's disease** strikes some people in their sixties or beyond—and sometimes people in their fifties. Its most noticeable symptom is extreme forgetfulness, which understandably causes irritability and the inability to make choices and follow through on actions.

If we live long enough we likely will face times of increased dependency and need. What recommendations would you give to family members of an older person who suffers from increased frailty and forgetfulness? How might they balance meeting the person's needs while maintaining her or his dignity?

It is important to remember that senility and Alzheimer's disease don't happen to all older people. It is also important to remember that intellectual decline does not have to happen with older people, nor is it a characteristic of aging. When a person has opportunities to continue learning, he or she will continue learning. The ability to learn may be as high at age eighty as it is at age twelve.

FAITH ACTIVITY

Respect for Aging Compose a prayer that could be included in a church service celebrating aging and older people.

FAITH ACTIVITY

Concerns of Older People
Research local, state, national, and Church organizations that serve older people. Find out what the organizations consider important concerns for this population. How do these concerns match up to the Church's ethic of life?

Economic Security Along with health matters, finances are a real concern for older people, even though in recent years, government programs and policies have been designed to increase their economic security. As mentioned in earlier chapters, older people are now less likely than children to be poor. Nonetheless, many older people exist on a **fixed income**. That is, they depend on Social Security and sometimes pensions as their only sources of income. This annual income remains nearly the same in the face of increasing costs for goods and services. Many older people who retire or lose their jobs face uncertain futures because they lack the ability to add to their income if pension plans or family support falters.

Safety and Isolation Rita Ungaro-Schiavone noticed that quite a few older people in her Northeast Philadelphia neighborhood were living alone. She discovered that they were capable of living on their own but that they needed help to get food into the house or to make trips to the doctor or drugstore. She decided to begin a parish program called "Aid for Friends." Some parishioners cooked extra meals for distribution while others dropped off a weekly supply of these meals to homebound persons, checking as they did so on the physical and emotional well-being of each person. The program proved to be so successful, and the need so great, that Aid for Friends spread to many other parishes and religious organizations in the Philadelphia area.

As a group, people in the United States are on the move. Older parents can find themselves living in Kansas City while their children are busy with work and their own families in Atlanta or San Diego. When friends their own age die or move to a warmer or drier climate or to live with their children, older people become increasingly lonely. As their mobility decreases, their need for assistance increases. In some communities, because they are physically more defenseless, older people living alone often fear for their safety. This is especially the case when the older person is homebound. In today's highly mobile and youth-oriented society, older people are often left out of the network of support and social interaction that usually helps people in a community. Mistreatment of older people living alone or in care facilities has become so widespread that it now has its own label—elder abuse.

Stereotypes Would you like to be reduced to the popular image of "teenager" held in our culture? Probably not. While you are a unique individual, you do have things in common with other teenagers. But you also have your own story—likes and dislikes, personality traits, strengths, and interests. Similarly, if we approach older people with openness, respect, and readiness, we are more likely to discover their uniqueness, which has been developing for many more years than our own. Contrary to common stereotypes, older people are more likely than teenagers to be different from one another, and older people are more similar to than different from the rest of us. Stereotypes based on age are as destructive as stereotypes based on race, color, or gender.

We often forget that our view of older people is heavily conditioned by our culture. Not every culture looks at old age negatively. In Asian countries, for instance, older people typically are shown great honor. Even during the early years of U.S. history, older people were considered distinguished and worthy of special honor. Early on, men and women actually wore white wigs to make themselves appear older and, thereby, more dignified.

Euthanasia and Suicide Some years ago a story made newspaper headlines about a man who shot and killed his sickly, elderly wife because he wanted to "end her suffering." More than any other age group, older people are affected by policies and pressures related to euthanasia. Ageism adds to an atmosphere supportive of euthanasia. Those who advocate euthanasia, the deliberate killing of sick, suffering or disabled people, typically point to problems that exist not because of aging itself but because of ageism. For instance, in a society in which being old is associated with lacking independence, older people fear "becoming a burden on their children." Many older people suffer from depression because of physical aches and pains, isolation, fear of losing mental alertness, or little support from their family, and community.

Problems such as these don't come naturally with aging; they are expressions of ageism. For instance, older people need not feel isolated, depressed, and burdensome. Certain commonly accepted values and practices create pressures among some older people to consider suicide or euthanasia as means of "mercy killing"—a way to end their own problems and to spare others from taking them on as a burden as well. These pressures are not caused by aging itself or even by problems often accompanying old age. Physical suffering can be addressed through proper medical care, and forgetfulness is less a problem in a supportive environment. Rather, they result from societal attitudes and practices toward older people—that is, ageism.

FAITH ACTIVITY

How Would You Like It? Imagine you are an older person. Describe in writing how you would like younger people to relate to you and to treat you. How would the older people you currently know like to be treated?

With everyone else in a family and community, older people are important links in the chain of human society. Diminished memory and increased dependence do not break the ties that bind older people to the rest of us. Suicide and euthanasia are affronts to both life and love.

> Whatever its motives and means, direct euthanasia consists in putting an end to the lives of handicapped, sick, or dying persons. It is morally unacceptable.

CCC, 2277

GROUP TALK

1. Make a list of problems associated with aging.

2. In what ways are these problems a result of aging itself. Are they in any way also affected by ageism—that is, by personal or societal attitudes, values, practices, and policies? Explain.

3. How would you respond to someone who said, "We should make suicide and euthanasia legal for older people. They should have the right to end their suffering if they want to."

The Christian View of Aging

Healing the rupture between society and its elderly members requires a major effort to change attitudes as well as social structures. In undertaking this task, we are not simply meeting the demands of charity and justice. We are accepting our own humanity, our link with past and future and, thereby, our link with the Creator.

> Catholic Bishops of the United States,
> *Society and the Aged*, no. 52

We find in the early section of the Old Testament heroes of the Hebrew people described as living superhuman life spans. Scholars suggest that the Hebrew patriarchs did not actually live to such great ages but rather that this was a way to show reverence and respect for them. In the Scriptures, aging is associated with wisdom and understanding; older people are to be cherished and accorded special care. The commandment "Honor your father and your mother" (*Exodus 20:12*) reflects this belief.

The Acts of the Apostles, which describes the rapid growth of the early Church, mentions a problem that existed in the fledgling Christian community—widows were being neglected. At the time, widows tended to lack economic security and needed explicit help from others if they were to survive. The first people mentioned in Acts charged with specific duties in the community were "seven men of good standing" appointed specifically to serve the needs of widows (*Acts 6:1–4*). Thus, care for widows who fall upon hard times was one of the first activities to which the Church explicitly dedicated herself.

Catholic leaders today make it clear that overlooking older people, ignoring their special needs and unique contributions, breaks our link both with the past and with our own future. Our personal attitudes and social structures need examining so that the bond between old and young can be more strongly knit together. If Jesus teaches us anything, it is that life means relatedness. To divorce ourselves from any group lessens our connection to life itself and ultimately to God.

Religion that is pure and undefiled before God, the Father, is this: to care for orphans and widows in their distress, and to keep oneself unstained by the world.

✝ James 1:27

FAITH ACTIVITY

Design a Program If you were to design a program for older parishioners, what would it include? Ask an older person: What would you like from the Church? Compare your proposal with what the older person would like and present it to your class.

Heather's Story

Reluctantly, Heather joined the volunteers from her school that would be visiting a care center for the next two months. Heather had been to a care center only once before, when she had gone along with a friend who was visiting her grandmother. Heather found that visit completely depressing, and she was anticipating a similar experience.

Initially, her expectations were realized. She was afraid to go near any of the residents for fear one would touch her. She had been given the name of Mrs. Ruth Lewis to visit. The woman was pointed out to her—sitting on a bench where she leaned on a walker and stared ahead. Mrs. Lewis appeared very frail and wore a sweater in the warm room. Heather was not looking forward to spending time with this person with the blank eyes and aged skin. What would she do with her? What could she talk about?

Surprisingly, when they got together Mrs. Lewis carried the conversation. She asked Heather about her family and her school and then told Heather about her own family. Perhaps because she felt so nervous, Heather talked away about herself and Mrs. Lewis told about an incident from her own school days as if it had happened yesterday.

After her second trip to the care center, Heather felt comfortable walking the halls and came to look forward to her visits. She even got the hang of helping Mrs. Lewis out of her chair and steadying her with her walker. When Heather's ten weeks were up, she held Mrs. Lewis's hand for a long time and assured her that she would come back to see her. When she kissed her good-bye, Heather felt as though she had met a beautiful person and had indeed made a special friend.

GROUP TALK

If you could arrange an interview with an older person, what kind of questions would you ask?

What do you feel you could learn from the interview?

FAITH ACTIVITY

Serving the Needs How does your parish serve the needs of older people? How does it utilize the services of older people? What opportunities are there for older people and younger people to get together? Share your information with the class.

Responding to Older Persons

Despite the claims of miracle drugs, aging is not going away. However, any shame associated with aging and the difficulties linked to aging can be reduced. And it's good to remember that older people are a storehouse of lived experiences waiting to be tapped.

Our Personal Response A key to young people gaining a more positive and realistic picture of older people is to spend time with them, as Heather did. As anyone who is close to a grandparent knows, a friendship that spans generations is special. However, with older people, as with people of all ages, it is important to keep in mind that they are precious in themselves, not because they are useful or helpful to us. Therefore, the first step toward justice for older people is fostering a spirit of compassionate care for them.

> I have learned that a culture which equates material possessions with success, and views the frantic, compulsive consumer as the perfect citizen, can afford little space for the aged human being. They are past competing, they are out of the game. We live in a culture which endorses what has been called "human obsolescence." After adolescence, obsolescence. To the junk heap, the nursing home, the retirement village, the "Last Resort."

Sharon R. Curtin, *Nobody Ever Died of Old Age*
(Boston: Little, Brown and Co., 1972),.195–196

Keys to Making Life Better for Older People

- Improved health and education for children and young people

- A strengthened spirit of morality and social concern among those who are young

- Expanded employment opportunities for young adults

- Increased support for families

Societal Changes In the United States, steps have been taken to put into place a "safety net" for older people. This has eased but not eliminated financial worries for many. Basic health care, although still a major expense, is now viewed as a right for all older people, although the medications they need are often their greatest financial burden.

Surprisingly, a key to meeting the safety and security needs of older people is to improve the lot of all children. That is, while older people have particular strengths, they also have their needs. In the future, the increasing number of Mrs. Lewises will depend more and more on the Heathers of the nation—for physical assistance, for contributing money to Social Security funds that support retired persons, and in general for weaving the social fabric upon which everyone depends. When one out of every five children in a country lives in poverty, it will become harder to provide long-term care for older people. In other words, the work of social justice, for old and for young, is all of one piece.

GROUP TALK

1. Explain and use examples to defend or refute the following statement: A key to meeting the safety and security needs of older people is to improve the lot of children.

2. Would you support a bill that called for the federal government to pay the full cost of prescriptions for people over sixty-five? Why?

The Dignity of Persons with Disabilities

Answer **agree, disagree, or uncertain** to the following statements. Choose statements that you believe are most significant. Explain your answers.

1. I know and socialize with a person or persons with disabilities.

2. I treat a person with a disability the same as I treat anyone else.

3. I am uncomfortable around people with physical or mental disabilities.

4. Our society has taken adequate steps to provide for persons with disabilities.

5. Children with emotional or mental problems should attend schools separate from other children.

Jesus spent time with many people whom today we would categorize as having a disability. Even so, our society is not known for exceptional care for persons with disabilities. Too often the response of many to persons with disabilities parallels what we sometimes seem to want from all marginalized people—that they be out of sight and out of mind. However, in a compassionate community, all of us are richer when we care for one another as sisters and brothers.

[Jesus said,] "When you give a luncheon or a dinner, do not invite your friends or your brothers or your relatives or rich neighbors, in case they may invite you in return, and you would be repaid. But when you give a banquet, invite the poor, the crippled, the lame, and the blind. And you will be blessed, because they cannot repay you, for you will be repaid at the resurrection of the righteous."

Luke 14:12-14

GROUP TALK

1. What groups of people do you think are marginalized in contemporary American society?

2. Why would you categorize these people as marginalized?

3. What types of programs and social changes would help them become fuller participants in society?

The Double Burden of Having a Disability

The true stories on the next page all paint a rosy picture of the experience of being disabled. They also portray friendly, easy relationships between people who have disabilities and those who don't. However, persons with disabilities often find that other people zero in on their differences and seldom look beyond them. Persons with disabilities can end up feeling set apart from the group, as if to be different in one particular way means to be different in all ways.

Snapshots of Persons with Disabilities

★ Alex is a familiar sight riding his wheelchair through the school halls. His classmates include him in activities, and Alex misses no chance to participate in whatever ways he can. On the sidelines at every game, he proudly wears the school's football jersey and serves as the team's honorary manager. He excels at computer skills, and his classmates don't hesitate to come to him for help running programs. When he encounters a difficulty, such as finding enough space for his wheelchair in the narrow lecture hall, he seeks help without complaint. At his school Alex is not "that boy in a wheelchair"; rather, he is Alex–classmate, computer whiz, football manager, friend.

★ Brad loves his work. Through a local agency serving persons with mental disabilities, he landed a job cleaning up the theaters at a nearby multiplex. Occasionally he gets to see the movies, although most of the time he sees only the last few minutes of them. Brad loves being at the center of the excitement. He greets moviegoers warmly, and generally people respond in a friendly manner. Occasionally, regular customers even ask him which movies he recommends. Brad's cheerful personality makes movie-going a more pleasant experience for everyone.

★ Blind since birth, Mrs. Fielder still managed to graduate from college with a teaching degree. She impressed the school's administrators so much with her knowledge of history and her teaching ability in her student teaching that she was hired to teach some of the most demanding senior high courses there. Students do not dare act out in her classes. Despite her disability, Mrs. Fielder has developed her own system for maintaining classroom order. Mostly students are spellbound by the "behind the scenes" stories she tells about great historical events. In some aspects of her job, she works differently from other teachers, and she requires a few special accommodations. Nonetheless, the strongest impression that the school community has about her is that she loves her work and her students, and her students love her.

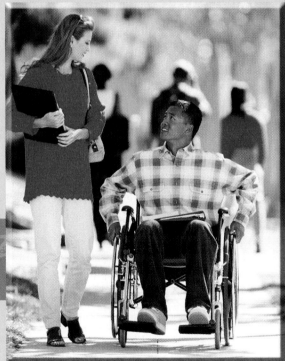

GROUP TALK

1. Think back to your first encounter with a person with a disability. How did you react? What did you feel?

2. What types of experiences with persons with disabilities have you had recently? How did you react? How did you feel?

3. Describe ways that people might respond to you if you were disabled in some way.

People are naturally fearful of the unknown. If we have few opportunities to be with people who are blind or severely hearing-impaired, with someone who has cerebral palsy or Down's syndrome, or with those who use wheelchairs for mobility, then we can easily be cautious and unsure about how to relate to them. As a result, people with disabilities often carry a double burden: coping with a disability while also dealing with rejection or peculiar responses from others.

Although disability is not a precise term, many more people in the United States are disabled than we might think. One estimate suggests that one in seven people in the United States can be classified as disabled.

It is important to remember that many people have invisible disabilities. For instance, a child may have mild mental handicaps or any number of learning disabilities. Sometimes people with invisible disabilities encounter more difficulties in life than those who are obviously disabled because others do not recognize their special needs and therefore place unrealistic expectations on them.

Most importantly, all of us are disabled in some way. More accurately, all of us are more or less able-bodied and only temporarily so. Some of us just happen to be more noticeably disabled than others. This third point sets us in the direction of responding positively toward others, whether we are among the noticeably disabled or not. None of us is 100 percent "able"; all of us have shortcomings. Alex (in the earlier scenario) cannot walk, but none of his classmates has mastered the computer as Alex has. By the same token who is more "disabled"—someone with minimal eyesight or someone blinded by hate? Even though we probably would not label them disabled, people can be emotionally handicapped as well as physically or mentally handicapped.

FAITH ACTIVITY

Living Experience Arrange to visit a residential facility for persons with mental or physical disabilities. Report on your experience to the class. Describe your feelings. Describe how the persons were living their lives.

Needs of Persons with Disabilities

The positive tone of the previous stories is not meant to minimize or dismiss the special needs of persons with disabilities or the immense burdens encountered by their families. Depending on the severity of the disability, caring for a disabled person, child or adult, can be a twenty-four-hour-a-day job. Meanwhile, parents and other caregivers cannot overlook other daily tasks involving the home, employment relationships, and possibly other children. Children and sometimes even adults can be unintentionally cruel to persons with disabilities and their families. Simple things like shopping become major undertakings. Finances are constantly strained. Siblings of persons with disabilities carry all kinds of added burdens, such as often taking on the role of being "little parents" to a disabled brother or sister. At the same time, siblings of persons with disabilities often develop into extremely caring persons who are especially sensitive to others' needs.

The needs of persons with disabilities and their families are great. A just and compassionate community seeks ways to ease their burdens through voicing support, sharing tasks, and planning programs that contribute assistance. In 1990, the U.S. Congress passed the **Americans with Disabilities Act**. You may have noticed in your local community the parking spaces reserved for persons with disabilities. An increase in the number of these spaces was initiated by the disabilities act. One of the most significant contributions of the act has been the realization that, where possible, the best way to help persons with disabilities is to make it easier for them to help themselves.

> ## FAITH ACTIVITY
>
> **Accessibility for the Disabled**
> Research what changes have been made in your community to help persons with physical challenges. What additional changes would you recommend to make your community more "handicapped accessible"? List these proposals on a chart.

The Christian View

> The central meaning of Jesus' ministry is bound up with the fact that He sought the company of people who, for one reason or another, were forced to live on the fringe of society. (*cf. Mk. 7:37*) These He made the special object of His attention, declaring that the last would be first and that the humble would be exalted in His Father's kingdom. (*cf. Mt. 20: 16, 23:12*) The Church finds its true identity when it fully integrates itself with these *marginal* people, including those who suffer from physical and psychological disabilities.
>
> Pastoral Statement of U.S. Catholic Bishops on People with Disabilities, 12

Persons with disabilities are often great teachers—modeling courage, patience, joy in the face of hardship, and the resourcefulness of the human spirit. They are gifts from God, embodiments of Christ's presence, as we all are. Therefore, an important lesson taught to us by people with disabilities is the value and dignity of the human person. None of us measures up to perfection, and yet Christians humbly celebrate that we are all created in God's image. This core Christian teaching applies to a person who is mentally or developmentally disabled just as it does to everyone else.

The U.S. Catholic bishops consider justice for persons with disabilities to be a right-to-life issue. Fear of those with disabilities promotes abortion. The killing of unborn children who may not be perfect promotes prejudice against people with disabilities. This holds true for considering euthanasia for the severely disabled.

The bishops point out that the right to life implies other rights, in this case the right to full participation in the human community. Therefore, the bishops call for examination of education, employment, housing, and accessible public buildings to determine whether or not persons with disabilities have the possibility of suitable participation. The bishops see justice for persons with disabilities as an outgrowth of Christian love, which affirms our common humanity:

> No acts of charity or justice can be of lasting value unless our actions are informed by a sincere and understanding love that penetrates the wall of strangeness and affirms the common humanity underlying all distinction.
>
> Pastoral Statement on People with Disabilities, 3

Special Beatitudes

Blessed are you who take time to listen to difficult speech, for you help us to know that if we persevere, we can be understood.

Blessed are you who walk with us in public places and ignore the stares of strangers, for in your companionship we find havens of relaxation.

Blessed are you who never bid us to "hurry up"; and more blessed, you who do not snatch our tasks from our hands to do them for us, for often we need time rather than help.

Blessed are you who stand beside us as we enter new and untried ventures, for our failures will be outweighed by the times when we surprise ourselves and you.

Blessed are you who ask for our help, for our greatest need is to be needed.

Blessed are you who help us with the graciousness of Christ, for oftentimes we need the help we cannot ask for.

Blessed are you, when by all these things you assure us that the thing that makes us individuals is not in our peculiar muscles, nor in our wounded nervous systems, nor in our difficulties in learning, but in the God-given self that no infirmity can confine.

Rejoice and be exceedingly glad, and know that you give us reassurances that could never be spoken in words, for you deal with us as Christ dealt with all his children.

Stan Carder, *A Committed Mercy*
(Grand Rapids, MI: Baker Books, 1995), 41–42

FAITH ACTIVITY

Special Beatitudes Imagine what it might be like to have a particular disability. Use the "Special Beatitudes" to write your own set of beatitudes that would reflect the perspective of a person who possesses that disability.

GROUP TALK

1. Besides physical handicaps, what are some ways that a person might be "disabled"?

2. List problems that you imagine parents of a severely disabled child might face.

   ★ What strains on their energies and spirits might they encounter?

   ★ What types of assistance do you think would be most helpful to them?

3. Name ways that having a severely disabled sister or brother might affect you.

Protecting Society, Respecting Prisoners

What is the relationship between social justice and criminal justice, the treatment of people in our judicial system? Aren't prisoners a big part of the problem and therefore not deserving of our consideration under a discussion of justice? In fact, social justice, which focuses on discrimination and unjust social structures, and criminal justice, which focuses on the arrest, trial, and treatment of people in the judicial system, are more closely linked than they might immediately appear. Jesus himself named prisoners (captives) as one group to whom he was sent.

The Spirit of the Lord . . .
has sent me to proclaim release to the captives . . .

Luke 4:18

As with the other significant issues raised in this chapter, we need to consider the Fifth Commandment's teaching on the right to protect ourselves and society, and the implications this has for just living. Since murder is the intentional killing of an innocent person, we might think that the legitimate defense is an exception to the commandment, but it's not. As Saint Thomas Aquinas states,

"The act of self-defense can have a double effect: the preservation of one's own life; and the killing of the aggressor. . . . The one is intended, the other is not."

Summa Theologica II-II, 64, 7, (*CCC* 2263).

Another aspect of this issue is that civic authorities have the right and duty to decrease and contain behaviors that jeopardized the safety or rights of others and the basic laws of society. This is part of their responsibility to safeguard the common good. So, governments have the right to punish those who break the law proportionate to the offenses they have committed. This punishment protects society but also provides the opportunity for the person who has committed a crime to "correct" or change his or her behavior. Prisoners are worthy of respectful treatment, for they are made in God's image and likeness and are called by Christ to conversion as all of us are. That being said, who is imprisoned and how they are treated is a justice issue, for there is great inequality in the U.S. system.

A Visit to a Big City Prison

Although it is in the heart of the city, the prison is a world unto itself. Never having been inside a prison before, you enter cautiously, filled with images and stereotypes gathered from years of watching TV cop shows and news reports.

Once past the metal detector and the seemingly endless series of locked gates, you enter a room where many prisoners are gathered to see a play to be performed by the prison drama club. Looking around the room, you begin picking out the guards from the prisoners. The two groups wear different uniforms, and there are many more prisoners than guards. Most of the prisoners are African American; most of the guards are Caucasian. However, the prisoners do not appear more hostile, more angry, more frightening, or more "criminal" than the guards. In fact, the prisoners generally appear more friendly and relaxed than the guards—perhaps because they are not "on duty" and you are a guest in their "home."

One prisoner named Smitty comes over to greet you. A kindly looking man, he appears to be something of a leader and wants to make you feel at ease. Older than most of the prisoners, Smitty serves as a father figure for many of them, often listening to and settling disputes. He also leads the Tuesday evening Bible study sessions.

Another prisoner, James, is prison librarian and has recently become a Catholic. He longs to talk about Jesus and the meaning of some of the parables. Like most of the inmates, James has been in the prison for a year awaiting trial. Of the approximately twelve hundred prisoners here, only about three hundred of them have been sentenced.

After the play, a dramatization of several poems by African American writers, the warden invites you on a tour of the prison. Entering "F" block, one of eight long corridors with small rooms with metal doors on either side, you receive stares from most of the men. Strangers don't often visit. The warden greets many of the inmates by name.

Stepping into one open cell, you introduce yourself and chat with a man sitting on his bed, the only furniture in the room. When you return to the corridor and the warden, you mention to him that the man in the cell seems like a good person. The warden responds, "He is a good person. He isn't here because he's not a good person. He's here because of what he did. He's awaiting the death penalty any day."

As you are leaving the prison, you ask the warden: "What are these men doing here?" The warden answers without hesitation: "For you, prison would be a hardship—you have something better to live for. For many of these men, prison is perhaps not the worst place to be—the outside world has little to offer them. Many of these men grew up with us; we're the only family they know and the only people who care about them."

As you leave behind the prison walls and enter the "real" world again, you wonder: What kind of society do we have that can offer so many people nothing better than life within prison?

FAITH ACTIVITY

Perspectives on Prisoners
Illustrate with a drawing or poem the contrast between how prisoners are viewed in our society and how they are viewed from a Christian perspective.

White- and Blue-Collar Crimes

Crime has to do with violating laws designed to protect people. There are **crimes against persons** and **crimes against property**. Some laws exist to maintain good order, such as driving on the right side of the road. You may be surprised to know that the most commonly occurring harmful crimes are not committed by people who fit most people's image of a criminal. Also, those who commit these crimes spend a proportionately small amount of time in prison. For instance, of all crimes against persons, one kills far more people than all others combined—drunk driving. Drunk driving is a middle-class crime, one that even so-called respectable citizens commit.

> In 2002 in the United States, an estimated 17,419 people died in alcohol-related traffic crashes. These deaths constitute 41 percent of the 42,815 total traffic fatalities. Drunk driving is the nation's most frequently committed violent crime, killing someone every 30 minutes.
>
> National Highway Traffic Safety Administration

Of all crimes against property, fraud and embezzlement are the most prevalent. Fraud and embezzlement are white-collar crimes, committed by persons in business or government in the course of their work. These types of crime tend to be treated less harshly in the criminal justice system. People who commit them often can afford bail money and quality legal services—keeping them out of jail until their trial and providing them opportunities to make as strong a case as possible. Even executives of large companies who have run those companies into the ground because of illegal and immoral practices while personally amassing great wealth often spend little or no time in prison.

In practice, therefore, those who commit crimes and go free and those who commit crimes and are in prison have not always been treated equally. A great difference exists between criminal justice for those who are poor and criminal justice for people who have wealth. Statistics bear this out.

> The inmate population has risen from 250,000 in 1972 to a record 2 million inmates in 2000. Just as African and Hispanic Americans are victimized at higher rates, so too are they incarcerated at higher rates:
>
> > – African Americans make up 12 percent of the U.S. population but represent more than 49 percent of prisoners[13] . . .
> >
> > – Hispanic Americans make up 9 percent of the U.S. population but 19 percent of prisoners[15] . . .
>
> Prison inmates have high rates of substance abuse, illiteracy and mental illness. . .
>
> > – 24 percent are incarcerated for drug offenses, and nearly half were under the influence of drugs or alcohol when they committed the crime.[17]
> >
> > – 70 percent did not complete high school.
> >
> > – As many as 200,000 suffer from some form of mental illness.[18]
>
> **U.S. Conference of Catholic Bishops,** *Responsibility, Rehabilitation and Restoration*

The answers to the questions "Who is in prison?" and "Why are they in prison?" may seem obvious: People who commit crimes are in prison, and people who commit crimes deserve to be in prison. These apparently obvious answers mask many mistaken ideas about prisoners and the entire criminal justice system. Such an answer can lead us to sit back comfortably and ignore our country's prisons, to view them as necessary inconveniences. While we sit back, new prisons are being built, often privatized for profit. The human reality of prisoners and their problems is easily buried in apathy and an "out of sight, out of mind" mentality.

A case can be made that our country's prisons serve as human warehouses; most of those in them are the marginalized people of our society. The vast majority of people in prisons are poor, uneducated, and members of minority groups. Most adult prisoners had their first taste of imprisonment in a youth detention center. Those who end up in prison usually have a long history of failure in their lives. Typically, they possess one or more of the "invisible disabilities" mentioned earlier in this chapter and reiterated in the statistics quoted by the U.S. Catholic bishops. There is a great need in most prisons for volunteers who can teach basic reading skills. Finding legitimate work is difficult when a person can't read street signs or fill out employment forms.

More often than not, prisoners come from unstable and even abusive family backgrounds—often having raised themselves or been taken in by a gang—or have had a parent in prison. They have had repeated failures in school and lack job skills or a record of long-term employment. Along with family, the school system, and the job market, prison becomes one more institution of a society that has not provided enough support to help them move anywhere but where they end up. In prison, a person's sense of self-worth and human dignity comes under constant attack. Again, this description of prisoners is not meant to excuse crime or simply to "blame the system" for society's ills. Prisoners who make it to a better life take responsibility for their actions and work hard to overcome the obstacles that society may put in their way.

GROUP TALK

1 One rationale for prisons is that they serve as a way to decrease crime.

★ For what types of crime and potential wrongdoers do you believe prison would serve as an effective deterrent?

★ For what types of crime and potential wrongdoers would prison not serve as a very effective deterrent?

★ Explain the reasons for the differences in your two lists. What surprised you when you read about the people who are in prison?

Pleas Bargaining and the Bail System Even though jailed offenders come mainly from a poor and disjointed socio-economic background, it may be argued nonetheless that those in prison have been found guilty by the best that our society has to offer—trial by a jury of their peers with adequate legal counsel. In reality, however, most inmates plead guilty and spend time in jail as a result of **plea bargaining**. In our overworked court system, plea bargaining speeds up decision making and allows timely access to trial for those who do not plea bargain. For individual defendants, guilty or not, a plea often becomes the best "deal" they feel capable of getting from a system that has given them few breaks in the past.

In our current system of justice the following scenario is possible. A man unable to raise bail is accused of a crime and sent to jail. He is later told that a court date will not be forthcoming for at least a year; but if he pleads guilty, he can get off with a sentence of six months, part of which he has already served. The accused person, guilty or not, might reasonably choose plea bargaining for the shorter sentence than spend an additional six months or so awaiting trial. Such a scenario may sound outlandish, but in fact it represents the norm in many prisons. Nationwide, over 50 percent of county jail inmates are awaiting trial, presumably "innocent" but unable to raise bail or hasten a court date.

Critical Awareness of the Prison System

Remember those who are in prison, as though you were in prison with them.

Hebrews 13:3

Prison officials are public servants; so are police officers, judges, and lawmakers. We want to believe that our criminal justice system is fair and just, that all people are treated equally under the law, and that those who are punished deserve what they receive. Few of us know the criminal justice system or life behind bars. Even when a newspaper exposé describes inhumane conditions in prisons, we shrug it off. It is as if, because of one mistake or one incident of mistaken identity, convicted persons become fair game for any degree of inhumane treatment because "they deserve it."

Casting blame on people who work in the criminal justice system is unfair. While mistreatment can occur any time one group holds absolute power over others, those involved in criminal-justice work have a difficult and thankless job. Some taxpayers want no money spent on prisons but want the system to be "tough on crime." Some don't want a prison facility in their neighborhood. In fact, people want to be shielded from the unpleasant reality that prisons exist at all. While no one wants to think about prisons, frustration at crime rates runs high. Those who end up in prison serve as scapegoats for all of our anger at the ugliness of crime. We want nothing to do with them. We want professionals to handle them, preferably harshly, and most especially to keep them out of sight. When practicing justice, however, we must face the realities of our system of punishment.

> The many forms of punishment for those who are convicted of crime in the United States vary, ranging from fines and probation to boot camps and chain gangs, to incarceration in jails and prisons, and finally to the death penalty... As incarceration rates have increased, so have other punitive measures. Mandatory minimum sentences are much more common as is the willingness to use isolation units. As of 1997, thirty-six states and the federal government have constructed "supermax" prisons. These facilities isolate prisoners considered most dangerous and confine them to small cells by themselves for twenty-two to twenty-four hours each day. Additionally, the death penalty is being used with increasing frequency. . . . These statistics and policies reflect legislative action at the federal and state levels that is adopted *by legislators seeking to appear "tough on crime" in response to often sensational media coverage of crime.*
>
> U.S. Conference of Catholic Bishops, *Responsibility, Rehabilitation and Restoration*

A first step toward making prisons work better is simply to become informed about prisons and the criminal justice system.

Second, similar to our attitude toward other groups mentioned during this course, we need to realize that prisoners are not all alike and that they are more like us than different. The difference is that circumstances surrounding their lives or their particular response to needs or wants brought them into conflict with civil authorities and the criminal justice system. This does not mean that people who commit crimes are harmless or that prisoners are innocent. Often, well-intentioned persons wanting to help a prisoner may quickly discover that he or she doesn't want their help or tries to "con" them. What it does mean is that we look upon prisoners as persons with God-given dignity, worthy of respect—not as inhuman "others."

On this point an interesting experiment took place at Stanford University some years ago. Researchers created a mock prison to test how people would respond when placed in the roles of prisoners and guards. After six days the experiment had to be called off. Even though conditions did not come close to duplicating the horrors of real prison life, the people involved started suffering severe psychological side effects. We might think the system works in the following simple manner: A person commits a crime, pays his or her debt to society, and then goes free. Such is far from the truth. A person who has been imprisoned is tainted for life, both by the experience itself and by society's attitudes and policies toward "ex-convicts."

GROUP TALK

1. What is your reaction to each of the methods of punishment noted by the bishops?

2. What questions do you have about just and reasonable punishment for prisoners?

The Foundations of Just Punishment

Criminal justice is an emotional issue strongly laced with fear. Sensational cases, such as the sniper attacks in Washington, D.C., and the surrounding area in the fall of 2002, point out our vulnerability when it comes to crime and result in new cries for greater punishments.

In *Responsibility, Rehabilitation and Restoration*, the U.S. Catholic bishops called for an approach to criminal justice based on the following foundations:

1. Protecting society from those who threaten life, inflict harm, take property and destroy the bonds of community.

2. Rejecting simplistic solutions such as "three strikes and you're out" and rigid mandatory sentencing.

3. Promoting serious efforts toward crime prevention and poverty reduction.

4. Challenging the culture of violence and encouraging a culture of life.

5. Offering victims the opportunity to participate more fully in the criminal justice process.

6. Encouraging innovative programs of restorative justice that provide the opportunity for mediation between victims and offenders and offer restitution for crimes committed.

7. Insisting that punishment has a constructive and rehabilitative purpose.

8. Encouraging spiritual healing and renewal for those who commit crime.

9. Making a serious commitment to confront the pervasive role of addiction and mental illness in crime.

10. Treating immigrants justly.

11. Placing crime in a community context and building on promising alternatives that empower neighborhoods and towns to restore a sense of security.

FAITH ACTIVITY

Social Justice Give an example that illustrates this statement: ". . . improving criminal justice must go hand in hand with addressing concerns of social justice."

The bishops' recommendations avoid the pitfalls of emotionally reacting to a difficult situation rather than rationally planning for the future. Following up on their foundations, the bishops called the Catholic faith community to a number of tasks, including:

- Teach right from wrong, respect for life and the law, forgiveness and mercy.

- Stand with victims and their families.

- Reach out to offenders and their families, advocate for more treatment, and provide for the pastoral needs of all involved.

- Build community.

- Advocate policies that help reduce violence, protect the innocent, involve the victims, and offer real alternatives to crime.

As with all struggles for justice, our action for social change needs to be accompanied by personal and spiritual conversion. The Catholic community cannot teach right from wrong or promote respect for life, mercy, and forgiveness without presenting the Gospel message. We respond to the promptings of the Holy Spirit by being open to what Christ has to say to us and how the cardinal virtues lead us to a morality that promotes life. The Holy Spirit active in the Church unites us in worship and in praying for the conversion that people as individuals and society as a whole need.

Capital Punishment Some people argue that if the threat of life in prison isn't enough to decrease crime, then we need an even harsher punishment—capital punishment. Following a brief period when it was outlawed by the Supreme Court, capital punishment has again been in effect in the United States since 1977. Capital punishment and the way it is administered raise many justice concerns. While the legal system provides lawyers for accused people who cannot afford one, those who are wealthy can obtain better resources and more talented and experienced legal representation. As a result, those who are condemned to die are nearly always poor, have had minimal education, and are in higher proportion African American.

The arguments for and against capital punishment are numerous. Those in favor of it contend that it decreases crime, is less costly than life imprisonment, eliminates people who are a threat, and makes a statement about how abhorrent certain crimes are. In reality, no hard evidence supports the claim that crime rates drop when capital punishment is allowed. And appeals and other legalities actually make it more costly than life imprisonment. Advances in DNA testing have resulted in clearing some people on death row, and in some states this has led to the reevaluation of all cases involving the death penalty. Studies also indicate that the death penalty is meted out unevenly, depending on race, economic status, geographic location, and other factors.

The Christian View of Capital Punishment

Capital punishment is an act of despair. In essence it says that there is no hope that someone can change or that a person's life is worth saving. The *Catechism of the Catholic Church* teaches that " as far as possible [punishment] should contribute to the correction of the offender" (*CCC* **2266**).

> *I have no pleasure in the death of the wicked, but that the wicked turn from their ways and live."*
>
> ✝ Ezekiel 33:11

The Catechism does not make a blanket condemnation of capital punishment. The reason for this is that the state has the responsibility to protect its citizens and promote the common good. If capital punishment is the only way to achieve these ends it is acceptable. (See *CCC* **2266–2267**) The Catechism also says that because modern states have available alternative means of protecting its citizens, "the cases in which the execution of the offender is an absolute necessity 'are very rare, if not practically non-existent'".

The U.S. Catholic bishops summarize the Church's problems with capital punishment, especially as it is administered in the United States, in this way: "Capital punishment is cruel, unnecessary and arbitrary; it often has racial overtones; and it fails to live up to our deep conviction that all human life is sacred . . . we cannot build a 'culture of life' by state-sanctioned killing" (*Responsibility, Rehabilitation and Restoration*).

GROUP TALK

1. Does capital punishment (a) diminish a sense of the sacredness of life or (b) make a statement about how precious life is? Explain.

2. What are the goals of capital punishment? Are the goals as you state them consistent with Catholic teaching on justice?

3. What are society's alternatives to capital punishment? Are they more or less effective in meeting the goals of criminal justice than capital punishment is?

›Faith in Action

Jesuit Volunteer Corps

Sponsored by: **MaryKnoll Missionaries**

Whether they volunteer as an immigrant advocate in Camden, New Jersey, or as a teacher in Godavari, Kathmandu, Nepal, their commitment is the same—empowering people who are poor to be free from the forces which oppress them.

> **The more time I spend in Jesuit Volunteer Corps the more I realize that simplicity is about more than just limiting material possessions. It's about accepting when people are not on time, being happy even when things do not go perfectly, and remembering the most important part of my job is spending time with people**
>
> Mary Zagar

As part of the Jesuit Volunteer Corps (JVC), more than 12,000 men and women have given one or more years of their lives, often delaying graduate school or jobs, to fulfill the JVC mission of serving the poor directly, working for structural change in the United States, and accompanying people in developing countries.

The first Jesuit Volunteers began their service in 1956 to the Native American community of Alaska in Copper Valley. Under the sponsorship of the Oregon Province of the Society of Jesus (Jesuits), the group grew, eventually reaching out to cities across the United States and to developing countries.

Jesuit Volunteers live simply and in community with other Jesuit Volunteers in low-income neighborhoods which helps them develop a consciousness of what it means to be poor. This lifestyle gives them the opportunity to share meals, discussions, and prayers, as a way of renewing and encouraging each other to continue their ministry. Volunteers are usually placed at non-profit, often grassroots agencies, as well as in schools and parishes. All volunteers are encouraged to examine the causes of injustice and to search for creative, long-term solutions and faith-filled responses. In turn, they are changed by the experience.

Mary Zagar, a graduate of the University of Maryland, prepared for a career in urban planning. After prayer and discernment, she decided that living with and helping people who are poor would give her the experience of inner-city community she wanted. As a Jesuit Volunteer, Mary worked at Emmaus House, a community center in an impoverished area of Atlanta, Georgia. She lived with seven other Volunteers and spent her time at Emmaus House working with senior citizens. "It was like being in a bubble of love," she said. "You don't realize how much people appreciate the small things. Like Mother Teresa said, 'We can do no great things; only small things with great love.'" Her year of service over, she is now pursing a graduate degree in urban planning at Tufts University in Boston.

GO ONLINE

Visit www.harcourtreligion.com to learn more about the Jesuit Volunteer Corps and for a link to their site.

Prayer

Begin by praying the Sign of the Cross.

Reader 1: Lord, you have examined my very heart and mind, and you know all about me. You know when I'm awake. You know when I'm asleep. You know all my thoughts and dreams. You hold my future in your hands.

Reader 2: Infinite are your thoughts about me. They are beyond my reckoning. They number more than the drops of water in the oceans or the grains of sand on their shores. You are always thinking about me. You even knew me before I was born. All my complexity was fashioned by you.

Reader 3: In the light of your piercing light, grant me a complete renewal. Refashion my soul in your image and likeness. May I be purified by your presence through and through, and be prepared for your eternal presence in heaven.

Based on Psalm 139

End by praying the Sign of the Cross

>Review

1. What is meant by a consistent ethic of life?

2. Contrast a culture of life with a culture of death.

3. What does the Church teach about the unborn?

4. Define *contemplation*.

5. With what did Pope John Paul II associate contemplation in order to ensure that it is not simply a passive gesture?

6. Define *ageism*.

7. List the areas of concern associated with old age that are mentioned in the text.

8. What does it mean to say that many older people live on a fixed income?

9. What does it mean to say that persons with dis-

abilities carry a double burden?

10. Define *invisible disabilities*.

11. What right do the U.S. Catholic bishops claim for persons with disabilities?

12. What are the two major categories of crime?

13. What are the typical characteristics of most people in prisons?

14. What is the Catholic view on capital punishment?

15. What does a social justice perspective contribute to our understanding of crime?

>Key Words

ageism (p. 134) Discriminatory attitudes and practices toward people based on their age.

Alzheimer's disease (p. 135) A progressive disease that may occur in older people, leading to confusion and impaired judgment.

Americans with Disabilities Act (p.145) Act passed by Congress in 1990 initiating changes to ensure that the rights of the disabled are not violated because of a disability.

crimes against persons (p.150) Killing or physically hurting someone.

crimes against property (p.150) stealing or damaging property.

culture of death (p. 127) Culture that fosters values and practices harmful to life.

culture of life (p. 127) Culture that values all human life.

euthanasia (p. 124) The deliberate killing of sick, suffering, or disabled people intended to "end their suffering."

fixed income (p. 136) The income that remains much the same year after year, such as Social Security or pension payments.

plea bargaining (p. 152) Pleading guilty to a charge or to a lesser crime in exchange for a recommendation of a lighter sentence than one usually given for the offense.

senility (p. 135) Irreversible brain damage that may occur in the aging process.

>Our Challenge

We humans are social creatures. We travel through life with others and in need of others. Likewise, others need us. Indeed, we are family—born and unborn, old and young, abled and disabled. We are all part of a seamless garment, and we are all called to have a consistent ethic of life. Differences can lead to injustices or to mutual enrichment. However, justice means being particularly attentive to those who are most vulnerable in our human family. While justice comes into play throughout our lives, at no time is our need for others more evident than at the beginning and end of life. Christian charity reminds us that not only do we share our lives with one another, we are also responsible one for another.

POVERTY IN THE UNITED STATES

A SCANDAL WE CAN OVERCOME

CHAPTER GOALS

In this chapter you will:

★ examine truths and myths about poverty.

★ address homelessness, business corruption, and terrorism as challenges of poverty.

★ learn why the Gospel challenges everyone to work to overcome poverty.

★ explore ways of responding to poverty.

★ consider how the Church speaks on behalf of immigrants.

Poverty: Truths and Myths

Answer **agree, disagree,** or **uncertain** to the following statements about poverty in the United States. Choose statements that you believe are most significant. Explain your answers.

1. Most people in the United States who are poor live on welfare.

2. People who are poor should be taken care of by private charities rather than by the government.

3. Because of special needs and disabilities, people beyond retirement age are more likely to be poor than younger people are.

4. A major cause of poverty today is an increase in single-parent families.

5. Welfare keeps people from taking responsibility for their lives.

6. Poverty is not a major problem in the United States; priority should be given to other concerns, such as terrorism.

The problem of poverty in the United States is complex, confusing, and controversial. Some of the most deeply ingrained beliefs about people who are poor are completely false or are partial truths that cloud over the painful reality of poverty. For a number of decades now, a heated debate has been going on in the country about how best to address the problem of poverty. Approaches to solving the problem sometimes shift in emphasis with each national election. In order to put a human face on those who are poor in the United States, let's first examine some common notions about poverty.

Who Are the Poor?

A popular image of poverty in the United States today is that of inner-city poverty, and for various reasons this image of those who are poor has found a place in our national consciousness. In the 1960s, the United States declared a "war on poverty," largely because of some heart-wrenching reports about the extent of poverty in the country and the harmful effects it was having on people. At the time, perhaps for the first time since the Great Depression, rural poverty received much attention. Pockets of people who lived in shacks or abandoned cars and buses on dirt roads were out of sight from the majority of people. Rural poverty was invisible poverty; people living away from the mainstream were "out of sight, out of mind."

And still today, for a number of reasons, people who are poor continue to be largely invisible. Why? Although rural poverty is still a big problem, it seldom makes the news anymore. So the rural people who are poor are forgotten, invisible.

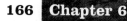

Images of Poverty

★ After an undistinguished high school career, Jamal worked off and on for a janitorial service for six years. He managed to have a place of his own for a few years. Lately, employment has been sporadic, leading him to return home to live with his retired parents. Therapy uncovered that Jamal suffers from severe chronic depression. Even with medication he has become increasingly reclusive and unable to work.

★ Hannah was introduced to crack cocaine at parties she went to with her boyfriend. Her boyfriend has since left her, but Hannah continues to indulge her habit every chance she gets. Her baby son was born prematurely and shows signs of problems caused by his mother's addiction.

★ Since arriving from Ukraine, Peter has worked as a carpenter's assistant. His wife works part time doing nails in a beauty salon. Because of a labor dispute, Peter has not worked now for over a month, and business at the beauty salon is slow. Peter and his wife have two children but no family or friends upon whom they can depend for help.

★ By saving what money they could from low-paying jobs, Salvador and Maria purchased a van which gives them more flexibility in finding employment. For a decent wage, they took jobs cleaning floors at the local hospital. Sometimes their shifts overlap by a few hours. On those evenings their three children sleep in their van in the hospital parking lot until their mother or father is free to take them home. During breaks Salvador and Maria check on the children to make sure they're okay.

★ After being abandoned by his mother, Rasheed grew up in various foster homes. When his latest foster mother forbade him from hanging out with his friends, Rasheed decided to live on his own—sometimes with a friend's family, sometimes in the park, sometimes in an abandoned building. Although he is only fifteen, in the past year Rasheed has attended only ten days of school.

★ When the steel plant closed, Jeff's hometown began to look like a ghost town. Eventually he landed a temporary job when a superstore opened up nearby, but business has been slow and work hours sporadic. Now his car needs extensive repairs, but Jeff cannot pay for them.

> "The common good...should make accessible to each what is needed to lead a truly human life: food, clothing, health, work, education and culture, suitable information, the right to establish a family, and so on.
>
> (cf. Gaudium et spes 26 § 2) *CCC* 1908

GROUP TALK

All the above scenarios portray people who are poor in some way. If they are to survive or flourish, all of them need some form of assistance, either short-term or long-term.

1. What kinds of programs would be most beneficial for each of the people mentioned above.

2. What role should government agencies play in assisting these people? In what specific ways could government best serve them?

3. What role can the Church play in helping these people?

Second, more people who are poor are now living in the same neighborhoods as people who are not poor. They reside in small towns and suburbs, attending the same schools as their less-poor neighbors. On the surface, they neither dress differently nor look different. They too are invisible. And last, thanks to the buildup of suburbs, the relocation of jobs away from downtown areas, and highway systems that cut over or around older neighborhoods, most of the people who are not poor can avoid encountering those who are obviously poor and living in clusters within major cities. We are called to think of all of the invisible people living in these situations "another self," out of respect for their human dignity, but how can we do that when we don't even "see them"? What can be done to make those whom we may overlook visible to us: Sometimes it's simple happenstance that provides us the chance to see differently.

Grand Canyon, a movie of the early 1990s, gives a clear picture of this third type of invisible poverty suddenly becoming visible. In the movie, a suburbanite driving his luxury car home at night on a Los Angeles expressway pulls off the road when he begins having car trouble. He enters the world of a Los Angeles ghetto. Stranded, he contacts a local garage from his car phone. Before the pickup truck arrives, a carload of teenagers pulls alongside the broken-down vehicle. The teenagers, brandishing weapons, torment the man waiting with his car. When a garage mechanic arrives, he convinces the youths to spare the man and let him do his job. After the tense incident, the mechanic movingly tells the wealthy suburbanite, "It's not supposed to be this way." Later, the mechanic and the driver become friends and travel to the Grand Canyon— a place that represents a simpler and healthier image of how the United States is supposed to be.

GROUP TALK

Put yourself in the place of the three sets of characters from the movie described: the driver, the mechanic, and the teenagers.

1. What is each character's or group's perspective on poverty in the United States?

2. How are their perspectives different? Why?

3. How do you think each character or group views the other characters?

"Us or Them"

> Everyone should be able to draw from work the means of providing for his [or her] life and that of his [or her] family, and of serving the human community.

CCC, no. 2428

The goal presented by the Catechism is illusive, even in the world's most prosperous and resource-rich country. In fact, people who are poor are much more "us" than "them." There is no one "face" of poverty in the United States. Statistics that attempt to identify who is poor can overwhelm us.

- Members of all races are numbered among those who are poor. Most people in the United States who are poor are white, but a larger percentage of the African American, Latin American, and Native American populations are poor.

- Most of the people who are poor in the United States do not receive welfare. Only about two-thirds of those eligible even apply.

- A large number work full time or part time and *still* are poor. In reality, on average, people labeled as poor in the United States work much more than people in other Western countries who are poor.

- Even before changes limiting the time people could receive benefits, most welfare recipients received government help intermittently rather than continuously. This suggests that they worked for a time but, for various reasons, did not or could not hold onto jobs.

- Studies of women on welfare indicate that most of them welcome programs aimed at helping them get off welfare and become gainfully employed.

- Finally, people who are poor are much more likely to be *victims* than perpetrators of crime.

Some economists refer to the U.S. welfare system as a safety net. They believe it helps keep poor people from becoming homeless people. While it is true that welfare often gives money to people who are jobless, many challenge the idea that recipients are in it for a free ride. Who would want to settle for such a limited existence just because it's free?

"Work Is Available for Anyone Who Really Wants It"

The traditional way out of poverty was relatively simple: Get a job. However, at least three factors related to the economy make this avenue to economic improvement not as open as it once was. For one thing, in this country the number of jobs for unskilled workers has greatly diminished. To understand why, first take a look at where your athletic shoes, toys, bicycles, sports equipment, and electronic equipment were made. Chances are, as will be noted in the next chapter on global poverty, most of them were manufactured in one of the Pacific Rim nations or Central American countries or in Mexico where labor costs are cheaper. Also think about all the tasks that once were done by people that are now done by machines.

FAITH ACTIVITY

Is Minimum Wage Adequate? An unskilled laborer usually begins a job at minimum wage. Assume that a worker is employed full time.

- What would be the worker's annual wages before taxes?

- Budget this person's annual expenses if he or she were living in your area.

- How possible do you think it would be to maintain a minimum standard of living with this income?

The Myth of the Welfare Queen

A Philadelphia newspaper reporter heard people talking about how some women on welfare receive their government checks monthly and lead "the good life" while the rest of us work hard to pay taxes to support them. Being an investigative reporter, David Zucchino decided to look into the reality of women on welfare in his hometown and write a book about it. Here is part of what he found:

If there were any Cadillac-driving, champagne-sipping, penthouse-living welfare queens in North Philadelphia, I didn't find them. What I found instead was a thriving subculture of destitute women, abandoned by their men and left to fend for themselves and their children, with welfare and food stamps their only dependable source of income. Their lives were utterly dominated by subsistence concerns. They spent hours each day foraging for food and clothing and securing safe housing for themselves and their children through punishing heat waves and bitter cold snaps. Out of sight of mainstream America, they survived from one welfare check to the next, making ends meet by picking through trash cans, doing odd jobs, borrowing from relatives, and shopping at thrift stores. They lived at the mercy of the welfare bureaucracy, which demanded documents and economic updates, while sometimes cutting off payments with little warning. Through it all they struggled to stay alive in one of the most dangerous places in America. North Philadelphia is cursed with one of the highest violent crime rates in the nation; its main industry and chief source of employment is the sale of illegal drugs.

David Zucchino, *Myth of the Welfare Queen* (New York: Scribner, 1997), 13-14

GROUP TALK

A twenty-three-year-old single woman with two preschool-aged children had previously shared an apartment with the father of her children. When he became abusive, she left with her children and temporarily moved in with a relative. She lacks education or training beyond high school, and she has no family members who can assist her financially. Imagine yourself in her situation.

1. What would life be like for you?
2. How would you wish to be treated by others?
3. How would you maintain your sense of dignity?
4. What kind of future would you envision for yourself?
5. What steps could you see taking to better your situation?
6. What kinds of community support would you like to have?

Second, employment opportunities for people who are unskilled no longer supply economic security. Ask someone who works at an employment office what kinds of jobs are now available for unskilled laborers.

Unlike forty years ago, jobs for unskilled workers pay minimum wage or barely above it, offer little hope for advancement, provide no long-term job security, and include minimum, if any, benefits. In other words, while there are some employment opportunities in today's economy for people who are unskilled, far fewer unskilled laborers make a decent living wage at the limited job opportunities that *are* available.

Third, many new businesses and industrial complexes are inconveniently located for potential workers who are poor. Over the past few decades, many manufacturing plants and other business centers have relocated away from areas where people who are poor live to wealthier areas. Suburban centers of employment often are not accessible by public transportation; they are, however, located more conveniently for executives and other upper- and middle-class workers who drive to work. Most workers with higher paying jobs travel by car from one suburb where they live to another suburb where they work. Put these factors together, and the results are few real opportunities for unskilled workers and a widening gap in wages between more-skilled and less-skilled workers.

FAITH ACTIVITY

Economic Security In small groups, look at manufacturing jobs in your state. Have there been plant closings in recent years? If so, find out how many employees lost their jobs. Find out where the products are now made that once were manufactured at these plants. Report to the class on your findings.

2004 U.S. Federal Poverty Guidelines

48 contiguous states and District of Columbia

Size of family unit	
1	$9,310
2	$12,490
3	$15,670
4	$18,850
5	$22,030
6	$25,210
7	$28,390
8	$31,570

For each additional family member, add $3,180

Christian Goals for Welfare Reform

To protect human life and human dignity

To strengthen family life

To encourage and reward work

To preserve a safety net for the vulnerable

To build public and private partnerships to overcome poverty

To invest in human dignity and poor families

Administrative Board of the U. S. Catholic Conference, Political Responsibility

GROUP TALK

1. What are your strongest images of people in the United States who are poor? Why do you think you hold such images? Why might people who are not poor prefer to view those who are poor as "them"?

2. What are some practical ways to implement the Christian Goals for Welfare Reform?

Recent Challenges of Poverty

Do not boast about tomorrow, for you do not know what a day may bring.

✝ Proverbs 27:1

Every historical age brings unique challenges to those who are poor and vulnerable. From a Christian perspective, their challenges are challenges for all of us. Today in the United States, the fear of losing everything and then living on the streets or in shelters or in cars often stalks the poor. During economically difficult times government programs aimed at helping people who are poor are typically the first to be eliminated. In particular, the events of September 11, 2001, have redirected funds away from those who are poor.

Symptoms of Poverty

Homelessness The sight of men sleeping in cardboard boxes over heating vents and women dressed in layers of clothing rummaging through trash cans has become part of the urban landscape of the United States. Who are these people? Is our society so hardened that it overlooks the irony that homeless and penniless people huddle within a few feet of tall buildings that serve as headquarters for multi-million dollar businesses? Besides being uncomfortable with this state of affairs, what can those of us who have a home and plenty of clothes do for those of us who do not?

◄ A homeless family eats Thanksgiving dinner in Washington D.C.

Accurate statistics for the homeless population are hard to come by. People who are homeless are not likely to respond to questionnaires sent through the mail or to show up at voting booths on election day or get counted in a census. In many cases, entire families are homeless, often due to economic factors such as job loss or inadequate income. Many people who are homeless suffer from drug dependency or from mental illness—which is most often dealt with on an out-patient basis and with medication, without the supervision that many mentally ill people need. Some social workers report that many homeless people do work, but their wages are insufficient to provide for themselves and their families. An alarmingly high number of homeless people are children who have to fend for themselves. Some of these children ran away because of extreme poverty or physical or emotional abuse. Others were actually sent away by their parents or not allowed to return once they left

One frightening aspect of accounts of people who are homeless is how much they actually resemble the population at large. Many other people fall into the category of being what some call **near homeless**—a paycheck, a mortgage or rent payment, or one family crisis away from losing their home. Do you have a relative who exhibits signs of emotional problems and is no longer able to work? Is that relative on the way to becoming homeless? Is the friend who drinks too much and has a family history of alcoholism destined to live later life in and out of shelters and treatment centers? Is the fifty-five-year-old neighbor who loses his job and is now too psychologically paralyzed to seek another going to be able to hold himself together until retirement age? Is the relative who can't seem to shake his wartime experiences going to survive the strain on his family's finances and his government pension?

As these scenarios suggest, the answer to the question *Who are the people who are homeless?* is that they are our friends, relatives, and neighbors who have come upon hard times. They are children whose families cannot cope with the challenges of our changing economy and who lack the support of a capable extended family or a caring community. They may be people who are addicted or mentally ill and cannot find a place in the system. They may be single young men or women whose education and skill levels rule out adequate long-term employment. They may be the person who has lost a job because of corporate downsizing. Who are the homeless? The answer is that *any one of us*, living in this world where there are no certainties, could too easily become one of the homeless.

FAITH ACTIVITY

Helping the Homeless Find out what organizations in your area help people who are homeless. Divide into small groups and have each address the approach one organization takes to deal with the problem. Are people who are homeless or formerly homeless involved in the organization? Report on your findings.

FAITH ACTIVITY

Business Scandal Research a large-scale business scandal that occurred in recent years. Discuss the impact that the scandal had on various groups of people.

Poverty and Business Corruption The new millennium brought with it a series of business scandals that wreaked financial havoc throughout the world. The media focused on corrupt practices of individuals in leadership positions and on their fall from power. However, corruption in business is not simply a matter of personal morality; it is also a justice issue. In other words, as is so often the case, those members of society who are poorest end up suffering the most when a nation's economy or the world's economy suffers a downturn. For instance, many retired people found that the savings they had set aside over a lifetime of work were no longer sufficient to pay their bills. They had invested money in retirement funds that depended on ethical practices and forthright reporting by major businesses. Deceptive accounting and dishonesty by firms whose assets exceeded those of many nations resulted in a sharp drop in investments, in jobs, and in confidence around the world. Charitable organizations also reported a decline in donations, leading to a cutback in the services they could provide.

We may take for granted the day-to-day workings of business. We might also presume that people at the highest levels of power take care that they use their power with consideration for those affected by their decisions. But sometimes they don't. When corrupt practices occur on a large scale, we come face to face once again with the reality of our interconnected, interdependent world. Invariably, the most vulnerable suffer the greatest hardship.

September 11, 2001 The terrorist attacks on the World Trade Center in New York City and the Pentagon in Virginia presented new problems for those who are poor. The Catholic bishops of the United States cautioned the country to not forget the "least among us."

Overcoming poverty in our own nation requires a continuing commitment as well. The needs of the jobless, hungry and homeless cannot be ignored or neglected. New spending in response to September 11 and a declining economy will place new pressures on international and domestic programs that serve poor and vulnerable families. The poor abroad and in our own country must not be asked to bear a disproportionate burden of the sacrifices that will have to be made.

U.S. Conference of Catholic Bishops,
A Pastoral Message: Living with Faith and Hope after September 11

Recognizing that the events of September 11, 2001, would have an impact on another vulnerable segment of the population, the Catholic bishops of the United States took a courageous stand on the treatment of immigrants among us and the national policies related to immigration. The bishops stressed the need to respect basic human rights, especially for refugees and immigrants. They also cautioned people to avoid blaming these newcomers as a group for any of the country's problems. In the name of national security, innocent people should not be harmed or discriminated against or prevented from settling in the United States. (See *Living with Faith and Hope after September 11.*)

GROUP TALK

1. What types of programs could help homeless people with their immediate needs?

2. How have the events of September 11, 2001 affected "the least among us?"

▼ Memorial to victims of September 11th terrorists attacks

INTERNATIONAL VICTIMS OF THE WORLD TRADE
SEPTEMBER 11, 2001

EL SALVADOR · HAITI · JAPAN · MEXICO · PHILIPPINES
ETHIOPIA · HONDURAS · JORDAN · NETHERLANDS · POLAND
FRANCE · HONG KONG · KAZAKHSTAN · NEW ZEALAND · PORTUGAL
THE GAMBIA · INDIA · KENYA · NICARAGUA · ROMANIA
GERMANY · INDONESIA · UNITED NATIONS · NIGERIA · RUSSIA
GHANA · IRAN · UNITED STATES · NORWAY · SLOVAKIA
GREECE · IRELAND · LEBANON · PAKISTAN · SOUTH AFRICA
GRENADA · ISRAEL · LIBERIA · PANAMA · SOUTH KOREA
GUATEMALA · ITALY · LUXEMBOURG · PARAGUAY · SPAIN
GUYANA · JAMAICA · PERU · SRI LANKA

Responding to Poverty

FAITH ACTIVITY

Addressing the Needs What institutions and organizations in your area are sponsored by the Catholic Church or were founded as Catholic institutions or organizations? Which of them addresses the needs of people "who are poor and vulnerable, the elderly, and immigrants"? As a class project, address one of the material needs of the institution.

[T]hough he was in the form of God, [Jesus] did not regard equality with God as something to be exploited, but emptied himself, taking the form of a slave, being born in human likeness.

Philippians 2:6-7

Because the Son of God became one of us, all people have been raised up with him. To leave any of our brothers or sisters in poverty is unacceptable.

Christianity and Poverty

In an earlier chapter, the case was made that not only does God side with those who are poor, he actually identifies with them. The popular Christmas season image of the Holy Family searching for shelter reminds us that from the beginning of his earthly life Jesus himself knew the hardship of poverty, and he transformed poverty by bringing new life out of it. Jesus taught us that God's kingdom belongs to the poor and lowly, those entering with humble hearts. Jesus experienced the thirst, hunger, and need of those who are poor; he identified with those living in poverty of every kind, and he proclaimed "active love" toward them a necessity for entering his kingdom.

▼People sleeping in homeless shelter in Denver, CO.

The Church recognizes this requirement of Jesus as being based upon the God-given dignity of all people. She claims a special right to speak out against poverty and assumes responsibility for working for changes that enable those who are poor to live the full life God intends for them. In this way she calls each of us to practice the virtue of justice.

> People who are poor and vulnerable, the elderly, and immigrants are not abstract issues for us. They are in our parishes and schools, our shelters and soup kitchens, our hospitals and charitable agencies. (The Catholic community has a national network present in virtually every part of the nation. It includes almost 20,000 parishes, 8,300 schools, 231 colleges and universities, 900 hospitals and health care facilities, and 1,400 Catholic Charities agencies. The Catholic community is the largest non-public provider of education, health care, and human services in the United States.)
>
> Administrative Board of the U. S. Catholic Conference, *Political Responsibility*

Catholic Social Teaching: Anti-Poverty, Pro-Child

> While 31 million Americans, including 12 million children, according to the U.S Census, suffer from hunger, the food that is wasted in the United States alone could feed 49 million people.
>
> *Maryknoll* Magazine (September 2002), 13

One common denominator running through the groups of people described in this chapter is the fact that the most vulnerable members of society suffer the most from poverty. But children, the most vulnerable age group, need to be given priority in anti-poverty programs. In 1991 the U.S. Catholic Bishops described a crisis of poverty that they then saw among the country's children:

> Children are the poorest members of our society—one out of five children grows up poor in the richest nation on earth. Among our youngest children, a fourth are poor. Children are nearly twice as likely to be poor as any other group. Among children, the younger you are, the more likely you are to be poor in America. And poverty means children miss the basics—the food, housing, and health care they need to grow and develop. They are deprived in a way that hurts and distorts their lives.
>
> U.S. Catholic Conference, *Putting Children and Families First*

FAITH ACTIVITY

Special Needs Children Research and list groups who help special needs children in your area. As a class, find out what you could do to help these children. Make it a Lenten or Advent project.

The bishops who sponsored this statement praised the work done by groups and individuals who seek to make life better for children. They asked the government to assist and support these efforts—especially in providing services for families. The bishops pointed out that government programs and policies turned around for the better the economic situation among older people. Now it was time for the government to implement such policies to aid children.

Eliminating Poverty

With rare exception, every nation on earth provides some assistance to its citizens who are poor. In the United States, welfare reform was initiated by the federal government in the mid-1990s. The resulting changes in welfare programs shifted administration of programs to the state level, limited the amount of time people could receive government assistance, and attempted to move people previously on welfare to a situation of economic self-sufficiency. But there continue to be people truly in need, and for many of them the combination of government aid and contributions from private charities remains insufficient to move them out of poverty. Does this country possess the resources to provide for their needs? If so, why does the scandal of poverty, in some cases rivaling that which is found in much poorer countries, continue to exist in the United States?

The degree of poverty that exists in our country is a scandal not a curse. A curse is out of our hands; a scandal is a condition we can do something about. Anti-poverty programs must aim against poverty and not against people who are poor. In its document, *Political Responsibility*, the administrative board of the U.S. Conference of Catholic Bishops reminds us that the goal of welfare reform should be decreasing poverty and dependency, not decreasing resources or programs.

Current social and economic realities suggest that large numbers of people who are poor require help if they are to move out of poverty or even survive. Eliminating poverty requires a delicate balance. First, we clearly need to provide for those who cannot help themselves. That is, we need to provide a "safety net" of goods and services for the most vulnerable members of our communities. Second, we need to assist those who can help themselves to become more self-sufficient. Failure to maintain this balance can lead to people falling between the cracks of the variety of services available to help people in need.

Welfare-to-work programs aim at helping poor people become more self-sufficient. Through welfare reform initiatives, the United States has committed itself to creating and expanding such programs. Welfare reform legislation limited the amount of time people could receive welfare payments—generally five years. To be effective, anti-poverty strategies must combine the two approaches to doing social justice

FAITH ACTIVITY

Anti-Poverty Programs Find out what you can about various anti-poverty programs, both government run and privately sponsored. Describe the aims of each program and how it seeks to achieve those aims. Explain whether or not you would support each program.

described in chapter 4—that is, involve individuals on the one hand, and on the other hand, address social and structural problems that contribute to poverty. An observation by economist Rebecca Blank is helpful here:

> The reason poverty is so high in urban ghetto neighborhoods is because a whole host of destructive forces has evolved over time, with institutional problems in the schools, reinforced by lack of nearby employment, reinforced by poorly maintained public housing structures that become centers for drug and gang activities, and so on. The problems in these neighborhoods are deeply structural and environmental at the same time that they are deeply behavioral. It is difficult to know how to break out of the vicious circle.

Russell Sage Foundation, *It Takes a Nation*
(Princeton, NJ: Princeton University Press, 1997), p. 289

Who Should Pay?   One aspect of the discussion about aid to people who are poor centers around who should help them, the government or private charities such as church groups. Currently, both government and private agencies help people who are poor. But many private charities such as the network of Catholic Charities organizations also receive funding from the government. In the Catholic social justice tradition, government support is not considered something to be avoided. Catholic tradition holds that programs should be run at the most local level possible and also that various aspects of society should work together to address problems.

Given the extent and the nature of poverty in the United States, centralized government might be the most efficient overseer of key anti-poverty initiatives. And, it's not only government officials and structures that can make a difference. Many people, including Catholics, encourage greater public participation in advocacy, legislative networks, and community organizations. When the people are involved and put a voice to their concern, they can have an impact. As we discussed in the first chapter, an important aspect of living by the Fourth Commandment is taking an active part in society. We can do this by working with local and national government leaders to promote the spirit of justice and solidarity in the organizations, structures, and attitudes of society.

▲Gang graffiti covers a door in San Francisco, CA

As Catholics, our involvement is two fold: social conversion through the action for structural change as described above and personal conversion on the way we think about, relate to, and treat those who are poor. As the Church's teaching on the Seventh Commandment reminds us, this personal conversion is rooted in the person of Jesus, who "became poor , so that

Haves and Have-nots

★ The U.S. Gross Domestic Product is 21% of the world's GDP.

★ The top one percent of U.S. wage earners earn about 39% of the total U.S. income.

★ If you were a person living in another country, how would you view the wealth of the U.S.? How do lower wage earners view top wage earners within the U.S.? Compare and contrast these two perspectives.

by his poverty you might become rich" (2 Corinthians 8:9). By taking on human nature, Jesus transformed it, making it possible for each of us to become more God-like, to share in his divinity, and to become rich through his sacrifice and gift of life.

Jesus calls us to give life as he gives life, to have the right attitude toward our possessions and how we use them; the cardinal virtue of temperance helps us with this. If our attachment to the things of this world is put in the proper perspective, then our ideas on what's truly important and needed for life are put into proper perspective. We'll then be better able to see those who are poor, and the structures and norms that contribute to their plight, through God's eyes. They will be visible to us as never before.

Changing attitudes is not easy, and we have the grace of the sacraments to help us. As we've mentioned before, the Eucharist commits us to the poor, When we receive the Body and Blood of Christ, we are nourished by the gift of himself he has willingly offered. We must willingly give of ourselves, and see Christ in the poorest among us. All are made equal by Christ's sacrifice and gift of new life, and if all are welcome at this table, how can all not be worthy of the food and shelter they need to live? Saint John Chrysostom told us, "You dishonor [his] table when you do not judge worthy of sharing your food someone judged worthy to take part in this meal." (See CCC 1397.)

GROUP TALK

1. Describe attitudes of people who are poor and not poor that need to be addressed if poverty is to be alleviated.

2. Describe behaviors among people who are poor and not poor to be adopted, changed, or discontinued if poverty is to be alleviated.

Migrants and Immigrants

Most communities in the United States now boast a population of people who recently arrived in the country. Often they speak Spanish, sometimes the French dialects of Haiti or parts of Africa, and frequently one of the Middle Eastern or Asian languages. Their country of origin may be in Latin America, Africa, the Caribbean, Asia, or the former Communist bloc of nations. A few years ago, a California bishop noted that "the Asian population in the United States today [7.2 million at that point] is equal to the population of Paraguay or Uruguay. . . . The number of Asians in the Archdiocese of Los Angeles alone is greater than the entire population of Guyana or Suriname" (Bishop John Cummins, "Acknowledging the Extent of Asian Immigration," *Origins*, vol. 27, no. 25). Bishop Cummins pointed out that "The prediction for the year 2025 is that the United States will be 25 percent Hispanic, and it will be 12 percent Asian."

Migration has become a worldwide phenomenon. Not everyone who migrates is poor, but typically people from poorer or politically unstable countries seek refuge in wealthier, more stable environments—most often to earn a living. Likewise, not every immigrant is a person living in crowded quarters or working hard at menial jobs, although many do in order to send money home to relatives.

Is there a stance that citizens of the United States can take toward immigrants to their country that would combine both justice and sensible immigration policy? In light of the topic of this chapter, the question more specifically is: How do we respond to those people who are poor who feel desperate in their own country and who seek an opportunity for betterment by migrating to this country?

Bishop Cummins observed that the national mood toward immigrants "shifts between hospitality and hostility. The pattern is cyclical, touched by graciousness in good times, by harshness in difficult economic circumstances. When job competition comes to the fore, newcomers are blamed for societal ills." The fear and anger that followed the terrorist attacks of September 11, 2001, likewise heightened hostile attitudes toward immigrants. In the face of shifting attitudes toward immigrants, Bishop Cummins finds Scripture reminding us, "We are called to be a welcoming Church." The *Catechism*, too, presents a major challenge to those among us who resist the settlement of immigrants among us:

> The more prosperous nations are obliged, to the extent they are able, to welcome the *foreigner* in search of the security and the means of livelihood which he cannot find in his country of origin. Public authorities should see to it that the natural right is respected that places a guest under the protection of those who receive him.
>
> *CCC*, 2241

Immigrants and the Economy

Have recent immigration trends helped or hurt the economy? Research indicates that wages and unemployment are no more a problem in cities with larger shares of immigrants than in other cities, which suggests that immigrants are not negatively affecting employment in these communities. Some immigrants work at jobs geared directly to members of their own community and so do not displace other workers. Many perform jobs that most native-born workers do not want and would not take, at least for the wages offered.

Immigrants who are in the country illegally fear deportation and tend to stay away from even those government services available to them. And the national debate over more or fewer government services for this group is shrill. Since they lack power over wages and working conditions, illegal aliens often receive below minimum wages and work in substandard conditions. Since the workers are in the country illegally to begin with, to whom can they complain?

> While it is difficult to point to any single event as the cause for the upsurge in anti-immigrant sentiment, several factors have played a role. These include the perception that U.S. borders are out of control and that undocumented migrants are flooding the United States to take scarce jobs and to access public benefits. This perception has little basis in reality; the undocumented typically fill jobs unwanted by U.S. workers and are ineligible for most benefits, even though they pay $7 billion annually in taxes and social security contributions. Moreover, 85 percent of immigrants come to the United States through legal means.
>
> Wendy Young, "United States Immigration and Refugee Policy: The Legal Framework," *Who Are My Sisters and Brothers?* (Washington, DC: USCCB, 1996), 45

Immigrant communities help create jobs by requiring goods and services themselves. But for a number of years now, a national debate has been going on about whether or not, and to what degree, immigrants who remain poor should be eligible for government services such as public schooling (how much, how long), health care, and public assistance. The trend recently has been toward reducing the amount of government assistance available to immigrants.

How easy it is to forget that "All Americans—even those known today as Native Americans—are either descended from immigrants or are immigrants themselves" (Jim Carnes,

"Us and Them," *Teaching Tolerance*, 1995, 44). The question is: What is the just response to the new immigrants among us?

GROUP TALK

Answer **yes**, **no**, or **uncertain** to the following statements. Describe the images or information upon which you base your answers.

* Immigrants take jobs away from citizens of the United States.
* Unskilled immigrants tend to work harder than unskilled citizens.
* The racial background of immigrant groups plays a part in governmental policies and popular attitudes toward them.
* The United States should restrict legal immigration to a greater degree.
* The United States should more carefully enforce its laws restricting illegal immigrants

Mexican Immigrants and Mexican Americans People migrate to the United States for various reasons. One story that illustrates a link between an immigrant experience and issues of poverty and justice is the ongoing story of Mexican immigrants and Mexican Americans. Over the past several decades, Mexicans have made up a large portion of both the legal and the illegal immigrants that have come to this country. History provides some perspective on this phenomenon.

◄ A map of Mexico, created in 1826

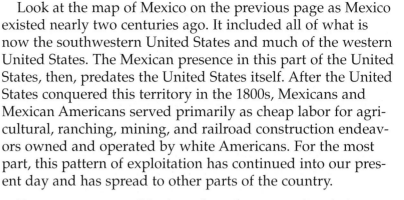

FAITH ACTIVITY

Formation of the UFW Research the role César Chávez played in the United Farm Workers union and report on it to the class.

Look at the map of Mexico on the previous page as Mexico existed nearly two centuries ago. It included all of what is now the southwestern United States and much of the western United States. The Mexican presence in this part of the United States, then, predates the United States itself. After the United States conquered this territory in the 1800s, Mexicans and Mexican Americans served primarily as cheap labor for agricultural, ranching, mining, and railroad construction endeavors owned and operated by white Americans. For the most part, this pattern of exploitation has continued into our present day and has spread to other parts of the country.

For over a century, Mexicans have been crossing their northern border to find work. Specifically, they want to find jobs that pay better than do those available in their own country. On this side of the border, Mexican workers have either been welcomed or discouraged from coming, depending on how great the need is for their labor. For various reasons, Mexican Americans as a group have been slower than European immigrants from a century ago to climb the social and economic ladder to success.

Why is this? One reason is that, after the European expansion to the west, Mexicans and Mexican Americans were often assigned negative labels: lazy, not very intelligent, carefree, and irresponsible. Second, almost all recent arrivals from Mexico and other Latin American countries have been peasants seeking work. The constant flow of new immigrants from these countries contributed to the image of Mexican Americans as being poor and uneducated, for many of the newcomers were not blending in with the dominant culture. Today, while stereotypes about Mexicans have either changed or become less common, the economic and educational status, the political power, and the opportunities for advancement of Mexican Americans have remained below those of European immigrants.

Cesar Chavez ▼

Traditionally, migrant farmworkers, many of them from Mexico, have been numbered among the lowest paid, least secure, and most poorly protected workers. They harvest crops seasonally, moving from location to location as different crops ripen, and therefore are never in one place for long. In parts of the country, such as California, there seems to be an endless pool of workers. If one migrant does not accept the wages and conditions offered, another one will. The plight of migrant workers was first brought to the attention of the general public by the novelist John Steinbeck. His novel, *The Grapes of Wrath*, gives a popular depiction of white migrant workers who traveled from the dust bowl of Oklahoma to work the fields of California during the Great Depression.

It took until the mid-1960s before there was a serious movement to unionize migrant workers. The person who spearheaded the drive to unionize was César Chávez, whose father had lost the family's Arizona farm during the Depression and been forced to work as a migrant. Like Dr. Martin Luther King Jr., Chávez used nonviolent protest techniques to win support for his cause. When he called for a boycott of California grape products, including wines, vast numbers of people in the United States agreed and refused to purchase these products. Support for the boycott was so great that after five years California growers recognized the United Farm Workers (UFW) union. Formation of the UFW represents a remarkable story of people who are poor working with people who are not poor to bring about change.

The Church Speaks on Behalf of Immigrants

Poverty levels are highest among the most recent immigrants, those who have come to the United States since 1990, while poverty rates among immigrants who arrived in the United States before 1970 more closely resemble those of the native-born population.

AmeriStat (July 2000)

It is really a surprise that, in this nation of immigrants, many citizens take a hard stand against immigration. Of course, countries need rules and policies regulating immigration, especially when people fear for the nation's security. However, in addition to concern for immigration laws and their enforcement, there must be compassion. Church leaders identify migrants as one group that deserves special attention and compassion. In 1995 the Catholic bishops of Florida addressed the crisis of increased migration going on throughout the world. The bishops went back to another historical period when large groups of people were on the move from country to country—the period following World War II. They quote from a post-World War II document, *The Émigré Family*, issued by Pope Pius XII:

> The *émigré* Holy Family of Nazareth, fleeing into Egypt, is the archetype of every refugee family. Jesus, Mary and Joseph, living in exile in Egypt to escape the fury of an evil king, are, for all times and places, the models and protectors of every migrant, alien and refugee of whatever kind who, whether compelled by fear of persecution or by want, is forced to leave his native land, his beloved parents and relatives, his close friends and to seek a foreign soil (*Exsul Familia*).
>
> *Statement on Immigration: The Flight to Egypt*

Are conditions in our world today similar to post-war conditions? Traditionally, a distinction was made between refugees and migrants. **Refugees** are driven out of their homeland under the threat of losing their lives because of warfare or political oppression. On the other hand, migrant workers leave a country voluntarily. Today these distinctions have become blurred. In some cases people, refugees, are leaving their homelands because of the threat of immediate physical violence. Other people, **migrant workers**, are leaving their homelands to avoid the threat of poverty and hunger. In both cases people are being uprooted because of real threats to their lives.

A bishop whose diocese hosts many migrants refers to one group as the **economic migrants**. He placed current patterns of migration in the broader context of today's global economy and asked: "Why in this new world is there free movement for goods and capital, but not for persons, especially poor persons? The wealthy seem to move and settle where they will" (Bishop Carlos Sevilla of Yakima, WA, "The Ethics of Immigration Reform," *Origins*, vol. 27, no. 43). Bishop Sevilla concluded that "the Church's teaching holds that there is a right to emigrate for economic reasons" and that anti-immigrant feelings that demean people in need are a sign of "a grave spiritual disorder." He proposed that "even when people are undocumented immigrants, there is a 'humanitarian zone' in which their human rights must be upheld and their basic needs supplied."

The Catholic bishops of Mexico and the United States have continued to stand with immigrants and migrants in their quest for a "place at the table" of plenty.

> We stand in solidarity with you, our migrant brothers and sisters, and we will continue to advocate on your behalf for just and fair migration policies. We commit ourselves to animate communities of Christ's disciples on both sides of the border to accompany you on your journey so that yours will truly be a journey of hope, not of despair, and so that, at the point of arrival, you will experience that you are strangers no longer and instead members of God's household.
>
> *Catholic bishops of Mexico and the United States,*
> *Strangers No Longer: Together on the Journey of Hope, #106*

FAITH ACTIVITY

Ministry to Migrants Investigate how the churches in your area minister to migrants. Find out what kind of education programs they provide, what type health care they offer, and what job assistance they give. Discuss your findings.

Immigration and the American Spirit

"Quite close to the shores of New Jersey there rises a universally known landmark which stands as an enduring witness to the American tradition of welcoming the stranger and which tells us something important about the kind of nation America has aspired to be. It is the Statue of Liberty, with its celebrated poem: 'Give me your tired, your poor, Your huddled masses yearning to breathe free. . . . Send these, the homeless, tempest-tost to me.' Is present day America becoming less sensitive, less caring toward the poor, the weak, the stranger, the needy? It must not!" (Excerpt from the homily of Pope John Paul II at Mass, October 5, 1995, Giants Stadium, East Rutherford, NJ.)

When the Holy Father graced New Jersey with his visit in 1995, he remarked that from its beginning, the United States has been a haven for generation after generation of new arrivals and prayed that America will persevere in its own best traditions of openness and opportunity.

> Give me your tired, your poor, Your huddled masses yearning to breathe free, The wretched refuse of your teeming shore. Send these, the homeless, tempest-tost to me, I lift my lamp beside the golden door!

Inscription on the Statue of Liberty
—Emma Lazarus

▼ Italian mother with her three children after their arrival on Ellis Island

GROUP TALK

In the year 2000, people born outside the country made up 10.4 percent of the total population of the United States. Latin Americans comprised over 50 percent of these, followed by Asians as the second largest group.

1. Does immigration at its current levels, and in the current form of multicultural emphasis, threaten the unity or enhance the character of the country? Explain.

›Faith in Action

The Youth Empowerment Program

Sponsored by: **The Coalition on Homelessness and Housing in Ohio**

More than 60,000 children and teenagers experience homelessness in Ohio every year and they are doing something about it.

> " I do YEP because I want to help make changes that will make things better for other kids. I am a homeless youth and I want to show people that youth are not all bad. No matter what our age, race, or class, we care about this community and can make a positive difference. "
>
> Ceira

The Youth Empowerment Program (YEP), a homeless initiative sponsored by the Coalition on Homelessness and Housing in Ohio (COHHIO) and funded in part by the Catholic Campaign for Human Development (CCHD), gives current and formerly homeless youth and youth aging out of foster care a chance to break the cycle of poverty and homelessness.

By organizing homeless youth into leadership advisory councils, YEP helps them put their own ideas into action. All council members have equal say and equal power. Members talk to other youth in shelters and invite them to participate. They give them food, toiletries, and computer training. But most of all, they offer support, something worthwhile to do, and somebody to listen to what they have to say. They offer them a sense of self worth and self-accomplishment achieved through giving back to their community.

Aimed at destroying stereotypes, YEP councils work to change the community's perception of homelessness. By acting on their ideas for change, these young people are able to make significant changes to local, state, and national policies. Recent successes include helping change policies in family shelters to admit teenagers so that families are not separated; assisting a local shelter to build a safer building with improved services for children and teenagers; partnering with national organizations to increase funding for homeless education to the amount of $60 million; and lobbying for a new state law in Ohio that addresses the rights of homeless youth to education.

YEP councils' participation in lobby days at the Ohio Capitol has included providing each legislator with a house built by a shelter youth group. These houses, made of building blocks, craft sticks, etc., come with a message, an impassioned cry for more funding for affordable housing programs. Whether it is testifying before the U.S. Congress for increased housing and education funds or advancing the cause of increased minimum wage in Ohio, these short-term projects are producing long-term social change in the communities of homeless children and youth.

Through advocacy, education, public awareness, and community service, YEP is training tomorrow's leaders to address the root causes of homelessness in their own neighborhoods across the state.

For thirty-five years CCHD has been building solidarity and offering a preferential option for and with the poor. CCHD does this by funding organizations that help poor and low income people help themselves. CCHD believes that the best way to end poverty is to involve the poor in creating long-term solutions.

◀ **Teens participating in The Youth Empowerment Program.**

Visit www.harcourtreligion.com to learn more about YEP, COHHIO, and CCHD and for links to their sites.

Prayer

Begin by praying the Sign of the Cross.

Leader: Jesus, you knew poverty first hand. We seek you in children, just as you called children to come to you.

All: Lord Jesus, help us to bring them your blessing.

Leader: We seek you in immigrants, just as you welcomed strangers.

All: Lord Jesus, help us to bring them your blessing.

Leader: We seek you in people who need welfare, just as you extended a caring hand to people in need.

All: Lord Jesus, help us to bring them your blessing.

Leader: We seek you in all those who find themselves poor, knowing that you are there.

All: Lord Jesus, help us to bring them your blessing.

Leader: Lord Jesus you invite all people to come to you and your message is for society's unaccepted as well as those it accepts. May we always uplift the downtrodden as followers and representatives of you.

All: Amen

End by praying the Sign of the Cross.

▶Review

1. What does *invisible poverty* mean?

2. List three reasons why poverty is still largely invisible in the United States.

3. Describe the employment status of most of those who are poor.

4. Give three reasons why fewer opportunities exist for viable employment for unskilled workers today than existed forty years ago.

5. Name three categories of people who make up the homeless population in the United States.

6. What does it mean to be among the *near homeless*?

7. Describe the justice implications of immoral business practices in large corporations.

8. Why does Catholic teaching propose that to be anti-poverty today means to be pro-child?

9. What two actions are required to eliminate poverty?

10. Define welfare-to-work programs.

11. How does Catholic social teaching view the role of government?

12. What reasons do the text give to make the case that illegal immigrants do not hurt the U.S. economy?

13. Give two reasons Mexican Americans as a group have been slower than some other immigrants to raise their social and economic status.

14. What was the result of the movement headed by César Chávez?

15. How are refugees traditionally distinguished from migrants? Why has this distinction become blurred?

▶Key Words

economic migrants (p. 186) People who come to a county seeking a better life for themselves and their families.

migrant worker (p. 186) A person who moves regularly in order to find work.

near homeless (p. 173) People with no savings or resources to carry them over during times of financial crisis.

refugee (p. 186) One who flees to another country or power to escape danger or persecution.

welfare-to-work programs (p. 178) Government assistance programs that provide aid while individuals are trying to learn a new trade or seek employment.

Our Challenge

The first step toward overcoming poverty and addressing the challenges of migration and immigration in the United States is accepting this challenge: We are sisters and brothers, all of us children of a loving God who is present and active in the world through the Holy Spirit. And because we are Christian, followers of the one who redeemed us, reconciled us with God, and gave us new life in the Holy Spirit, we are called to care when some of us go to bed hungry, are cold, are sick with no money for help, are homeless with no place to go, and are stranded with no way home. The Gospel challenges us to help.

The next chapter will continue our discussion of poverty, with emphasis on global poverty. In that chapter we will explore in more detail the Christian response to poverty. We will also make the necessary connection between Christian life and the Church's liturgy, especially the Eucharist.

CHAPTER 7

GLOBAL POVERTY

MAKING INTERDEPENDENCE WORK

CHAPTER GOALS

In this chapter you will:

* examine global poverty and its threat to health and life.

* determine why certain countries are poor.

* explore the Gospel through the eyes of the poor.

* recognize that through the Eucharist we are spiritually nourished and challenged to respond to the hungry.

Examining Global Poverty

what's your opinion?

Answer **agree**, **disagree**, or **uncertain** to the following statements. Choose statements that you believe are most significant and explain your answers.

1. Serious hunger and starvation are rare occurrences in the world today.

2. Enough food exists to feed the world's population adequately.

3. Before helping others, we should take care of people in our own country who are poor.

4. Changing our lifestyles (for example, the amount we consume) can help people who are poor.

5. Increased aid from wealthy countries is the best way to help poor countries.

6. Underdeveloped countries would do well to model their economies and lifestyles after the United States.

Maria's story on the next page is similar to the stories of many young people who live in the Southern Hemisphere. If she remains on her family farm, Maria will live her life on the edge of starvation or disease caused by poor nutrition and inadequate health care. If she seeks her fortune in the big city, chances are that she will end up in a physically and emotionally demeaning employment situation or working for minimal wages making products for consumers in the Northern Hemisphere. Working conditions in factories in underdeveloped countries typically damage young people's health and shorten their productive years—and their lives. Even working gruelingly long hours, Maria probably would not earn enough to assist her family or to provide for herself when she is replaced by another young girl with greater stamina and smaller fingers more suited to certain kinds of work.

In 1999 the World Bank sponsored a series of sessions with people from around the world who were poor; the results were published in 2000 as *Voices of the Poor: Crying Out for Change*. The purpose of the project was to gain a sense of the pressing concerns of people who are poor and of what it feels like to be poor. The people described strikingly similar experiences of poverty. In addition to material deprivation and overall physical ill-being, they spoke about the constant worry, fear, and frustration they felt, which instilled low self-confidence and a sense of powerlessness.

Where and when do we begin responding to the stories of poverty around the world? To begin with, we need to develop two perspectives. First, we have to acknowledge the extent of poverty. A second prerequisite to responding to global poverty is a matter of attitude. It's important to keep in mind that poverty and hunger are not natural. If some people are suffering needlessly it is not because "that's just the way it is." People are poor or hungry because of choices people make. Poverty can be overcome, but only if people change their priorities and make different choices.

There are two ways that international agencies measure poverty. The first is **income levels**, and the second is the **physical quality of life index**. Statistics are available that reveal the number of people worldwide who lack adequate resources to overcome their poverty. The physical quality of life index measures factors other than insufficient income that accompany poverty. When this index (PQLI) was first adopted it focused on three indicators of poverty—infant mortality, life expectancy, and illiteracy. For instance, in some parts of the world average life expectancy is over eighty years. However in a large section of the world, life expectancy remains below fifty-five years.

Maria's Story

My name is Maria Olana. I am a *campesina*—a peasant girl. I live on a small farm seventeen miles outside of Santa Rosa de Copan, Honduras, with my parents and six brothers and sisters. I once had two other brothers and another sister, but they died. The most recent death was my very young sister Rosa. This past winter, Rosa had diarrhea and weighed only seven pounds when she died. I cried and cried. When Rosa got sick, we went to our friend Cortia, who helps cure us. She told us that there was a cure for Rosa, but it would cost 100 lempira or about fifty U.S. dollars—we just didn't have the money. We also can't afford the medicine to cure the dengue fever, which my father has all the time. Sometimes it's so bad, he can't even work.

Our farm is on a steep hillside. We have one *manzana*, or about one and one-half acres, of land. We do not own the land—we lease it from Mr. Mendez, who lives in Santa Rosa. When times are good, we have plenty to eat. Our farm grows corn and beans, and we raise some chickens. Banana and orange trees nearby give us fruit. My father sells some corn and eggs to buy rice, material for clothing, and a few tools. Times are not good now, though. The rains this year were extra heavy, and much of our corn crop was washed down the hillside. Many of our chickens have died, and all we have to eat are a few beans and some bananas. My father put in a new corn crop, but some kind of insect seems to be eating the corn before it gets very big.

We would love to get some of the rich land in the valley so that we could grow more, and our crops wouldn't keep being washed away by the rains. But all the valley land is owned by the fruit company. My oldest brother, Carlos, used to work for the fruit company in the pineapple fields. Last month, though, Carlos lost his job. The people at the fruit company told him that because of a recession, people in North America were not buying as many pineapples, and fewer people were needed to work the fields.

A man from the government came to see us last week. He told us about a new kind of corn that we could plant that did not grow as tall as the corn we are used to. He said that the short plants would be less likely to wash away and that they also produced about three times as much corn. My father was very excited until he found out that in order to use this corn, he would have to buy chemicals to fertilize the plants and protect them from diseases. "The new plants would give us a chance to get ahead," my father said. But we all knew there wasn't any way we could get started with the new corn.

In tough times like this, all that is left is to dream. I have heard that it is possible for young girls to get jobs in the city. I went to school two years ago, and I was told I was very smart. I really liked school, but my father needed me on the farm. He says that girls need only to know how to cook, gather firewood, and make clothes. Someday I will find a way to make life better for my children than it has been for me.

Adapted from "Maria's Story," C. Joy and P. Regan, *World Hunger: Learning to Meet the Challenge* (New York: Impact on Hunger, 1983), pp. 85–86. The story was created by the Impact on Hunger organization to reflect documented family situations in Honduras and other developing countries.

GROUP TALK

1. Review the seven major themes of modern Catholic social teaching in Chapter 3. Which themes apply to Maria Olana?

2. If Maria came to live with your family as part of an exchange program, what would you want to say to her? What words of hope would you offer her that her dream could come true?

3. If you went to live with Maria's family as part of an exchange program, what do you think the experience would be like? What effect do you think it would have on you?

Rich Countries Versus Poor Countries

The WorldWatch Institute reports that the world's **840 million hungry people** are matched by the same number of overfed people in wealthy countries.

Maryknoll Magazine (September 2002), p. 13

The wealthiest **20 percent** of the world's population consumes **68 percent** of its commercial energy; the poorest **20 percent** uses less than **2 percent**.

United Nations Development Programme

According to the United Nations, **85 percent** of young people (ages 15–24) live in the world's poorest countries. Over half of the world's young people are unemployed and many others make barely enough to survive. Young women are particularly disadvantaged.

FAITH ACTIVITY

Living in Poverty In magazines and books, look for information about what it means to be poor from the perspective of people who are living in poverty. Write about how they experience their situation.

The majority of the world's people who are poor live in Africa, especially sub-Saharan Africa, and in parts of Asia and Latin America. However, just as there are people who are poor in countries with more financial wealth such as the United States, so too there are wealthy people in countries where poverty is prevalent. The extent of poverty is so great in some countries that it is accurate to say that whole countries are poor. That is, in some countries, living without electricity, without running water, and in shacks with dirt floors describes the way of life for most people. Professional health care is scarce, so that even minor illnesses can be life threatening. Most people attain only minimal levels of education. Governments are so strapped with debts that they can do little to help their suffering citizens. One unfortunate indicator of nationwide poverty is the extent of hunger-related illnesses and death.

Hunger: When Poverty Threatens Health and Life

When you arrive home from school today, you will probably ask, "What's there to eat?" A trip to the refrigerator will, no doubt, provide a quick and satisfactory answer to that question. For about one-fifth of the earth's people, however, trying to answer the question "What's there to eat?" consumes most of their day and a large part of their income.

Sadly, what the poorest fifth of the world's population receives to eat cannot satisfy their hunger. Their health and strength is gradually depleted. They end their day with gnawing hunger pains and with the realization that getting enough food to survive will be their main task again tomorrow. Because hungry people experience many days of poor nourishment, they are more likely to become sick or diseased than well-fed persons are. Death is no stranger within the families and neighborhoods of hungry people. They live every day on the narrow edge between life and death.

Just before mealtime we might say, "I'm hungry." Yet we all know that the hunger we feel is not what people concerned about "world hunger" are referring to. The hunger experienced by the world's poorest people refers to chronic **malnutrition** and undernourishment.

Malnutrition: A Lack of Necessary Nutrients When we were young, we probably tried to read the strange-sounding words on the side panels of cereal boxes. They stated, "Satisfies the minimum daily requirements for the following vitamins and minerals. . . ." We probably took it for granted that we were on our way to meeting our daily nutritional needs with our cereal, milk, and juice. In fact, most of us in North America receive adequate nutrition.

By contrast, the 20 percent of the world's population who are hungry do not receive minimum daily requirements of proteins, vitamins, and minerals vital to good health. Because these people can afford nothing else, the bulk of their diet consists of one type of food—usually rice, corn, or millet. For six out of ten people in the world, rice is the staple of their diet. Although nutritious in itself, rice alone cannot provide complete nourishment. As we learned in our middle school health classes, proper nutrition requires a varied diet. Consequently, a poor diet leaves the world's hungry people malnourished. When this condition persists, they suffer from chronic malnutrition.

Chronic malnutrition leads to protein-deficiency diseases that eventually result in death. Lack of vitamin A causes blindness. Iron deficiency leads to anemia, which results in a feeling of tiredness and sluggishness and reduces energy and motivation. Life expectancy among chronically malnourished

people is in the forties, while well-nourished people today can expect to live on average into the high seventies. Naturally, chronic malnutrition is most damaging to young children and pregnant women. Young children are most likely to die or to become brain-damaged from malnutrition.

Undernourishment: A Lack of Sufficient Calories

While malnutrition refers to the quality or type of diet, **undernourishment** refers to the quantity, or amount. Calories provide needed heat and energy for the human body. Undernourished people lack a diet that meets minimum caloric requirements. As a result, their bodies must feed on their own tissues. Here is a description of the physical results of undernourishment:

> When food intake drops below energy expenditure, the body must draw upon its own tissues for energy. When this energy drain continues too long, the person starves. The body burns up its own fats, muscles, and tissues; kidneys, liver, and endocrine systems often cease to function properly; blood pressure and pulse fall drastically; edema [swelling from excess fluid] usually happens, skin acquires the consistency of paper; . . . hair grows on the forearms and backs of children; lassitude and confusion set in so that starvation victims often seem unaware of their plight, . . . and the body's immunological defenses drop. . . . Once more than 40 percent of the body weight is lost, death is virtually inevitable.

Medard Gabel, "Ho-Ping: Food for Everyone,"
World Hunger: Learning to Meet the Challenge
(New York: Impact on Hunger, 1983), 15–16

GROUP TALK

1 What would be different in your life if you were chronically malnourished or undernourished?

2 If you survived, how would your future differ from what you now look forward to?

In developing countries, 91 children out of 1,000 die before their fifth birthday. By comparison, in the United States 8 children in 1,000 will die before turning five years old.

More than 800 million people in the world are malnourished–777 million of them are from the developing world. And 177 million of them are children.

Each day in the developing world, 30,100 children die from mostly preventable and treatable causes such as diarrhea, acute respiratory infections, or malaria. Malnutrition is associated with over half of those deaths.

Bread for the World

About 24,000 people die every day from hunger or hunger-related causes.

The Hunger Project, United Nations

Famine and wars cause just 10 percent of hunger deaths, although these tend to be the ones you hear about most often. The majority of hunger deaths are caused by chronic malnutrition. Families simply cannot get enough to eat. This in turn is caused by extreme poverty.

The Institute for Food and Development Policy

Besides death, chronic malnutrition also causes impaired vision, listlessness, stunted growth, and greatly increased susceptibility to disease. Severely malnourished people are unable to function at even a basic level.

United Nations World Food Programme (WFP)

Causes of Hunger

All famines are complicated by politics; no famine [in the twentieth] century . . . occurred in a democracy.

Steven N. Krentel of World Vision

When we see images of starving people on television or in newspapers, chances are that there is a backdrop of wasted land where neither crops nor livestock could survive. Once-fertile ground has been reduced to a desert. Do droughts, famines, and floods cause the conditions leading to hunger?

For most of human history, drought and flooding have plagued us. Nonetheless, these natural occurrences need not lead to large-scale human suffering and death. Social systems can usually meet the challenges of nature. An example of organizing society to work with nature comes from the Bible. When Jacob's son Joseph was in Egypt, he (Joseph) advised the pharaoh to store up grain during the seven years of plenty to meet the needs of the seven years of drought. (See *Genesis 41:28–36*.)

FAITH ACTIVITY

World Hunger Visit www.harcourtreligion.com for links to one of the groups referenced in the chart and other sites that deal with world hunger. Choose one of the sites to review. What further facts are presented on the site? Share these in class and create a new chart for your classroom.

FAITH ACTIVITY

Famine Research Ethiopia, Ireland, or another country or part of the world that has experienced famine. Find out what factors led to the famine. To what degree were causes environmental? Did politics play a role in the problem? If so, how? How did the international community respond to the crisis? Report on your findings.

Invariably, where modern famines have occurred, political and social conditions have contributed significantly to the problem. Famine is more often a byproduct of war, social upheaval, and other human activity than it is of nature. Drought itself has links to human behavior. For instance, recent studies suggest that air pollution originating in the United States and other heavily polluted areas has contributed to diminished rainfall in the parts of Africa now experiencing an extended drought.

Why Are So Many People Hungry?

Imagine ten children at a table dividing up food. The three healthiest fill their plates with large portions, including most of the meat, fish, milk and eggs. They eat what they want and discard the leftovers. Five other children get just enough to meet their basic requirements. The remaining two are left wanting. One of them manages to stave off the feeling of hunger by reducing physical and mental output, though she is sickly, nervous and apathetic. The other dies from a virus which he is too weak to ward off.

Arthur Simon, *Bread for the World* (Mahwah, NJ: Paulist Press, 1984), 18

OUT OF TEN CHILDREN

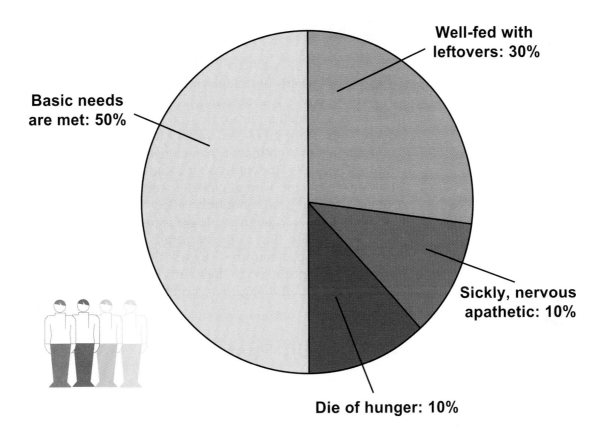

Well-fed with leftovers: 30%

Basic needs are met: 50%

Sickly, nervous apathetic: 10%

Die of hunger: 10%

This bleak picture leads to the question, "Why are people in our world chronically malnourished and undernourished?" The answer is simple: People are hungry because they are poor. For example, peasants working on lush plantations can be too poor to feed their families what they themselves are helping to harvest. Some countries with severe hunger problems export food to other nations because they need the revenue that these exports bring. And keep in mind that hunger-related problems continue to exist even in rich countries, such as the United States.

GROUP TALK

If you were in charge of an ad campaign designed to address the problem of world hunger, what slogan would you use? Who would your audience be for this ad campaign? What would be the rationale for using your slogan?

Characteristics of Poor Countries

D eath, ill health, and deprivation are common in countries where poverty is rampant. While each country with a large population of people who are poor has its own identity and set of problems, most of these countries share a common mix of identifiable characteristics. Knowing common features generally present in poor countries can help us seek solutions to the problem of global poverty. Countries with extensive poverty are commonly called "undeveloped" or "underdeveloped" countries. There is truth to this label, but it can also be misleading. Four characteristics commonly found in underdeveloped countries suggest that historical and global factors have contributed to their current condition. A global response is needed to improve conditions there.

A Colonial Past

At the end of World War II, there were two independent countries on the continent of Africa. In 1957 there were four. By 2004 fifty-four countries in Africa and on the surrounding islands were independent.

While colonialism is nearly a thing of the past, many less-developed countries were once colonies. A colonial past does not automatically condemn a country to poverty. Hong Kong, Canada, and the United States have fared quite well as former colonies of England—in many ways taking on the characteristics of the empire in the global marketplace. Through colonization, many of the cultural refinements and scientific advancements of Europe were brought to the Americas. Nonetheless, to understand poverty today, it is necessary to step back a few hundred years, and in some cases only a few decades, to note the negative impact colonialism can have.

Colonialism, as explained in Chapter 2, refers to certain countries, often European, controlling other countries. One reason to conquer other territories was to benefit the homeland, using colonies to provide natural resources, markets, or in some cases labor. Cities, transportation systems, agriculture, and industry were established to promote commerce with the homeland. Even today, most underdeveloped countries remain dependent on a few wealthy countries and trade exclusively with them rather than with one another. As a result, they remain **economic colonies**.

High-minded colonialists might claim that colonialism was good for conquered lands—bringing them the benefits of European civilization, religion, and development. However, the bottom line was always how this venture into a far land would help the political aims, business interests, and citizens of the controlling country. A side effect of colonialism was that people who were colonized had their language, culture, and identity relegated to secondary status or wiped out. It is no surprise that the effects of colonialism outlived actual colonial periods.

A Closer Look

A Former Colony's Fall into Poverty

If we tried to imagine what an underdeveloped area looks like, we would probably conjure up a town like Potosi, Bolivia. At an altitude of 15,000 feet above sea level, Potosi is difficult to reach. The roads leading to it are bad. The native Indian people who live there squeeze out a skimpy living from the poor soil. The only other major source of employment is a tin mine in the mountain which overlooks the town. Housing is poor, and running water and electricity are a luxury in the area. . . .

However . . . in the 1600s, in the heyday of Potosi, they say that even the horses were shod with silver. At the height of its boom, the town had a population equal to that of London and larger than that of European centers like Madrid, Rome, or Paris. Potosi attracted silks and fabrics from Canada and Flanders, the latest fashions from Paris and London, diamonds from India, crystal from Venice, and perfumes from Arabia. Something really valuable in the 17th century was referred to commonly as being "worth a Potosi." . . .

The entire economic and social life of Potosi was based on wealth from a single commodity—silver. This silver was mined by the native Indian population and shipped directly to Spain. Potosi silver financed, in large measure, the development of the Spanish empire in the 17th century. . . . The underdevelopment of Potosi, then, began with the abuse of its people and resources through the European colonial system. The Latin American economy was geared by the Europeans to meet their own needs, not those of the people local. . . .

Development Education Centre, "Development and Underdevelopment," Development Education Viewpoint, 1 (Toronto: Development Education Centre, 1975)

GROUP TALK

As a group, write a journal entry for a citizen of a nation that is a colony of another country.

1. Describe what you think your life would be like.
2. What feelings might you have?
3. What hopes and fears would you expect to have?

Population Growth

Underdeveloped countries have higher rates of population growth. There are reasons for this: As people become wealthier and more economically secure, they tend to have fewer children. But, when people face poverty conditions, they depend on many births to help ensure that at least some children survive to adulthood. Children increase possibilities for income, add to a family's support system, and provide for parents when they are old. Large population growth can result from poverty as well as increase poverty.

The Catholic Church is not necessarily against taking steps to limit population growth, but opposes abortion and artificial birth control as means of achieving this goal. Instead of these methods, the Church calls on wealthier nations to help in promoting education, improving health care, and advocating other forms of development in poor countries. In this way, people who live in these countries will be able to sustain themselves and provide for their families. Where limiting population growth is appropriate, the Church also supports the use of those methods known as Natural Family Planning.

Is There Too Little Food, Land, and Water? Population growth in underdeveloped countries raises the question of the earth's ability to feed its population. Most experts agree with the following assessment: "If the present world food production were evenly divided among all the world's people, with minimal waste, everyone would have enough. Barely enough, perhaps, but enough" (Arthur Simon, *Bread for the World*, 18). This viewpoint is hopeful but not encouraging. Food cannot be evenly divided, and waste occurs in large proportions. So, while we can say that there is enough food in the world, it is also true that scarcity of food is a major problem.

Landowners in both underdeveloped and developed nations who own large plots of land are more likely to use their land as investment for **cash crops** or leave land unplanted and accept a subsidy from the government for doing so than are farmers who own smaller plots of land. Because much of the land in poorer nations is owned by investment landowners, much of the cultivated land in underdeveloped countries is now given over to the production of cash crops rather than to **food crops**.

> One of the greatest injustices in the contemporary world consists precisely in this: that the ones who possess much are relatively few and those who possess almost nothing are many. It is the injustice of the poor distribution of the goods and services originally intended for all.
>
> Pope John Paul II, *On Social Concern*, 28

If enough food does exist to feed everyone in the world, then the problem of hunger is one of caring and distribution more than production. That makes world hunger a moral problem more than a technological one—that is, a problem of justice. The material problem of hunger most strongly affects people in underdeveloped countries; the moral problem of hunger must be dealt with by people in developed nations.

We do possess the ability to feed everyone. However, this would require a change in priorities by the world's population. People would have to be considered first over profits and politics, some change in eating habits would be required, and a definite change in how we view one another would have to take place. On a practical level, food scarcity calls for increased food production, a reduction in waste, and attention to methods of food consumption. It also calls for a settlement of political differences and an end to governmental corruption that stands in the way of distributing food to those who need it most.

Scarcity of water may cause more problems worldwide than scarcity of land. Water is used for drinking, cooking, bathing, and crop irrigation—and it is essential in holding off hunger and diseases. For many people in poor countries, finding drinkable water is a daily struggle. Sometimes the solution is as straightforward as digging a well, installing a community water tap, or devising a simple irrigation system. These and more elaborate ventures require planning and community cooperation. They also require money, which many undeveloped countries simply do not have.

GROUP TALK

List the resources and luxuries you have that make it possible for you to enjoy adequate food and water. Then imagine how your lives would change as one, and then the next, and so on, disappeared from your everyday lives.

Multinationals and Single-Export Economies

Living in a comparatively wealthy country, we know that there exists a great demand for products available only from underdeveloped countries and for products that can be manufactured inexpensively by using poorly paid workers. We know too that underdeveloped countries are under great pressure to rely on one product or on a few products as their primary source of income. These products are meant to be exported and not to be used locally.

Countries that rely heavily on exporting only one product—**single-export economies**—or a few products, for example, coffee or bananas, occupy an unstable position within the global economy. If a fruit company does not find a favorable situation in one country or from its workers, then the company can easily threaten to harvest bananas in a neighboring country. When demand for a particular item goes down, a country dependent on that one export has no other resources to help it weather the accompanying financial downfall. Strapped with debt and overrun with citizens desperate for employment of any kind, the country is in no position to hold out for justice for its workers.

Multinational corporations—corporations that possess assets in many countries—are the first to benefit from this arrangement. Sometimes their budgets exceed the whole budgets of the countries in which they are located. The directors of such corporations are expected to make money for company stockholders. Keeping labor costs down is one way of increasing profits. Countries where the standard of living is low to begin with provide a labor pool of workers who have little choice but to work for whatever wages are offered them.

Sometimes both a company and a country benefit from a multinational corporation's business ventures. However, the livelihoods of ordinary people are often displaced, leaving people to abandon the way of life that had sustained them for centuries—frequently forcing them to leave the countryside or familiar village for life in a city or on a mega-farm or ranch. In this case, a company and a few well-placed local citizens benefit at the expense of cheap labor provided by people whose wages will not raise them and their families out of poverty and hunger.

FAITH ACTIVITY

Impact on Global Poverty Rank the following from highest to lowest in terms of their impact on global poverty: international businesses, international agencies (for example, the United Nations and the World Bank), wealthy countries, the governments of underdeveloped countries, societal and structural problems in underdeveloped countries, actions of people who are poor. Explain your rankings and what role each group could play in solving global poverty

The Social and Political Climate

Not everyone in underdeveloped countries is destitute. These countries often have a small minority who, along with multinational companies, control practically all the wealth in the country. They may live in great luxury, with servants and Swiss bank accounts, even though they are surrounded by great poverty.

The great inequality between rich and poor in underdeveloped countries raises questions about how best to help those who truly need help. The fact that a country reports an increase in its Gross National Product does not mean that those who are poor are benefiting. Sometimes it can mean simply that the rich get richer. However, it would be unfortunate if the gross inequality and corruption in underdeveloped countries would serve as an excuse not to seek ways to diminish the tremendous suffering that is common there.

Partially a legacy of a colonial past, underdeveloped countries traditionally tend to be **oligarchies.** Political power might shift from one faction to another within this elite, and leadership might at times be more dictatorial or more democratic. However, faced with extensive problems, governments in underdeveloped countries seldom have a history of stability and often lack wide or deep-seated popular support. In this situation, a country's military takes on the role of policing its own citizens rather than protecting the country from external threats, and international businesses wield a great deal of power since they hold out the promise of wealth for some.

FAITH ACTIVITY

Rich and Poor Use reference sources, find out the Gross National Product, life expectancy, and other measures of wealth and health for two countries in two parts of the world. Which is richer? Besides standard of living, what distinguishes the countries? Develop a poster with this information and share it with the class.

Burden of Debt A burden of debt to developed countries plagues most underdeveloped countries. International agencies exist that grant loans to countries to aid in their development. Often the welfare of the majority of citizens is not a primary concern when agricultural or industrial programs are initiated. Rather, the belief prevails that increasing the Gross National Product will somehow benefit everyone in the country. Given the governmental instability in many countries, sometimes the leaders who actually received the loans are no longer in power. Sometimes the projects are never built, and no one can officially account for what happened to the money. Often the needs of people who are poor are often neglected as governments of underdeveloped countries try to establish a place in the global marketplace.

In safe and healthy societies, a set of institutions exists to support social well-being—a standard currency, healthcare facilities, schools, banks, and law enforcement. In underdeveloped countries, people carve out a support system in families and local communities as best they can, since wider institutions are seldom stable enough to be counted on for long-lasting support.

GROUP TALK

1. Would you refuse to work for a company that explicitly exploits cheap labor, such as employing children to work in factories? Why? What examples from Jesus' ministry and principles of Catholic social teaching would you use in your argument?

2. If you discovered that one of your favorite products was manufactured using exploited labor, would you discontinue buying that product? What examples from Jesus' ministry and principles of Catholic social teaching would you use in your argument?Explain.

3. If you were part of an international task force on poverty, what programs, policies, and legislative action would you recommend?

A Christian Perspective on Poverty

Scripture makes it clear that people who are poor hold a special place in God's heart. Mary, the Mother of the Son of God, refers to herself as a poor servant girl. Her song of praise at the beginning of the Gospel according to Luke indicates the joy that is found in the Lord who singles out the lowly, reverses things, and fulfills his promises recorded in the Old Testament.

[F]or he has looked with favor on the lowliness of his servant.
Surely, from now on all generations will call me blessed. . . .
He has brought down the powerful from their thrones,
and lifted up the lowly;
he has filled the hungry with good things,
and sent the rich away empty.

✝ Luke 1:48, 52–53

Throughout Latin America, people tell stories of Mary appearing to the poor, offering a message of hope. Some of these apparitions have been officially recognized by the Church. The most famous of these, the appearance of Our Lady of Guadalupe, occurred in Mexico in 1531. At that time Mary appeared to a native of Mexico named Juan Diego. Mary appeared as an Indian princess on a hill that had been a shrine dedicated to an Aztec goddess. She asked that a chapel be built in her name, and eventually one was. Our Lady of Guadalupe is a symbol of hope to the native people of Mexico. In 2002 Juan Diego was canonized a saint by Pope John Paul II.

▼ *The Virgin of Guadalupe* by Miguel Cabrera

Poverty and Scripture

Church leaders throughout the world apply to their particular setting Christ's message of Good News to people who are poor. An example of an area particularly troubled with poverty is northern Brazil. Some time ago the bishops of that region described the deplorable living conditions of most of their people and offered a vision of how they would like to see their world:

> We want to see a world in which money is placed at the service of human beings and not human beings at the service of money. We want to see a world in which all will be able to work for all, not a divided world in which all persons work only for themselves. Therefore, we want to see a world in which there will be only one people with no division between rich and poor.

Richard Shaull, "The Marginalization of a People,"
Heralds of a New Reformation (Maryknoll, NY: Orbis Books, 1984), 102

Recent popes and other Church leaders have often played the prophet's role, affirming that hunger and need should not exist and deploring that everything possible is not being done to eliminate these ills:

> Countless millions are starving, countless families are destitute, countless men are steeped in ignorance; countless people need schools, hospitals, and homes worthy of the name. In such circumstances, we cannot tolerate public and private expenditures of a wasteful nature; we cannot but condemn lavish displays of wealth by nations or individuals. . . .

Pope Paul VI, On the Development of Peoples, 53

The Seventh Commandment and Poverty Since those who are extremely poor have practically nothing to be stolen, how can the Seventh Commandment—which forbids theft—help them in their struggle to overcome poverty? People don't usually steal from people who are homeless. You've learned in the previous chapters that this commandment is about much more than stealing; it's about creating situations in which our neighbors (in the broadest sense of the word) do not have access to the things they need to thrive; it's about equal access to the goods of creation and protecting those goods so that people everywhere can benefit from them now and in the future.

The Book of Leviticus speaks of an application of the Seventh Commandment meant to assist those who find themselves poorer than their neighbors and other family members—the **jubilee year**. According to Leviticus, every fifty years steps are to be taken to eliminate debt and to restore the Israelites to their original condition as free people and as landowners on an equal footing with everyone else. Leviticus

bases its call to jubilee on the proclamation by God that he alone is the true owner of the land. For their part, people are "aliens and tenants" on God's land. (See *Leviticus 25:23*.) If God, who desires the well-being of all his children, ultimately owns the earth's goods, then the Seventh Commandment has implications for all those with material possessions in abundance, not just for those who overtly take from others. In the spirit of jubilee, societies should take steps to help those who fall upon hard times.

The jubilee year was one of many juridical measures prescribed in the Old Testament directing people to "open wide your hand to your brother, to the needy and to the poor in the land" (*CCC* 2449). (See *Deuteronomy 15:11*.)

"Hence, those who are oppressed by poverty are the object of *a preferential love* on the part of the Church which, since her origin and in spite of the failings of many of her members, has not ceased to work for their relief, defense, and liberation through numerous works of charity which remain indispensable always and everywhere" *CCC* 2448.

The Church is involved not simply in meeting the needs of people on a physical level, she also is concerned with their spiritual well-being. People have a right to live a life in which they can make a free response to God's call; all people have a vocation, no matter their economic state in life. Therefore, the Church seeks to help people overcome whatever factors—physical or other forms of deprivation—that would prevent them from their true development as human beings beloved of God.

The Gospel Through the Eyes of the Poor

How does the Church reach out to the poor today? Latin America is one of those areas of the globe where many people are extremely poor. Traditionally, it has also been overwhelmingly Catholic. Prior to the late 1960s, the Church was more closely identified with the wealthy few who held power in Latin American countries. For the most part, Church leaders believed that if they could help educate and inspire good Christian leaders, then everyone—including those who were poor—would benefit.

However, when Latin American bishops gathered in 1968, they took a different approach to common problems. Namely, they asked: What would it be like to read the Gospels through the eyes of those who are poor? This simple but challenging question led to the beginning of a movement that has challenged religious thought ever since.

The Latin American bishops noticed that far too many of their people were dying before their time, that they spent lives filled with hardship and suffering, and that certain elements within the social order contributed to their problems. In response to this situation, the bishops realized anew the Christian truth that the Gospel message not only offered hope for salvation after death, but should also challenged people to respond to God's grace and work for his reign of justice, peace, and love. The Gospel, then, challenges us to connect the personal call to the social call, and to work for liberation—for social changes that improve and respect the dignity and rights of those who are poor and their lives. The bishops proposed a different starting point for theology. They sought to "theologize" with people who were poor, not for them. They determined that theology must combine reflection on the Gospels with action initiated by and on behalf of those who are poor. As you might have noticed, this message reflects Catholic Social Teaching as described earlier in this book.

FAITH ACTIVITY

Speak on Hunger Prepare a speech on what you think Jesus would say to the world today about how we deal with hunger. Decide who your audience would be. Share the setting you chose and the speech with your class.

Jesus, the Bread of Life The reality of so many starving people in the world is an ongoing challenge to all Christians. Not sharing food with people in need runs counter to what Jesus stood for. Anyone who has ever visited a Jewish delicatessen or attended a Seder meal in a Jewish home knows the importance of food in the Jewish tradition. In that regard, Jesus was very much a product of his Jewish culture. Clearly, Jesus appreciated the importance of food and of "breaking bread together" as an essential human experience. In calling himself "the Bread of Life" Jesus was tapping into the natural human longing for the refreshment that comes from eating and applying that longing to the joy of eternal life. Refer to the following chart for a few of the references to food in the New Testament.

A Heavenly Feast

Isaiah 25:6	Heaven itself is described as "a feast of rich food, a feast of well-aged wines."
John 2:1-11	Jesus' first public miracle took place at a wedding feast.
John 6:1-13	One of Jesus' most famous miracles involved providing bread and fish for the crowds that followed him.
Luke 14:7-24	Jesus compared his kingdom to a banquet.
Luke 8:41-42, 49-55	When he brought Jairus's daughter back to life, Jesus immediately told her parents to give her something to eat.
Matthew 26:26	Before his death, Jesus shared a meal with his disciples.
Luke 24:13-35	After Jesus was raised from the dead, he appeared to the disciples on the road to Emmaus; when they arrived at the town, he shared bread with them. They recognized him in the breaking of the bread.
Luke 24:41	Jesus appeared to the eleven Apostles, asking them, "Have you anything here to eat?"
John 21:5	Jesus stood on the shore and asked the Apostles who had been fishing, "Children, you have no fish, have you?"
John 21:12	Jesus invited the Apostles to "Come and have breakfast."

FAITH ACTIVITY

Holy Event Have you ever experienced a meal that you might call a holy event? If so, write a paragraph explaining what made it so special.

Global Poverty 213

Challenge to Hunger Write an essay titled "The Eucharist: Challenge to World Hunger" in which you make a connection between the Eucharist and hospitality to strangers, concern for hunger, and the global community.

The Eucharist and Hunger The Eucharist is the heart and summit of the Church's life. This means that everything flows from and moves toward the celebration of Christ's Paschal mystery in the transformation of the bread and wine into his Body and Blood. The essential signs of which are bread and wine. In the Eucharist, Christ uses these simple signs of life-sustaining nourishment to commemorate his work of salvation accomplished by his life, death, and Resurrection. Every liturgical celebration makes present Christ's work of salvation, transforming us into his Body on Earth. Along with the other sacraments, the Eucharist supports us during our pilgrimage in life. Participation in the Eucharist also makes us long for the heavenly banquet that awaits us and strengthens us to, "Go in peace to love and serve the Lord."

In the Eucharist, Christ gives himself to us. In doing so he revives our love, strengthens our charity, and beckons us to be more merciful. That is, through the Eucharist we are nourished spiritually and revitalized in our efforts to respond to those who are hungry, crying out for food. To recognize Christ's Body and Blood, we must recognize him as well in our brothers and sisters who are poor. For that reason, the Eucharist is both comfort and challenge.

GROUP TALK

1 If you were a bishop, a priest, or someone else concerned about justice:

* How would you divide your time between business/government leaders and people who are poor?

* What kind of justice program would you promote that would include the concerns of community leaders and people who are poor?

2 Describe how elements of the Mass manifest (a) nourishment through Christ and (b) the need to care for others.

Responding to Poverty and Hunger

> Jesus shares the life of the poor, from the cradle to the cross; he experiences hunger, thirst, and privation. Jesus identifies himself with the poor of every kind and makes active love toward them the condition for entering his kingdom. (See *Mt 25:31-46*)
>
> *CCC* 544

An old movie portrays a lifeboat built for only eight people bearing twelve passengers. If all twelve remain aboard, the lifeboat is in danger of sinking. What should be done?

Some writers suggest that our earth is like that lifeboat. We have to make choices. Either some people must be left to die or the entire boat will capsize. A model called **triage** has been proposed as a way of deciding who will receive food from the earth's limited resources. Triage, a system first employed by the French during World War I, places wounded soldiers into three groups: (1) those who can survive with little or no attention, (2) those who can survive but need immediate attention, (3) those who can survive only with intensive treatment. Under triage on the battlefield, the third group is left untreated until the first and second groups are cared for. Of course, during the wait they might die.

Applying the battlefield triage model to those who are hungry around the world implies that some people should simply be left to die. Those who support this model suggest that when we try to help those who are hungry, all we succeed in doing is creating an even greater strain on the earth's limited resources. So, they reason, people suffering from chronic malnutrition should not be helped because too many people means not enough food for everyone. Of course, the Catholic Church condemns and rejects this type of triage and the attitudes behind it. As the Fifth Commandment reminds us *all* people are worthy of preservation and love because of their God-given human dignity; they are made in the image of God and redeemed by Christ. No matter how healthy or sick, they and their life are a gift from God that must be protected. And when we lead others to demean or undervalue human life by what we do or don't do, we participate in sin. This means that everything flows from and moves toward the celebration of Christ's Paschal mystery in the transformation of the bread and wine into his Body and Blood.

Declaring War on Poverty and Hunger

Every Gospel tells the story of Jesus feeding a multitude of people with one child's basket of food. Chapter 6 of the Gospel according to John tells us that Jesus fed five thousand people with the bread and fish carried by one small boy. To feed all those in the world today who are hungry also requires a great miracle. The need is so great, and our baskets are so small.

During much of World War II, certain products were measured out (rationed) and were often difficult to obtain in the United States. For the most part, citizens didn't mind. They knew that the soldiers had to be taken care of first. So they learned to waste less and to stretch the resources they had. They also began again the practice of growing their own food in "victory gardens." People saved even small things, such as aluminum gum wrappers, so that these items could be put to use in the war effort. If sacrifices could quicken the war's end, people at that time were willing to make them.

Wars cause a great deal of suffering, death, and destruction, but so does hunger. Catholic Relief Services reports that "every year 20 million people suffer hunger-related deaths and millions more experience the irreversible effects of childhood malnutrition: permanently impaired mental and physical development and diminished work performance." This means that every year, hunger is a greater killer than World War II, in which 17 million soldiers died worldwide.

If drastic measures were called for during that war, then equally drastic measures are called for in our current war against hunger. We can feed the multitudes who are hungry, but only with intense and sustained effort. The "basket" we have to share with others is not just our physical resources but our faith, determination, and ingenuity as well. Prayer and mutual support within the Church are needed to sustain us in our commitment to overcoming poverty. We know that our efforts can be successful because the Holy Spirit is working through us.

Overconsumption and Poverty "Don't waste that food—think of the starving children in China!" In the past parents have used this response to coax their children into finishing their vegetables. The idea is still worth considering: Does our waste help to cause hunger elsewhere? Does overconsumption in the developed countries contribute to the poverty that is widespread in underdeveloped countries? If those who are well-fed were to change their eating habits and adjust their lifestyles, would these changes benefit the people of the world who are hungry?

Patterns of consumption do have an impact on the world's food supply. For example, grain can be used to make alcohol or to feed cattle or to be eaten directly. Alcohol is a non-necessity, and more grain produced in the United States feeds cattle than feeds people. There are choices to be made. To make a difference, people who personally avoid waste and overconsumption must also work for societal changes and political action. Here's a simple example of how societal change can benefit underdeveloped countries:

If high school students throughout the United States decided to fast for a day and contribute money saved to help poor people, they could raise thousands of dollars. However, if they combined their sacrifice with efforts to influence government and business policies to benefit workers in poor countries, their impact would be many times greater. For instance, an increase of only one cent per pound in the price of raw coffee translates into more than sixty-five million dollars a year increased revenue for coffee-exporting countries.

Military Spending: Guns or Food?

No discussion of hunger would be complete without mention of military spending. We are becoming more aware that the world has limited resources. Unfortunately, when choices are made, most countries choose guns over food. For instance, in many underdeveloped countries, food storage is a major problem. The money needed to buy a modern military tank could be used instead to build modern storage facilities for rice, thus saving over four thousand tons of rice annually. Every minute, thirty children die of starvation or from lack of medications. In the same time, the world's governments spend over a million dollars on the military. In fact, one-half of 1 percent of what the world's militaries spend in one year would pay for all the farm equipment needed for underdeveloped countries, so that within ten years the people within these countries could raise enough food to adequately feed their own people.

Hunger kills as certainly as war does. Money and energy for weapons production have been bought at the expense of food production and distribution. The ability to overkill the human population has been won at the price of underfeeding millions of people.

FAITH ACTIVITY

War on Hunger If you declared a personal "war on hunger," what might you do differently? Make a list of specific changes you might make or specific activities you might undertake. Include possible steps leading to societal change or changes in governmental policies. How does prayer and working together as part of the Church sustain efforts to overcome hunger?

International and National Development

One-fourth of the world's economic output is produced by the 500 largest corporations. These corporations employ one-fourth of 1 percent of the workers of the world. International trade and aid agreements are sometimes designed to help wealthy nations either directly or indirectly, often placing profit over people. Consider what can happen at a time of

drought in a large part of the world. If the United States, which produces over half the world's grain supply, cuts back its grain production to raise the price of wheat in order to sell large quantities at high profit to another developed nation, great numbers of people in other countries will die of starvation.

Countries that are poor require a stronger voice in the international arena if their concerns are to be addressed by other countries and decision-making bodies. Leaders in underdeveloped countries often call for *trade*, not *aid*, as the best way to help their people. In categories described earlier in this course, trade—greater power on the international marketplace—offers more of a long-term solution to poverty than charity does. Of course, changing rules of international trade to better favor underdeveloped countries can lead to loss of control among developed countries that now hold the power in trade.

Nationally, development in poor countries must reflect the needs, strengths, and particular characteristics of specific areas involved. In particular, imitating wealthy and highly industrialized countries is not always helpful. For example:
- Mexico City has an efficient, inexpensive, and greatly used subway system. The United States, in contrast, has made a greater commitment to private transportation than to public transportation. If Mexico City, with its large population, were to imitate the United States in its emphasis on private transportation, the results would be disastrous.

- In farming, bigger is not always better. Large-scale farming is usually **energy-intensive**. On the other hand, small-scale farming is usually **labor-intensive**. The Green Revolution demonstrated the pros and cons of energy-intensive farming. Begun in Mexico, this development project gained worldwide publicity in the 1960s by introducing high-yield strains of various grains. Unfortunately, it also caused unemployment among the rural labor force, since their work

GROUP TALK

1. If your school sponsored a World Food Day event that included the option of skipping lunch and contributing lunch money to an anti-hunger organization, would you participate? Why?

2. Would you support a trade agreement that would benefit workers in underdeveloped countries but that would raise the price of consumer items in your country? Why?

3. Discuss the pros and cons of the following statement: *The United States should take the lead in fighting hunger by cutting back military spending and contributing the difference to world food programs.* Would you sign a petition bearing this statement? Why? Discuss the statement in light of Catholic teaching on justice.

was no longer needed. Because this energy-intensive method relied heavily on machinery, fertilizer, and other products, the project was best suited to larger farms. As a result, many of the unemployed farm workers migrated to already overcrowded cities.

Why Help People Who Are Poor? When asked "Why do you help them?" a priest involved in finding housing and work for immigrants, who entered the United States illegally, simply answered: "Because they're here." We face a similar question when we admit the presence of so many people who are poor around the globe: "Why help them?"

On a purely selfish level, the world—our world—becomes a better place when it is populated with people who are not starving, poorly educated, physically deprived, or desperate. This world would be a safer, friendlier, healthier, more beautiful world all around. Only hope-filled people, especially when hope is shared, possess the faith, character, courage, and motivation needed to make a better world for everyone.

But that is not our motivation as people of faith. The world is made up of family—sisters and brothers inseparably bound together as children of one God. As you probably know from your own experience, the family unit hurts whenever any of its members are hurting. Our faith calls for compassion and caring and action. We are one human family who needs to watch out for one another, provide for one another, experience what the other experiences, and will a change. This is what the Christian principle of solidarity is all about.

God is our loving Father, and the poor are incredible images of him with worth and dignity. He intends that we work to overcome the sinful injustices that prevent people from living out their God-given dignity. Christ wants us to take on the needs of others as if they are our needs. Will we cooperate with him to help our brothers and sisters?

FAITH ACTIVITY

How Does It Feel? Compose a prayer, poem, or work of art that reflects the struggles, fears, and hopes of a person who is poor.

In wealthier countries, "development" has a different meaning. There it means developing a different set of priorities and a consistent commitment to overcoming poverty, even when it exists in communities that we don't encounter regularly.

❯Faith in Action

Food fast

Sponsored by: **Catholic Relief Services**

Giving up burgers and fries for a meal may be hard for many young people, but across the United States thousands of young people participate annually in a twenty-four-hour hunger awareness retreat that combines fasting, prayer, service, and educational experiences.

> " Food Fast is always an awesome experience. When you are able to look past everyone repeating, 'I'm starving,' you can learn about, connect with, and serve people who are less fortunate. "
>
> –Kate Kirbie, Little Flower Parish

Sponsored by Catholic Relief Services (CRS), Food Fast is anchored in the four principles of Catholic Social Teaching that have bearing on our lifestyle choices—Life and Dignity of the Human Person, Dignity of Work and the Rights of Workers, Option for the Poor and Vulnerable, and Solidarity. Food Fast is designed to help young people learn about poverty and hunger around the globe as they raise money to help those who are suffering.

The experience of fasting in solidarity with the poor gives Food Fast participants a real understanding of what it feels like to be hungry and raises their awareness about the issue of hunger and things they can do to help. For example, they learn that for the $5 it costs them to eat at a fast food restaurant, a Rwandan family of five could buy enough corn meal, oil, and salt to feed them for three days.

Members of the Kingdom Construction Company (KCC), the youth group from Little Flower Parish, South Bend, Indiana, followed themes of "letting go" from the story of the rich man in Mark 10 and "I thirst" from the gospel account of Jesus' crucifixion during their 2005 Food Fast. After learning sessions on hunger, fasting, and Catholic social teaching, they bought food, prepared it, and served a feast for 125 people at Hope Rescue Mission.

As part of their 2005 Food Fast, youth group members from St. John Vianney Parish in Kirkland, Washington, provided a full meal to sixty-five homeless people who were camped on their church's front lawn in a tent city. They heard about poverty first hand from a Maryknoll missioner who spoke of his experiences in Kenya, and they decorated and distributed 500 lunch sacks to parishioners and collected them the following week as part of Operation Sack Lunch, a program that feeds the homeless of Seattle.

By working together Food Fast participants learn that when they "think locally," they are "acting globally" to end hunger and deprivation.

CRS is the official relief and development agency of the Catholic community in the United States.

◀ **Teens participating in Catholic Relief Services.**

GO ONLINE

Visit www.harcourtreligion.com to learn more about the CRS's program and for a link to its site.

The Magnificat, Mary's song of praise;

Begin by praying the Sign of the Cross.

My soul magnifies the Lord, and my spirit rejoices in God my Savior, for he has looked with favor on the lowliness of his servant.

Surely, from now on all generations will call me blessed; for the Mighty One has done great things for me, and holy is his name.

His mercy is for those who fear him from generation to generation.

He has shown strength with his arm; he has scattered the proud in the thoughts of their hearts.

He has brought down the powerful from their thrones, and lifted up the lowly; he has filled the hungry with good things, and sent the rich away empty.

He has helped his servant Israel, in remembrance of his mercy, according to the promise he made to our ancestors, to Abraham and to his descendants forever.

✝ Luke 1:46–55

End by praying the Sign of the Cross.

Review

1. Where do the majority of people of the world who are poor live?

2. Name two ways that international agencies measure poverty.

3. Name two conditions that are the result of serious hunger, and explain the difference between the two.

4. What is the primary reason why people are hungry?

5. Besides political and economic enslavement, what side effects resulted from colonialism?

6. What is the relationship between poverty and population growth?

7. What does it mean to say, that underdeveloped countries usually exhibit gross inequality?

8. What are economic colonies?

9. How have Church leaders played a prophetic role regarding world hunger?

10. What is a jubilee year? How does it apply the seventh commandment to helping those who are poor?

11. In what sense is the Eucharist a challenge to world hunger?

12. Explain the battlefield triage approach to world hunger.

13. Name three societal changes that could assist underdeveloped countries.

14. What is the Christian response to a world food crisis?

15. What does it mean to say that the nations of the world must choose between guns and food?

Key Words

cash crops (p. 204)–Crops grown to be exported in order to raise money.

economic colonies (p. 202)–Poorer countries dependent on a few wealthy countries to purchase their limited selection of crops or products.

energy-intensive (p.218)–Large-scale farming that depends more on heavy machinery, chemical fertilizers, irrigation systems, and pesticides than on people.

food crops (p. 204)–Crops grown to feed the people within a country.

income levels (p. 194)–Comparative amounts of money earned annually by individuals or families.

jubilee year (p. 210)–The Old Testament law stating that debts should be canceled and land restored to its original owners every fifty years.

labor-intensive (p. 218)–Small-scale farming that depends more on workers than on machines to do the farm work.

malnutrition (p. 197) –A state resulting from a diet lacking the nutrients vital to good health.

oligarchy (p. 207)–A country ruled by a few members of an elite group clearly distinct from the vast majority of the population.

physical quality of life index (p. 194)–The combination of a country's average infant mortality, life expectancy, and literacy rates.

single-export economies (p. 206)–Budgets based on one product as the main source of income.

triage (p. 215)–The practice of placing people into one of three groups based on their likelihood of survival and treating first the two groups most likely to survive.

undernourishment (p. 198)–Amount of food is less than what can sustain life.

>Our Challenge

The next time we gather with our family or friends to enjoy a meal, we might pray for the many people struggling to provide meals for their own families. Jesus is the Bread of Life. The next time we participate in the Eucharist, we might pause and remember that in doing so we are joining with the poor of the world who are also members of Christ's mystical body and that we have an obligation to them. We can commit ourselves to learning about one organization that addresses the problem of hunger and consider ways we can contribute. Our actions taken to eliminate poverty and hunger and to help make the world more like the kingdom of God are essential steps on our Christian journey.

RACE

CHAPTER 8

BEYOND STEREOTYPES TO THE AMERICAN DREAM

CHAPTER GOALS

In this chapter you will:

★ learn the roots and characteristics of prejudice.

★ analyze thinking that divides humanity according to race and cultural backgrounds.

★ examine how racism and racial prejudice affect society.

★ discover the Church's stand against racism.

Eliminating Prejudice

what's your opinion?

Answer **agree, disagree, or uncertain** to the following statements. Choose statements that you believe are most significant. Explain your answers.

1. I treat people and respond to people the same, regardless of race.

2. I would not mind if a family of a different race moved in next door.

3. I believe that people of different races should not marry each other.

4. Members of minority races should receive special consideration in educational and employment opportunities.

5. Public figures who tell racial or ethnic jokes should be severely criticized.

6. Every racial and ethnic group has had its share of difficulties. No one group or groups should be singled out as being victims of racism.

Often without much to back them up, we have likes and dislikes about things such as foods, styles of dress, speech patterns, ways of spending summer vacations, and methods of relating to others. Typically, our likes and dislikes are based on limited experiences. Usually they reflect what we have been comfortable with from our earliest years. We can feel so strongly about our beliefs and viewpoints that we hold onto them in the face of solid evidence to the contrary. Preferences and strongly-held positions are not what we mean by prejudice. We slip into **prejudice** when we make judgments that are unfounded or based on limited experience. Usually we are not even aware of the shaky foundation upon which we make prejudicial judgments. For example, saying "students at that school are all spoiled rich kids" based on hearsay or an encounter with two people is an unfounded generalization.

Characteristics of Prejudice

When directed toward groups of people, prejudice means more than likes and dislikes. Prejudice involves at least three characteristics that, together, harm both those who are victims of prejudice and those who are prejudiced.

Stereotyping Stereotyping is an attempt to make things "fit" into an oversimplified, incorrect, prejudiced opinion. Making generalizations is both a natural and a helpful use of human intelligence. If a person is scratched by a kitten, and that is the person's only experience of kittens, he or she might be afraid of kittens, or of all cats. Likewise, a near-drowning incident might keep a person from going near water for the rest of his or her life. We generalize; that is, we take one idea or experience and apply it, in general, to other situations.

Consider the following stories of race.

Julee left her native India ten years ago when she was six. Nonetheless, she continues to wonder how to respond to her classmates who tell her, "We think of you as being just like us. You don't seem Indian."

In a predominantly white school, Antonio and Aquella, two black students, spend their free time with other black students. In the beginning of the year, a few other students questioned this arrangement. Within a month, however, it was accepted by everyone as simply the way things were going to be.

For a few months now, Oun Mi, who is Korean, has been dating Patrick, who is Irish. Oun Mi's parents expect her to marry someone who is Korean and would never accept a non-Korean boyfriend for her.

Kathy, who is white, sees in a magazine a political cartoon portraying an Arab man as a terrorist. Kathy presumes that this is an accurate portrayal of all Arabs. In fact, she has never met anyone of Arab descent.

As they approach the mall, Darnell, who is black, jokes with his white friend Nick. "You know when I go into the stores, I'm watched more closely than you are." "No, they're suspicious of all young people, Darnell," Nick insists. "Seriously, Nick, all black people are lumped together as troublemakers by most white and Asian store owners."

Nhai struggles to get average grades. Her math teacher, who is white, questions her progress. "You're doing poorly, Nhai. I expected you to work harder and to do better in math. All the Asians but you are doing great work."

"Another business operated by Pakistanis," Mike points out as he leaves the convenience store with his friends. "If we're not careful, soon Americans won't own anything anymore."

The school has had a Black Cultural Club for many years. Asian and Hispanic students have recently sponsored events to celebrate their heritage. Feeling slighted, a group of white students approach their religion teacher requesting that she serve as moderator of a new "White Students Club."

GROUP TALK

1. Are all of the above incidents illustrations of racism? Why?

2. Have you, for any reason, ever felt like an outsider or experienced the sting of prejudice or discrimination? If so, describe the experience. How did you react?

3. Recall an experience that you have had with a person of another race.

   * What happened? (Where did the incident occur? How old were you at the time? What led up to the incident? How did you feel?)

   * How did this experience influence your attitude toward members of that race in general? Where are you today in terms of your view of members of that race? If your view has changed, what led to that change?

Sometimes our minds need to make swift and sweeping judgments or connections. But we have to be careful with this normal and healthy human skill, especially when it comes to people. When we base our opinion of an entire group of people on our experience of a few, we are stereotyping. Stereotypes can even be embedded in a family or community. For instance, many people from New England may have certain impressions of people who speak with a southern accent without ever spending much time with Southerners. Some people from California may hold certain beliefs about people from the east coast. Stereotyping means (a) generalizing about an entire group based on some characteristics of a few and (b) limiting our understanding of certain people to preconceived notions we have about them. A true picture of life is always much richer and more complex than stereotypical thinking suggests. Therefore, we must always be open to new and better information if we are to overcome stereotyping.

"My Truth" or "The Truth"

Prior to World War II, Nazis published propaganda that presented so-called scientific proof that Jews were racially inferior to "true" Germans.

During the 1800s, British cartoons portrayed Irish people as closely resembling monkeys in order to support discriminatory practices against them.

Before the U.S. Civil War, some supporters of slavery argued that Africans enslaved and brought to the United States were "fortunate" to be introduced to Christianity and civilization. Thus slavery was presented as actually being beneficial for slaves.

Often, during wars, enemy soldiers and civilians are considered less than human and given derogatory nicknames; thus it is easier to justify taking their lives. Furthermore, in military language, the killing of innocent people is referred to as "collateral damage." The term hides or de-emphasizes the human lives lost.

GROUP TALK

Name three stereotypes held by some people in your school or community. Imagine one of these stereotypes being applied to you. How would you feel if you were the object of such stereotyping?

Close-mindedness If we were to say "People on welfare are lazy" and hold firmly to that belief in the face of all the studies and statistics that prove otherwise, then we would be close-minded. Other examples of close-mindedness are:

- A white student walks into a classroom filled with many Asian students and concludes, "I don't want to be in class with Asians. They all work too hard."

- A store security guard watches a young black woman more closely than young white women customers.

In both cases, the persons involved are prejudiced insofar as they operate out of preconceived notions and are closed to all information except that which supports their prejudice. While we can work only from our own experiences of other people, it is also important to realize that our base of experience is limited. We practice prejudicial thinking when we close ourselves off from new information about other people and groups, other ideas, other possibilities.

Intense Negative Feelings Fear is really the main characteristic, the *source*, of prejudice. Prejudice is about hatred and anger, and hatred and anger are about fear. Prejudice is not just a matter of likes and dislikes. It is, in the end, a matter of intense hatred toward persons or groups of people. For example, we may dismiss acts of violence committed by members of our own social group but react strongly to similar acts by members of a different group. The slogan "My country right or wrong" illustrates such prejudicial thinking.

With its intensity of feelings, prejudice divides people into "us" and "them," insiders and outsiders. Prejudiced people hate others simply because of what they look like, where they came from, or what they believe. While all of us find comfort and security in identifying with our particular group, that identification and loyalty need not lead to hatred of others groups.

In the 1800s in the United States, four groups singled out as outsiders by dominant powers were African Americans, Native Americans, Catholics, and Jews. Members of each of these groups suffered at the hands of others who had strong negative feelings toward them.

FAITH ACTIVITY

Ethnic Hatred Write a brief report on an international conflict in which racial or ethnic hatred plays a role. Emphasize how loyalty and patriotism need not lead to hatred of others groups.

Classic examples of "us" and "them" thinking in the twentieth century were the Nazis in Germany, the Japanese in their treatment of Koreans prior to World War II, and the racial-discrimination policies known as apartheid in South Africa.

More recently, following the September 11, 2001, terrorist attacks, some people in the United States who either were or appeared to be of Middle Eastern descent experienced prejudicial treatment.

Numerous international conflicts today are fueled by group hatred. In the United States, the Ku Klux Klan, the neo-Nazis, the skinheads, the Aryan Nation, and other hate groups fear and hate non-white people and people of religious backgrounds other than Protestant. They view others as a threat to their "power" and way of life. Indeed, hate groups support violence against anyone who happens to be a member of a group they dislike.

One evening a middle-aged white person is standing alone at a bus stop. A black teenager approaches the person, who stiffens and is fearful of the youth's intentions. The teenager asks, "Do you know how soon the next bus is supposed to come?"

A Middle-Eastern family, parents and children, prepares to board an airplane. An airport security agent singles them out for an extensive search and treats them with hostility.

A woman shops at a market owned by an Italian family rather than one closer to her home which is owned by a Korean family because she wants to "buy American."

GROUP TALK

Working in small groups, apply to each case the characteristics of prejudice, and decide whether or not prejudice is involved.

Emmett Till

In 1955 Emmett Till, a fourteen-year-old black teenager from Chicago, was spending the summer with relatives in Mississippi. Outside a store in the small town he allegedly whistled at a white woman. That night some white men came and dragged Emmett out of his house, tortured him, mutilated his body, and tossed it in a river. Emmett's mother brought her son's body home to Chicago and held an open-casket viewing so that people could see the horror Emmett endured. The men who committed the crime admitted to it but were not found guilty by the jury made up of like-minded people. Emmett's death helped spark the civil rights movement that transformed the nation over the next few decades.

Roots of Prejudice

Where does prejudice come from? The roots of prejudice begin in early childhood experiences. We are not born with prejudice. We are taught it—sometimes directly, more often indirectly. However, we can overcome prejudice. The fear behind prejudice is often the fear of anything different, the fear of anyone "different" from us. If we are insecure, we may feel threatened by others who are different from us. When we feel secure, we can be open to other people and groups, to new ideas, to new ways of looking at things and to new ways of doing things. Certainly there are things in life about which we need to be cautious, but it is not skin color or a person's religion or someone's country of origin that need to be feared. God created everyone with equal dignity. And prejudice defies and denies that human dignity.

Overcoming prejudice takes courage. Sometimes it means going against long-held beliefs or the perspectives of people close to us. The opposite of prejudice is not simply tolerating differences: "You do your thing, and I'll do mine." Rather, the opposite of prejudice is actively seeking to learn about, feel connected to, and care about those who are different from us—all of whom are God's children. In a word, the opposite of prejudice is compassion.

Family Tree Think back on your own family's history of the last few generations. Draw a family tree as far back as you can go. Did your family's ethnic or racial background play any role in their understanding of the American dream? Explain. Do you think that your ethnic or racial background plays a role today in your view of or your achieving of that dream? Explain

GROUP TALK

① Think of a prejudice that you have. What do you think are the origins of this prejudice?

② "Children who have not yet learned who society's most frequent victims are will pick their own. I had no interest in playing with dolls or dressing up, so I was labeled a 'tomboy' My little brother, born brain-damaged, was called a 'retard.' An auburn-haired friend of mine remembers hearing, 'I'd rather be dead than red in the head.' Indeed, anything that makes a child 'different' is justification for slander: glasses, braces, thinness, fatness, tallness, shortness, poverty, or wealth. By the time most children are big enough to ride a bicycle, they know who the outsiders are and they know what to call them."

Sara Bullard, *Teaching Tolerance* (New York: Doubleday, 1996), 8

★ Do you think children tend to divide people into "us" and "them"? Why?

★ If you were a parent, how would you seek to help your children move toward greater acceptance of differences?

★ How would you rate yourself on dealing with the outsiders of your school or community?

How Different Are We? Many people in the United States feel uncomfortable talking about race. Even when we don't have intense feelings ourselves, public discussion about race issues often brings out anger, pain, guilt, disagreements, and frustrations that we would just as soon not deal with. Underlying this is the belief that open discussion about race is absolutely necessary if we are to heal—and become "one nation, under God."

> Many people believe that to not be racist means one must be color blind—that is, not recognize or place significance on a person's racial background and identity. But to ignore the significance of race in a society where racial groups have distinct historical and contemporary experiences is to deny the reality of their group experience.

Margaret L. Andersen and Patricia Hill Collins, *Race, Class, and Gender*
(Belmont, CA: Wadsworth Publishing Co., 2000), 50

GROUP TALK

1. Should we be color blind, dismissing racial differences, or should we try to identify and talk about racial and ethnic differences? What are possible dangers in each approach?

2. Can you envision a future in which being color blind is the normal state of affairs? What would need to happen to bring about such a future? Explain why you would or would not want such a society.

3. If you could change the racial situation of the United States in any way, how would you change it?

One Immigrant's Story

In 1935, when Elizabeth was twelve, she and her family left their native Czechoslovakia and immigrated to the United States. They settled in a city in the northeastern part of the country. At first Elizabeth viewed herself as an outsider, a "foreigner" who spoke no English and dressed differently. She had an olive complexion, darker than that of most people she saw in magazines or at the movies.

As time went by, Elizabeth began to feel more and more at home in her new country. She adopted the ways of her new land much more quickly than her parents did, who themselves started to appear "foreign" to Elizabeth. By the time she reached adulthood, Elizabeth had learned many of the lessons of the United States. One important lesson she learned and accepted was that she belonged to a low social class. Another lesson she learned was that she was white.

When black families started moving into her neighborhood, Elizabeth and her husband purchased a house ten blocks away in an all-white neighborhood. Except for brief periods taken off to have her children, Elizabeth worked as a seamstress. She would never think of socializing with the bosses at the company; nor could she imagine her own children ever achieving such high positions. She was friendly but did not socialize with the few African American women who worked at the factory. Elizabeth's understanding of the American dream was that her children would be able to work hard and live a decent life. She encouraged her sons to consider becoming barbers or auto mechanics. She never questioned whether that same dream was shared by or available in the same way for the children of the African American women with whom she worked. Nor did she question that the children of the bosses and owners at the factory had opportunities and privileges not available to her own children. For Elizabeth, the United States was a land of opportunity. She would encourage her children to do their best.

GROUP TALK

A number of decades ago, Elizabeth felt that an important lesson to learn was that she was considered white.

1. Do you believe that this was an important lesson for her? If so, in what sense?

2. Do you believe that being of a certain race makes a difference in the United States today? Why? In what way or ways?

Race as a Social Construction

One important aspect of Elizabeth's story is that when she came to the United States, she did not "know" that she was white, as opposed to black, or African American. She learned this identity by observing what it means to be white and to be black in this country. Similarly, some black Americans tell of being high school exchange students in Europe or of studying in other parts of the world. They discover that in many countries they are not "black" in the sense that the term means in the United States. Indeed, some African Americans have chosen to live in France or other countries in order to escape the racism that they experienced in the United States.

At times people of color in the United States talk about constantly living with a "dual consciousness," that is, a consciousness of being themselves and also of being of a particular race. Here is one person's experience of dual consciousness:

> I love the United States of America, and I love living here. But as an actor and as an individual, I find myself in a dual position. Like others from Latin America, I am part of an alien nation within a larger nation. . . . The fruits of our labor are prized and needed, but we are kept apart due to our language and culture. They like our food and admire our colorful art, but do not accept us as peers.

Ramon Novarro, in *The Fire in Our Souls: Quotations of Wisdom and Inspiration* by Latino Americans, edited by Rosie Gonzalez (New York: Penguin Books USA, 1996), 51

Race is a social construction. It is the kind of thinking that attempts to divide humanity according to skin color and body characteristics. Census reports and other surveys that try to identify people by race illustrate how hazy our idea of race can be. People who have identified themselves as "Hispanic" are either wholly or in part of European, Native American, or African heritage. The "Asian" classification can include—among others—people from Iran, the Indian subcontinent, Vietnam and Cambodia, China, Korea, and Japan. Interestingly, Lebanese, whose country of origin is in Asia, can be designated as "white." Perhaps most telling about the way people in the United States view race: A person who is 75 percent white and only 25 percent African American can be classified as "black." Only recently did the census bureau begin allowing people to identify themselves as multiracial.

Certainly, there are differences among ethnic groups and people from different cultural backgrounds. For example, people from Sweden typically have lighter skin color and lighter, straighter hair than people of southern Africa.

Research into the question of race continually arrives at certain conclusions:

- We humans are much more alike than different. That is, we share a common family tree, and, for most of humanity's existence, we have been much alike in physical characteristics. As the Judeo-Christian tradition has always taught, and as DNA fingerprinting suggests, we are, in fact, one human family.

- The term race is so loaded with culturally imposed views that it is virtually impossible to separate the meaning we assign to the word from any real differences that actually exist.

GROUP TALK

Working in small groups, complete the following activities and then share with the class.

1 Name a number of ethnic groups, and list characteristics that are popularly associated with each one.

2 For each characteristic, identify whether it typically has a positive, negative, or neutral meaning.

3 Explain and analyze your lists. For instance, is a Spanish accent viewed by most people in our society any differently from how an Asian accent, a Midwestern white accent, or an African American accent is viewed? Does the word *black* call up certain views or attitudes not connected with the word *white*?

The preceding discussion about racism is really about how we view race in our particular culture. How people label themselves often says as much about their view of race as it does about their actual background. For the most part, historically, the race question in the United States has been a matter of black and white and, especially in the western part of the country, white and Latino, and white and Native American. Today the United States is obviously multicultural; eventually, whites will be members of a minority group. Besides expanding as a multicultural country, more and more individuals have blurred racial and ethnic identities. For example, when pro-golfer Tiger Woods burst on the scene in 1996, people were confused about how to classify his one-quarter black, one-quarter Thai, one-quarter Chinese, one-eighth Native American, and one-eighth white heritage. Woods has described himself as cablinasian, a term meant to stand for a mixture of Caucasian, black, Indian (Native American), and Asian. In doing so, he challenged the standard racial categories used to describe people in the United States.

▼ Tiger Woods

Racism

So far in this chapter we have discussed prejudice, including **racial prejudice**. The question of racism is much more complex than whether or not certain individuals hold negative stereotypes about, or are unfriendly toward, members of other races. Individuals of any race or ethnic background can be racially prejudiced.

Racism, on the other hand, is part of the makeup of an organization, a community, or a society. For this reason, it can go undetected. For instance, a greeting-card store that has no cards depicting people of color is probably not overtly racist. *Overt* racism is conscious, premeditated, intentional harming of another because of race. *Covert* racism happens without harm being directly intended. Covert racism is much more dangerous than racial prejudice. For one thing, with racism we often cannot identify any one person or group who is responsible. Instead, policies, commonly accepted practices, and deeply ingrained values and expectations seem to be responsible for racism. Covert racism can be mistaken as simply "the way things are."

Racism = Prejudice + Power

Racism points to differences in *power*, *potential*, and *privilege* within a society. That is, a discussion about racism seeks to determine whether standards in a society, that is, what counts as "the norm," make belonging to one race more valuable and privileged than belonging to another. Or it might involve elevating one culture over another when that is not appropriate. Investigation into racism involves a search for difficulties that people might face because of their race.

Do certain racial groups possess power within a society that other groups do not? For instance:

- Do white children and Native American children generally have the same educational opportunities?

- Can Latino teenagers find jobs the same as non-Latinos?

- Is one race or ethnic group represented among leading politicians and civic leaders more than others?

- Is the racial makeup of those who own and manage businesses different from the overall racial makeup of the community?

- Are members of various races represented among both the wealthiest and poorest segments of society?

- Can people accused of crime receive a fair and equal trial regardless of their race?

- Are characteristics popularly connected with one racial or ethnic group held in as high esteem as characteristics connected with other groups?

- Are faulities such as hospitals, supermarkets, affordable housing, quality schools, and businesses equally available in communities regardless of their ethnic makeup?

Racism: A Function of Society As the questions about power indicate, racism is not simply a matter of some individuals strongly disliking people of other races. Individual racial prejudice alone does not account for unequal power and privileges between races. Individual sin and social sin (sinful structures) are distinct but, as racism demonstrates, closely connected.

History shows how the racism of individuals is reflected in the structures of society. During World War II, blacks and whites served in the military—living and dying for their country. But when black soldiers returned from the war to army bases in the South, they were not allowed to enter most clubs and restaurants there. Certain professions, such as that of professional baseball players, were also denied them. On the other hand, white soldiers could go wherever they wanted to go and pretty much do whatever they chose and were qualified to do. It was not until 1947 that Jackie Robinson broke the color barrier in baseball, and the armed forces were not desegregated until 1948.

Racism essentially refers to subordination based on race. As the following author's definition points out, racial subordination can occur because of the actions and attitudes of individuals. However, it can also result simply because of the way society is structured—its institutions.

> Racism is any action or attitude, conscious or unconscious, that subordinates an individual or group based on skin color or race. This subordination can be enacted individually or institutionally.
>
> Clyde W. Ford, *We Can All Get Along* (New York: Dell Publishing, 1994), 11

Racism exists when members of certain races have more power and privileges than members of other races. As the author suggests, this condition of racial inequality, or racial subordination, results either from the actions of individuals or from the power of society's institutions. Racism that is part of the very fabric of society (its social structures) is known as **institutional racism**.

FAITH ACTIVITY

Group Power Do certain racial groups within our society possess power that other groups do not? Find evidence to support your point of view. Debate this question with others in your class.

Institutional racism is a subtle, indirect, often unconscious expression of racism. Institutional racism shows itself when a white police officer pulls over a young black man driving a Jaguar, presuming that the car is stolen. It shows itself when the police officer holds the man longer and subjects him to more questioning than he would a white or Asian driver, even after the young man produces proof that he owns the car. Institutional racism shows itself when schools and healthcare facilities in mainly African American, Hispanic, and Native American communities are well below the standards of those in other communities. This results in children receiving poor health care and below-average education simply by accident of where they are born. It shows itself when Hispanics born in the United States do not accept Hispanics who come here from another country, or when the U.S.-born Hispanics, in turn, are not accepted by other ethnic groups.

These examples of institutional racism are not just the result of conscious choices on anyone's part to be racist. They are also unconscious reflections of the racial situation in the United States. As racism is racial prejudice at work in situations where power and privilege are unevenly divided, so institutional racism is inequality at work in the very structure of a society.

GROUP TALK

1. How would you react if you were a soldier returning to your country and certain places of entertainment and employment were closed to you? What would you do if you were a member of a race who was not restricted in these ways but knew such restrictions existed for others?

2. Determine whether or not the following situations are examples of institutional racism. Explain your choices.

   * A noted heart doctor, an African American woman, is mistaken for a cleaning woman at the hospital where she works.

   * A bank has an unwritten policy of refusing home loans to people who live within a certain area of a city, an area made up entirely of Hispanics and African Americans.

   * When the one Native American student at a school walks into the cafeteria, his classmates yell out their version of an Indian battle cry.

   * When a non-Italian and an Italian student get into a heated argument, another student chimes in, "Don't fight him, Will. His uncle is probably in the Mafia."

   * An Iranian American girl finds that many of her classmates do not include her in their social gatherings.

The Biblical View

How long has racism and prejudice plagued humankind? The Old Testament tells the story of God's chosen People, the Hebrews—the Israelites—who came to be known as the Jews. The Hebrew people were originally a mixed crew of wanderers, lacking in power, who were constantly bumping up against more powerful groups. Later, the Israelite people were not only victims of racism but responded to it in kind. One scripture story shows the intolerance of some Israelites toward another nation and also offers a lesson about how God expects us to treat "the other."

The story of Jonah is found in the book of the Old Testament that bears his name. God asks the prophet Jonah to go to the city of Nineveh to preach to its citizens. At the time, Nineveh was the capital city of the Assyrians, aggressive enemies of Jonah's people. The idea of doing anything to help the Ninevites so repelled Jonah that he disobeyed God and set sail in the exact opposite direction. In the section of the story with which we are all familiar, Jonah was tossed overboard and swallowed by a large fish.

Three days later, Jonah was spat up onto the shores of Nineveh. Reluctantly, he preached God's message to its citizens, hoping that they would not heed the message and thus incur God's wrath. To Jonah's dismay, the Ninevites did repent, and God saved them. God then taught Jonah a lesson by destroying the shade tree under which Jonah had been sitting. God let Jonah know that he cares for all people, for he has carefully created and crafted each one of us.

Lessons from Jonah:

- God does not lovingly create any people for them to be hated, given up on, or destroyed.

- God's vision of people is absolutely inclusive, absolutely compassionate.

- God is not a God only of one group but of everyone.

- All people are sisters and brothers under God.

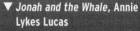

▼ *Jonah and the Whale*, Annie Lykes Lucas

Jesus Teaches Radical Love

In the New Testament, the understanding of stranger shifted for the Jewish people and other followers of Christ. We see Christ in each person we see, similar or different from us. "The other" is Christ himself. Therefore, the way we treat those who are different from us—indeed, those whom we would just as soon ignore—indicates precisely our love for or rejection of Christ.

Jesus has this to say:

For if you love those who love you, what reward do you have? Do not even tax collectors do the same? And if you greet only your brothers and sisters, what more are you doing than others? Do not even the Gentiles do the same?

✝ Matthew 5:46-47

In his day, Jesus confused many of his fellow Jews by treating Jews and non-Jews alike. When he met people in need, Jesus concerned himself with their pain, not their nationality, religion, race, or skin color. A prime example of Jesus breaking cultural and religious barriers is the story of the Samaritan woman at the well. The Gospel of John records Jesus' conversation with the woman, his assurance that he is the living water from which she would not thirst again. (See *John 4:4–42*). Jesus respected the dignity of this woman from Samaria, a land where Jews of mixed blood and different ritual practices lived. She was considered not only a "foreigner" but unclean as well. Jesus extended his offer of new life to her as he had those in Galilee.

After his Resurrection and Ascension, Jesus' Apostles and disciples began to understand the universality of their mission to proclaim the Good News to all nations. Empowered by the Holy Spirit, they were able to extend Jesus' message of mercy, love, and equality to people of other areas. One of the most striking characteristics of the early Christian community was that it included everyone:

"The broadening of Christianity to include the gentiles was begun by St. Peter, who said, "...in truth, I see that God shows no favors. Rather in every nation, whoever fears him and acts uprightly is acceptable to him" (Acts 10:34-35). The growth of the Christian family marks the shift in the early Church to an emphasis on the universality of Christianity. Through Pentecost, God "gathers into one the dispersed children of God" (John 11:52), focusing the efforts of the Church on building unity among human beings."

The U.S. catholic on Migration One Family Under God, 3

This unity of all human beings is the foundation of the Catholic Social Teaching theme: Solidarity of the Human Family. We are one human family no matter what national, ethnic, or racial background. Near or far, we are brothers and sisters. We must respect that unity and the equality that comes from sharing the same human dignity.

The Church and Racism

Every form of social or cultural discrimination in fundamental personal rights on the grounds of sex, race, color, social conditions, language, or religion must be curbed and eradicated as incompatible with God's design. [GS 29:2]

CCC, #1935

As members of the cultures in which they have lived, Christians have not been unaffected by prejudice or racism. Yet, overwhelmingly throughout her history, the Church has responded to the love of Christ and the Holy Spirit's prompting to spread the Gospel message. This has led the Church to seek unity and to recognize the God-given worth of all people. For example, Pope Saint Gregory the Great, who died in 604, lived at a time when to Romans "the other" meant in particular the non-Christian tribes of northern Europe. One such group, the Angles, was from England. According to legend, one day while walking through Rome Pope Gregory

A Closer Look

The Gift of Life

For decades, animosity has characterized the relationship between Jews and Palestinians in the Middle East. Suicide bombings and retaliatory raids have been the backdrop of daily life. In the midst of this great divide, stories of unselfish giving have sparked a small light of hope that people can rise above racial and political chaos.

In the summer of 2001, a thirty-three-year-old Palestinian man from East Jerusalem was shot in the head during a drive-by shooting. While his family believed the attackers were Israeli settlers, this did not prevent them from making a difficult decision. When the Palestinian was declared brain dead, his family was asked to donate his organs. The man's heart, lung, liver, and pancreas were transplanted into four Israelis, and his kidney was given to a young Palestinian boy. The father of the young man who received the Palestinian's heart asked to meet the family and said, "It is really touching, especially in these days when relations are so tense. This noble family comes and teaches us that it is possible to do things in a different way."

A year later, another transplant story was in the news. A sixteen-year-old Palestinian girl had been blind for four years, despite several surgeries to correct the problem. After an Israeli man died, his family donated his corneas to the young Palestinian. Within a day, she recovered her sight.

GROUP TALK

How are the above stories examples of the radical love with which God loves us?

witnessed a young English boy about to be sold into slavery. He told his companions, "I do not call them Angles, but angels." Pope Gregory recognized that a young northern slave in tattered clothes on an auction block was a *child of God* deserving of respect.

The history of the European occupation of the Americas is, at times, a ruthless and bloody one. The ruthlessness included acceptance and promotion of slavery of people from Africa and in the Americas. Some European Christians contributed to the devastation in the Americas, including acceptance of slavery. On the other hand, many French and Spanish missionaries risked death to share the Good News of God's love with Native Americans. Often these Christian missionaries provided the only voice insisting on respect for and kind treatment of native people in the Americas.

In her teachings on the Seventh Commandment, the Church has made her position on slavery clear: human beings are not things to be bought, sold, traded, or kept in slavery. Any action that leads to treating humans as merchandise in these ways is morally wrong.

The Church—A Multiracial, Multicultural Community

Because of the mission from Jesus to love one another and because of her global makeup, the Church today stands as an important voice against racism. The Good News of Christianity has blended, with most cultures and language groups on earth. As a result, today's Catholic Church is truly a multicultural community. In the United States alone, for centuries there have been both black and white Catholics. From the earliest days of European contact with this part of the Americas, there have been Spanish-, French-, and English-speaking Catholics. For most of her history the Catholic Church in the United States has been an immigrant Church. Today many immigrants—Hispanics, Latinos, Haitians, Vietnamese and other Asians, and Africans—add to the mix of cultures in the U.S. Catholic Church.

In their 1979 pastoral letter on racism, the U.S. Catholic bishops referred to racism as both a "fact" and a "sin." By calling racism a fact, the bishops point out the reality that racism exists within our nation. The people of the United States need to deal with that. By calling racism a sin, the bishops remind us that we need to respond to rid the country of racism with the same zeal with which we would respond to any sinful condition. In dealing with the topic of equality and differences among people, the *Catechism of the Catholic Church* reminds us that there are ". . . *sinful inequalities* that affect millions of men and women" and that "[t]hese are in open contradiction of the Gospel" (1938).

Catholics Across the World

According to the Vatican's *Annuario Pontificio* for the year 2004, at the end of 2002:

· There were more than **1.07 billion Catholics worldwide**; **17.2 percent** of the world's population.

· **Fifty percent** of the world's Catholics live in the Americas; **26.1 percent** are in Europe; **12.8 percent** are in Africa; **10.3 percent** live in Asia; and **0.8 percent** live in Oceania.

· Catholics make up **62.4 percent** of the population in the Americas, **40.5 percent** of the European population, **26.8 percent** of the population in Oceania, **16.5 percent** of the African population and **3 percent** of the Asian population. (*The Official Catholic Directory* reports that Catholics make up **23 percent** of the U.S. population.)

A Closer Look

Fighting Prejudice

Bertha Bowman was born on December 29, 1937, in Mississippi. She become a Catholic when she was nine and attended a school staffed by the Franciscan Sisters of Perpetual Adoration. The life and work of the sisters impressed her so much that, at age 15, she joined them and was given the name Thea.

Sister Thea's relationship with God was shaped through her family, religious community, prayer, and reading of the Scriptures. Her courage, knowledge, and right judgment guided her in sharing the message of God's love through a teaching career. After 16 years of teaching, she became the consultant for intercultural awareness in the diocese of Jackson, Mississippi. Sister Thea gave presentations across the country–gatherings that combined gospel preaching, prayer, storytelling, and singing. Her programs were directed to break down racial and cultural barriers. She encouraged people to communicate with one another so that they could understand other cultures and races.

In 1984, Sister Thea was diagnosed with terminal cancer. During an interview, Sister Thea stated, ". . . I think one difference between me and some other people is that I'm content to do a little bit. Sometimes people think they have to do big things in order to make a change, but if each one of us would light the candle, we'd have a tremendous light." One of her favorite songs was "This Little Light of Mine."

Thea lived a full life; she fought evils that drive people apart–prejudice, suspicion, and hatred. She fought for God and all people. She died in 1990.

GROUP TALK

1 Look through the Gospels to find other sayings of Jesus that speak of love. Apply these sayings to racism or our interaction with members of other races.

2 What do you see your parish doing to become more inclusive and friendly toward those who enter its doors? What more could it do? What could you do?

Responding to Prejudice

We have much to learn about ourselves and about others, and the changing face of our nation offers us many opportunities to do so. Racial and ethnic differences make our world a beautiful, exciting place to live. But prejudice and discrimination mar the beauty of the world we live in.

Steps Toward Getting Rid Of Prejudice
1 Value everyone as a person created in the image of God.
2 Know yourself.
3 Pray for the grace to overcome prejudice and participate in the celebration of the Eucharist to strengthen the Body of Christ in you so that you can better see Christ in others.
4 Become informed.
5 Treat others as you would have them treat you.
6 Seek reconciliation; this includes reconciling with God and the Church through the sacrament of Penance.
7 Speak out.
8 Get involved.
9 Keep a sense of humor.

How do we get rid of our prejudices? Look at the steps in the chart on this page. Step one is the Christian foundation for all that follows; it is the reason to get rid of prejudices and racism. Step two acknowledges that eventually hatred destroys us. We hurt ourselves when we hold onto prejudices that we may not even be aware of until we truly look at ourselves. Self-awareness, and along with that, self-acceptance, is an important step to any change. To begin overcoming prejudices toward others, we must spend time looking in a mirror.

Step three is essential. We are not alone, and we need not rely only on ourselves. We help ourselves and others when we call on Jesus to guide us and strengthen us in living as he did, loving all people because we are all children of our loving Father in heaven. Equally important is the perspective and hope we gain from the community of faith to which we belong. We are members of the Church, the Body of Christ on earth. We learn, grow, and celebrate together, and we experience the Holy Spirit in and through this community. Because the Church is so diverse, and many parishes today reflect that diversity, taking part in our local faith community gives us the opportunity to interact with people of different cultures and backgrounds, to grow in mutual respect.

The fourth step means cultivating a spirit of welcome, creating a space within ourselves where strangers can become friends. To do that, we must learn about other cultural groups and do so with an open-minded and compassionate attitude. We may discover reasons for the anger and frustration, hopes and joys of others that we never realized before. In the words from the Native American tradition, "Never judge others until you have walked a mile in their moccasins."

The fifth step means applying the wisdom of the Golden Rule to our relationships with people of other cultural groups. We can learn basic communication skills so that we can speak to, learn from, and interact with a variety of people. And even when we fail in our attempts to connect with others, we need to seek reconciliation with them as best we can—step six.

Overcoming prejudice and racism is not accomplished by indifference or inactivity. According to the seventh step, we need to speak the truth with courage. For example, it takes courage to befriend someone whom our friends may dislike. Courage is also needed to take steps to change social arrangements that oppress people.

Those at the forefront of social change say that the best way to overcome prejudices and racism is for people to work together to achieve common goals—step eight. Martin Luther King Jr. realized that all people in the United States suffer because of racism and the economic and social forces that ignite it. If all of us get involved to make the country better, prejudices and racism will lose their destructive power.

The last step—a sense of humor—may appear strange after the heavy tone of the others. It is not meant to deny the serious nature of prejudice or racism. It simply means—don't be too quick to take offense. It takes work to get rid of the sins of discrimination and racism. But the right kind of humor can break up tense situations and bring to light the silliness of much prejudicial thinking.

Discrimination in North America Following the discovery of the New World, Europeans enslaved millions of people in South America. African slaves first were brought to the Americas in 1619. In the thirteen colonies, there were also whites who were slaves and subject to the same laws and punishments as African slaves. Both black and white slaves could own livestock and work to buy their freedom. As time went by, the "servant codes" in the U.S. South came to apply only to black slaves.

The early English settlers in the Americas would never have survived without the help of the Native Americans. Yet Native Americans were subsequently mistreated by the white settlers. Most were displaced, assimilated, or killed.

GROUP TALK

Many jokes make fun of or belittle members of a particular race or ethnic group. On the other hand, some comedians can diffuse racially tense situations with humor. Think of examples of humor that make a stand against prejudice and racism. Examine what makes one type of humor good and another bad and hurtful.

"I Have a Dream"

"I have a dream that one day this nation will rise up and live out the true meaning of its creed: "We hold these truths to be self-evident: that all men are created equal." I have a dream that one day on the red hills of Georgia, the sons of former slaves and the sons of former slave owners will be able to sit down together at the table of brotherhood. . . . I have a dream that my four children will one day live in a nation where they will not be judged by the color of their skin but by the content of their character. . . .

This is the faith with which I return to the South. With this faith we will be able to hew out of the mountain of despair a stone of hope. With this faith we will be able to transform the jangling discords of our nation into a beautiful symphony of brotherhood. With this faith we will be able to work together, to pray together, to struggle together, to go to jail together, to stand up for freedom together, knowing that we will be free one day. . . .

From every mountainside, let freedom ring.

When we let freedom ring, . . . we will be able to speed up that day when all of God's children, black men and white men, Jews and Gentiles, Protestants and Catholics, will be able to join hands and sing in the words of the old Negro spiritual, "Free at last! free at last! Thank God Almighty, we are free at last!"

Martin Luther King Jr., "I Have a Dream" speech,
the March on Washington (August 28, 1963)

In the 1940s, psychologists Kenneth and Mamie Clark did research with four-year-old children. They gave children white dolls and black dolls with which to play. Without fail, both black children and white children said that the white dolls were "nicer." Unfortunately, even with the changes brought on by civil rights and the increase of African Americans in important positions in U.S. society, more often than not young children still select white dolls as "better" and "nicer" than black dolls. As one author remarks:

Something is clearly wrong when young children, as soon as they get a look at the world we've made, are disappointed with the color of their skin.

Sara Bullard, "Teaching Tolerance," Southern Poverty Law Review (Tuscaloosa, AL), 11

One African who learned about this choice for whiteness over blackness in the United States noted that before Europeans established colonies, in Africa "whiteness"—for example, white skin—meant weak and sickly. We must recognize that, while views on race and skin color are deeply ingrained in our society, perspectives on race are not universal and can change. To live the Gospel, we must change and remove restricting stereotypes from our hearts and patterns of living.

Stopping the Hurt Racism hurts:

- When unemployment among young people rises, unemployment among black youths increases considerably more than the average.

- Studies indicating that women are paid less than men also reveal that on average women of color are paid even less than their white sisters.

- When prison overcrowding occurs, when hunger and homelessness reach widespread proportions, or when older people must struggle to keep up with rising inflation—then African American, Native American, and Hispanic populations suffer more than others.

Justice includes admitting that members of certain races are commonly denied rights and privileges not denied members of other races. Certainly, wonderful success stories can be told about members of all races in the United States; the "American dream" has worked for many people of all races. Also, race is not the only factor in determining power, privileges, and opportunities. Nonetheless, simply because of their race, many people have a great struggle surviving and finding a place in U.S. society. In other words, racism very definitely exists in the United States. Overcoming racism is a work of justice, and until that work is done, the words "with liberty and justice for all" will not be true.

An old rabbi once asked his students how one could recognize the time when night ends and day begins. "Is it when . . . you can tell a dog from a sheep?" one student asked. "No," said the rabbi. "Is it when . . . you can tell a date palm from a fig tree?" another student asked. "No," said the rabbi. ". . . It is when you look into the face of any human creature and see your brother or your sister there. Until then, night is still with us."

Quoted in Dorothee Soelle, *The Strength of the Weak* (Philadelphia, PA: Westminster Press, 1984), 41

GROUP TALK

1. Name one thing you personally could do among your friends and classmates to bring about a greater understanding of racial differences.

2. Name specific ways that racial prejudice and racism are present and active in the United States.

3. Name underlying causes of the racial prejudice and race discrimination that exist in the United States.

›Faith in Action

Catholic Schools Opposing Racism (COR)

Sponsored by: **Queen of Peace High School**

A violent, racially-motivated hate crime committed by Catholic high school students in a Chicago neighborhood in 1997 brought teenagers together with civic leaders at a televised town meeting. They were asked "What can we do to see that this doesn't happen again?" Catholic Schools Opposing Racism (COR), initiated by Queen of Peace High School, is an answer to that question.

> Diverse cultures and beliefs too often separate us from one another. As a participant in COR, I have seen how important and necessary it is to put faith into action. I have learned to share the love of Jesus by welcoming others with compassion and open arms, knowing that even in our differences we are God's people.

Dwan Logan

COR is a network of the forty-one Catholic high schools in the Archdiocese of Chicago founded to take a stand against racism by building racial and cultural bridges. By consciousness raising and sensitivity training, COR teaches students how to respect and honor the differences of all persons of every race and culture, and how to treat one another as brothers and sisters.

Since 1999, students in more than 300 elementary and secondary schools have celebrated COR Commitment Day during African-American Heritage Month. Young people and their teachers say the COR Prayer and Pledge in a shared mission to create a world of racial harmony.

COR activities have included conferences, festivals, concerts, plays, immersion experiences, and shared suppers. The Just Stories conferences and festivals offered stories by professional storytellers and interactive workshops that celebrated diversity and posed race-related questions in creative ways. As one student said, "It was a way to hear God's word from a different perspective, a different viewpoint."

Teacher in-service programs, sponsored by COR, such as "The Shifting Face of Racism Today," provided educators with concrete examples of how their school communities can work against racism and for inclusion and diversity.

The Kaleidoscope Curriculum by author Susan O'Halloran and sponsored by COR, is available to all schools and offers lessons and activities geared to developing respectful behavior.

COR is sponsored by Queen of Peace High School, a Sinsinawa Dominican-sponsored school; Angels Studio, a communications ministry of the Chicago Province of the Society of the Divine Word; and the Augustine Stewardship Fund Trust of St. Norbert Abbey.

GO ONLINE Visit www.harcourtreligion.com to learn more about COR and for a link to its site.

Begin by praying the Sign of the Cross.

Leader: God our Father, we thank you for American jazz and Italian opera, for the earthy drum beat of Native American song, and the swirling energy of Ukrainian dance, for the peaceful strains of Japanese music, and the spiritual intensity of Arab chant.

All We pray that we may discover your face in the many colors and cultures in our world.

Leader: Help us follow your Son, Jesus Christ, and do what we can so that there will be fewer experiences of hatred or mistreatment because of race, creed, or ethnic background.

All We pray that we may discover your face in the many colors and cultures in our world.

Leader: May your Holy Spirit within us lead us to build bridges and break down barriers, so that your varied world will be a holy world. Amen.

All Amen

End by praying the Sign of the Cross.

>Review

1. Name and give an example of each characteristic of prejudice.

2. What is a hate group?

3. What is the root of prejudice?

4. What does it mean to be color blind? What are the alternatives?

5. What does it mean to say that race is a social construction?

6. What is dual consciousness?

7. What question may be addressed to reveal the presence of racism?

8. How is racism different from racial prejudice?

9. Define institutional racism.

10. In what way did Jesus go against dominant cultural norms in his treatment of others?

11. What did the U.S. Catholic bishops mean by calling racism both a fact and a sin?

12. Why is the Church today uniquely suited to speak out against racism?

13. Name the guidelines given for breaking down prejudice.

14. What was Martin Luther King Jr.'s vision of the American dream?

15. Why is overcoming racism a work of justice?

>Key Words

institutional racism (p. 239)–Racist actions and attitudes ingrained and operating in organizations of a society.

prejudice (p. 226)–Narrow-minded opinion based on a false premise.

racial prejudice (p. 238)–A strong negative feeling that a person holds toward members of another race.

racism (p. 238)–Subordination based on race; discrimination or oppression based on race.

stereotyping (p. 226)–Generalizing about an entire group of people and limiting our view of members of a group to narrow preconceptions.

>Our Challenge

Astronauts are granted a unique view of our world. In relating their experiences while in space, they often mention that they sense a "oneness," not only of the planet itself, but also of all the passengers on "spaceship earth." Astronauts often realize what important religious figures throughout the ages have proclaimed: We are all one.

Experts who study "peak experiences" suggest that most of us at some time in our lives also experience that the world is one and that we are all members of one family. Perhaps deep down we know that when one person suffers, we all suffer, and that seeking the good of all people is good for each of us. Prejudices and racism cloud over this bright view of humanity, which is in fact the view that Jesus wished for his followers. All people are created in the image of God and are equal in dignity. God calls us to cooperate with his plan and work to eliminate the sinful injustices that perpetuate racism and prevent people from living the full dignified life in the Spirit that God intends.

When we examine our prejudices and participate in overcoming racism, we are doing Christian service—collaborating with the Holy Spirit in the work of overcoming the sin of racism and helping to bring greater unity to the world. In so doing, our efforts contribute to the world reflecting more and more the Body of Christ.

CREATED IN GOD'S IMAGE

CHAPTER 9

WOMEN AND MEN

CHAPTER GOALS

In this chapter you will:

* ★ explore how men and women have equal dignity as created in the image of God and consider the teachings of the Sixth Commandment and Ninth Commandments.

* ★identify signs of sexism in the world today.

* ★consider the Church's response to sexism.

* ★discover how the Catholic Church speaks out against prejudice toward homosexual persons.

Men and Women Created in God's Image

what's your opinion?

Answer **agree, disagree, or uncertain** to the following statements. Choose statements that you believe are most significant. Explain your answers.

1. Women and men possess the same dignity and were created to be partners in the work of creation.

2. Men are as likely as women to be poor.

3. Women and girls are now as free as men and boys to ask someone out for a date or to propose marriage.

4. In coed high schools, girls tend to be less assertive than boys in speaking up in class and in taking leadership in school activities

5. I have had serious discussions about homosexuality.

6. Homosexual persons are usually pictured realistically in movies.

7. If a friend of mine was homosexual, I would be very upset.

8. Homosexual persons suffer from injustice in our society.

The Bible makes it clear that men and women are intended by God to live in harmony and created with equal dignity. However, people suffer when gender differences are mistreated or misinterpreted on personal or societal levels. *Sexism* is a term for attitudes and practices ingrained in a society that lead to people hurting because they are women or men. Since women and men are meant to support and nurture each other, both sexes suffer because of sexism. Sorting out how people may be hurting unnecessarily because of social perspectives and practices is difficult but important for creating a more just society.

Different and Equal

Welcome to biology 101: men and women are different. However, are they different not just physically, but psychologically, intellectually, emotionally, and spiritually as well? Ask yourself these questions: Do women typically view an occasion such as a sporting event or a movie differently from how men tend to view it? Do most mothers form a bond with their children unmatched by the bond between fathers and children? If infant boys and girls were left on their own, would they develop differently? Would they end up mirroring notions about male-female differences popularly held in North American culture?

Snapshots of Men and Woman

- Emma likes Noah. She would enjoy inviting him to go with her to a movie some Saturday night, but she fears this would frighten him off. Instead, Emma convinces her friends to hang out with her near Noah and his friends. She flirts with Noah, hoping that he will ask her out.

- The mother of two young children, Sarah has not worked outside her home for six years. Although her husband works regularly, he has always kept tight control of the family's money. For years now, Sarah has hidden money from her husband so that she can buy things for the children, things he considers unnecessary. Recently, Sarah's husband has become abusive toward her. Her main concern is the children. She doesn't see how she could care for them financially if she leaves her husband. She spends all her time trying to keep peace in the house so as not to upset her husband.

- On the morning of career day, Derrick attends the presentation on the nursing profession. He discovers that he is one of two boys along with thirty girls interested in becoming nurses. Concerned that nursing is not considered appropriate work for a man, Derrick leaves and attends the session on becoming a police officer.

- Like her two brothers, forty-year-old Jenny has children of her own. Since her father's death, Jenny has taken responsibility for caring for her increasingly dependent mother. Although Jenny's older brother has a larger house than she does and a job with more flexible hours, their mother expects Jenny rather than one of her sons to arrange doctors' visits and to provide a home for her. Although it is a burden on her own family, Jenny concludes that it is her responsibility as a daughter to care for her mother in this way.

- Seung Ah was the first female regional sales representative for her company. During her first full-scale company meeting, the eight other sales reps went out for a few drinks after dinner. Seung Ah joined them only to hear the conversation sink into telling crude sex jokes. When she complained that the jokes were belittling to women and made her feel uncomfortable, one of the male sales reps replied, "What's the matter? Can't you take a joke?"

- Twice during the soccer match, ten-year-old Ricardo was knocked hard to the ground, and twice he got up and continued to play. Bruised, limping, and in pain, Ricardo played to the end. When the game was over, his coach told him, "You played like a real man today Ricardo. I'm proud of you."

GROUP TALK

1. Do you think that all of these stories are realistic? If not, what specific aspects of the stories do not ring true for you?

2. Does each story represent a problem resulting from a distortion of what it means to be a man or a woman in our society? Explain.

3. Describe stories from your own experience that illustrate challenges that come with being a man or being a woman today.

Created in God's Image 257

Church teaching holds that differences between men and women are not just physical because, "*Sexuality* affects all aspects of the human person in the unity of his body and soul" (See *CCC* 2332). That is, a woman doesn't stop being a woman anywhere deep in her psyche. Neither does a man stop being a man at any point within himself. *Sexuality* affects all the various facets of what makes a person who he or she is (*CCC* 2332). The physical, moral, and spiritual differences among females and males represent a complementarity while maintaining equality.

Being male or female is part of God's plan for us, and it encompasses all of who we are as images of God:

God created humankind in his image,
in the image of God he created them;
male and female he created them.

✝ Genesis 1:27

We learned at the beginning of this course that God created humans to be special, to share in his life and love and in his work of creation. He told our first parents to be fertile and to populate the earth as part of his plan to share his love with humanity. Thus, sexuality and relationship were at the heart of who people were from the very beginning. Humans were not created to be solitary beings, and the partnership between man and woman is the first form of communion and connection among people.

The Sixth and Ninth Commandments deal with how this sexuality is lived out in our relationships and what behaviors and attitudes honor or degrade the gift of sexuality. It's important to consider these issues because they have an impact on how people view themselves and others. The way one integrates and expresses his or her sexuality is to be guided by the virtue of chastity, which stems from the cardinal virtue of temperance. Everyone is called to chastity, the proper integration of sexuality reflecting the unity of body and soul and the responsible expression of that sexuality. Chastity involves self-mastery, patience, discipline, and grace. We need to rely on the Holy Spirit to increase this virtue in us and to transform, when necessary, the ways we view ourselves and our sexuality so that we avoid sinful behavior. We'll consider some justice issues related to the Sixth Commandment later in this section.

"Each of the two sexes is an image of the power and tenderness of God, with equal dignity though in a different way."

CCC 2335

Sexual Difference and Justice Justice for men and women calls for recognition that men and women are different. Women's identity and "women's experience" do differ from men's identity and "men's experience." However, two cautions are in order: (1) we need to be careful about being too rigid in identifying differences between the genders, and (2) we need to examine how personal or societal values and practices might support injustice.

It is impossible to separate completely what men and women are by nature, compared to what they are by upbringing and cultural conditioning—nurture. At least part of how we view ourselves comes from deeply ingrained societal perspectives, some of which can be harmful. For instance, boys can't use "girls are by nature better at cleaning up and doing the dishes" as a way to get out of helping around the house. Men lose out if they believe that "a real man" must be strong and not seek help from others.

Men and women have equal dignity as created in the image of God, and both females and males needs to acknowledge and accept their sexual identity as something God-given, good, and unique to each. Equal dignity does not imply lack of difference; in fact, the opposite is true. Because of the equality of the genders, women's voices should be heard in the public arena as strongly as men's; and men should be as actively involved in the care of children as women are. Harmony, in families and society in general, results when both men and women contribute their unique gifts and work hand in hand.

FAITH ACTIVITY

What Does It Mean? Look through magazines that depict men and women in ads or articles. Select three pictures that portray a particular view of what it means to be a man or a woman. For each, write a paragraph describing that viewpoint. Is the viewpoint potentially harmful in any way?

Sexism—When Attitudes and Practices Lead to Injustice

As racism refers to discrimination and injustice based on race, so sexism refers to discrimination and injustice based on gender. For instance, if women's ways and women's roles are viewed as having less value than men's, then we have sexism. Attitudes and behaviors that place unreasonable restrictions on members of one or both genders are an expression of sexism. For example, men and women should be treated equally in the workplace. Sexism results when power and privilege are placed mainly in the hands of members of one gender. Sexism is at work when what counts as valuable and important favors members of one gender over the other. Like racist attitudes, sexist attitudes become ingrained into the fabric of a society.

Since a just society is based on harmony and equality, it follows that both men and women suffer when sexism is present. However, women are typically the more obvious and immediate victims of sexism. For instance, a study of U.S. lawyers found that only a small percentage of women lawyers advanced to levels of power in major law firms. The study found that women lawyers were often described differently from the way men were. Specifically, a female lawyer would be described in less professional terms. She would have "good people skills," while a male lawyer exhibiting the same behavior would be praised for being "good with clients." The two statements describe the same qualities, but the wording of the description applied to the male lawyer is more likely to imply professionalism and authority than does the wording describing the female lawyer.

Nonetheless, both men and women can suffer from sexism. Both can be burdened with expectations and restrictions simply because of their gender. Both men and women experience pressures that can restrict their development as persons and rob them of their God-given human dignity.

Patriarchy—When Male Power Dominates Historians point out that in most cultures women's way of thinking and viewing things has been given a secondary status. That is, decision-making power and determining what is considered most important rested in the hands of a select group of men. Men's activities and ways of thinking were privileged over women's. A society in which the dominant power resides in the hands of a select group of men is known as a **patriarchy**, a word that literally means "rule by the fathers."

FAITH ACTIVITY

Sexism in the Media Survey TV shows, commercials, popular songs, or music videos to determine how men and women are portrayed. Report on your findings. Would you label any of these portraits sexist?

Pope John Paul II was particularly sensitive to the way women have been relegated to an inferior position. In response, he declared that "it is time to examine the past with courage, to assign responsibility where it is due in a review of the long history of humanity" ("Letter to Women"). He noted that: "Women's dignity has often been unacknowledged and their prerogatives misrepresented; they have often been relegated to the margins of society and even reduced to servitude." He pointed out one problem that has historically led to a devaluing of women—namely, we tend to emphasize "sensational events" over "the daily rhythm of life."

GROUP TALK

1. What does it mean for you to be a man or a woman? What aspects of your understanding of manhood and womanhood result from nature or from nurture? Explain.

2. Would the cultural system that you would like to live in be predominantly masculine, feminine, or a combination of both? What might a cultural system be like that was built on each of these different viewpoints?

3. Looking back on your school career, do you believe that boys were treated differently from girls? Over time, did the actions or opinions of boys come to be treated differently from those of girls? If you answer "yes" to either question, give a specific example to support your answer. Explain.

Signs of Sexism

Expressions of Sexism Today

Pick up a magazine or watch a television show from over fifty years ago and it is immediately evident how greatly conditions for men and women have changed. The late 1960s saw what was called the "women's liberation movement," and indeed since then doors have been opened to women that were closed to them before that time. We take it for granted now that men and women should receive equal pay for equal work and that wives and husbands are equal partners in making family decisions. Nonetheless, if we look at the situation of women throughout the world, we discover that people are still hurting because of harmful social values and conditions. Here are three expressions of sexism that need to be addressed today.

The Feminization of Poverty The trend for a number of decades now has been the **feminization of poverty**. That is, women, and children dependent upon women, make up the largest percentage of people living in poverty. When poverty increases, women and children are affected the most.

> The face of poverty is increasingly a feminine face, where 70% of the 1.6 billion people who live in poverty are women and girls.
>
> Kavita N. Ramdas, President and CEO of the Global Fund for Women

Many reasons can be cited why women are more likely than men to be poor. First of all, women often earn less than men for the same type of job. Second, jobs traditionally labeled "women's work" usually pay less. These workers include salesclerks, secretaries, domestics, childcare workers, janitorial workers, and non-professional nursing home workers. Third, if a woman

FAITH ACTIVITY

Suffering from Sexism In a short essay, suggest ways that men might suffer from sexism and attitudes toward gender. What are ways that women suffer from sexism and gender attitudes? Do you believe that discrimination against men is a more, less, or equally serious problem today than discrimination against women? Explain.

is working in a position that could lead to a better paying job, she often hits a "glass ceiling." This is a term that refers to the barriers that women face in moving up or being promoted to a higher-level job. Finally, a rising number of families are headed by single women (divorced, widowed, separated, and unmarried). In many cases, these women receive no support from husbands or the fathers of their children. In poorer countries, men have a better chance of finding work than women do—especially if women have child-care responsibilities as well. The above factors added together result in the feminization of poverty.

The Power Gap When we look at positions of power in our communities, schools, businesses, churches, and government, we arrive at the overwhelming conclusion that men are still dominant in modern society. For example, no woman has ever been president of the United States, most cabinet members are still men, and few women are senators or governors. This imbalance exists despite the fact that women in the United States have had the right to vote since 1920 and currently make up a majority of potential voters.

Statistics reveal a similar absence of women in key power positions in other areas of life. For instance, in education the majority of elementary school teaching positions are held by women while the majority of university professorships are held by men. In medicine most doctors are men; most nurses are women. In business most executives are men; most office workers are women. This does not mean that certain types of work are less important than others. Rather, it indicates that in our society positions are typically viewed differently. Nurses and elementary school teachers arguably provide services as important as doctors and university professors. Yet positions women tend to hold are not valued as much, are not paid as much, and are not given as much authority.

The United States is currently experiencing changes that could affect this power gap between the genders. Women now outnumber men in law schools, medical schools, and colleges in general. Some educators fear that boys are now lagging behind girls in educational achievement even at early ages. As with all areas of justice, the goal is collaboration and equality, not domination of one group by another.

FAITH ACTIVITY

"Glass Ceiling" On the Internet, search for statistics that provide evidence whether or not a "glass ceiling" exists in contemporary society. Share your findings with the class.

GROUP TALK

1. Do you think it matters whether or not women hold positions of power in government, education, the entertainment industry, and business in general? Explain.

2. Why do you think that in the United States women and girls are now succeeding better academically than men and boys? Have you found evidence of this trend in your own educational experience? Do you envision a change in social relationships in the future due to this development?

Relationship Violence, Brad and Marci started going together in junior year. Two months into the relationship, Marci went to a party without Brad. She spent the evening talking to friends and classmates, both boys and other girls. When Brad saw her the next day, he was furious. "What were you doing talking to other guys! Don't be going to parties without me. And stop spending time with those loser friends of yours."

Marci felt bad. If she truly loved Brad, she shouldn't do anything that would make him jealous. His anger and jealousy showed how much he loved her. Marci stopped going to dances because Brad thought they were stupid. Instead of attending school football games she and Brad spent weekend nights watching videos together or with his crowd.

Marci tried her best to be attentive to Brad. Every once in a while, however, he would flare up. Once at lunch when she was talking to friends he grabbed her by the arm and pulled her away from the group she was with. She felt that he wanted her entire life to be centered around him. But isn't that what love is all about?

Relationship Violence

An emergency room nurse noticed that a number of women came to the hospital with their husband or boyfriend sporting unusual bumps, bruises, or sprains. Invariably the woman would say that she was hurt in a fall. The nurse got the hospital to initiate a program whereby women who came to the emergency room with any kind of suspicious injury would be interviewed separately from the husband or male partner. Often in this more secure setting the woman would confide that she in fact had been abused. Partner abuse usually goes unreported. Often the victim feels as though it is her fault. More often than not, the victim is a woman.

Dating violence, stalking, spousal abuse, and rape are obviously horrendous distortions of what male-female relationships should be. Researchers have tried to understand why these problems occur as frequently as they do. They are thwarted in their attempts by the tendency to cover up the problem by all the parties involved. Studies indicate a connection between **relationship violence** and a patriarchal mindset. For instance, many adolescent boys believe that it is okay and acceptable for them to be aggressive toward girls. Often these same boys misread what girls want or expect from them, especially when alcohol consumption is thrown into the mix.

Not surprisingly, a study of college students found that when partners believed that they should be mutually responsible to each other then relationship violence was less likely to occur. In other words, the mutuality, equality, and harmony intended by God are the foundation for wholesome relationships between the genders. Genesis reveals that the first form of communion between people is that between a man and a woman. Any discussion on violence against women needs to include pornography and rape as a violation of the dignity of women and as sins against chastity and the Sixth Commandment. Pornography reduces women (and men) to objects. Besides the horrible physical and psychological harm it causes, rape "deeply wounds the respect, freedom, and physical and moral integrity to which each person has a right" (*CCC* 2356).

Many of the values promoted by mainstream society can create attitudes toward sexuality that make pornography and rape seem acceptable to some. There is a need for modesty and temperance in speech and thought, and following the Ninth Commandment requires us to struggle against inappropriate desires and longings that can lead to actions that dishonor the gift of sexuality. Practicing the virtue of modesty in the ways we think, act, and dress can lead to the decency and discretion that counter behaviors that are contrary to the dignity of women and men. When we view our own bodies as integral to who we are, we are more likely to see the unity of body and soul in others and thus treat them with respect.

Relationship violence that occurs within families is commonly called **domestic violence**. Catholic teaching asserts that the family is meant to be a "domestic Church," not a place of domestic violence. The Catechism describes this concept in these words: "The Christian home is the place where children receive the first proclamation of the faith. For this reason the family home is rightly called 'the domestic church', a community of grace and prayer, a school of human virtues and of Christian charity" (*CCC* 1666).

The Fourth Commandment speaks directly to the mutual and life giving relationships that make up a family.

- Children are to honor and respect their parents for the many gifts of life they provide: taking care of them physically and emotionally to the best of their ability.

- Parents help their children spiritually, too, as they move along in their journey of faith. By example, through discussion, and in study, parents educate their children about what it means to be Catholic, how and why to pray, what is good and just, how to respond to God's grace, and what it means to live a life of virtue.

- When a mutual respect exists among family members, parents are able to encourage their children's vocations, remembering that the first calling of all Christians is to follow Jesus.

- Children show their respect by being thankful for all that their parents do, acknowledging them and their sacrifices, obeying them, and helping them in whatever ways they can.

- As we read in a previous chapter, this means especially caring for the older generation as they become less capable of caring for themselves.

As a domestic Church, the family provides a solid foundation for a healthy society. Nurtured in a spirit of good will, humility, and abandonment to the providence of God, all baptized people are thus better equipped to fashion a more just world.

GROUP TALK

1 Do you agree with each part of the following argument? Explain why or why not.

(a) Women as a group have long been treated as inferior to men.

(b) Women as a group have suffered because of being placed in this inferior position.

(c) Women continue to suffer because of certain cultural attitudes and practices.

(d) Active steps should be taken to ensure that women play a stronger role in shaping the present and the future.

2 One concern faced by parents is overseeing the use of media by children—the Internet, television, and popular music. (The Catechism itself urges moderation and discipline in their use [2512].) What guidelines would you recommend to parents regarding their children's exposure to the media?

The Church Responds to Sexism

We reaffirm the fundamental equality of women and men who, created in the image of God, "are called to participate in the same divine beatitude [and] . . . therefore enjoy an equal dignity" (*CCC* 1934). The life and teachings of Jesus as well as many recent Church pronouncements speak to the need for collaboration of men and women.

Jesus and Women

Jesus treated everyone he met—Jews and Gentiles, the righteous and sinners, men and women—with profound respect. He did so at a time when such mutuality was uncommon, even considered "sinful." For instance, in chapter 4 of the Gospel according to John, Jesus speaks with a Samaritan woman at a community well. In doing so Jesus broke three cultural restrictions in place at the time. First, he spoke in public to a woman who was not his wife. Second, she was a Samaritan, a member of a group typically avoided by devout Jews. Third, he asked her to spread the news of his message to her towns-people. In effect the Samaritan woman became the first known missionary to non-Jews. Inviting a woman to proclaim the Good News may not sound radical today, but, at the time, Jesus was proposing a radically uncustomary role for a woman.

Jesus also had both women and men friends, again contrary to common practice of the time. As a matter of fact, after his Resurrection Jesus appeared first to one of his women friends. She likewise did not let being a woman stand in the way of her sharing the Good News:

Now after he rose early on the first day of the week, he appeared first to Mary Magdalene, from whom he had cast out seven demons. She went out and told those who had been with him, while they were mourning and weeping.

✝ Mark 16:9–10

▼ **The Crucifixion with Mary Magdalene by Luca Signorelli**

Jesus spoke out strongly against those who would "lord it over" others. He envisioned a community instead in which members would serve one another humbly. In the Gospel according to Matthew, after proclaiming the dual commandments to love God and love neighbor, Jesus criticized those leaders who "love to have the place of honor at banquets and the best seats in the synagogues, and to be greeted with respect in the marketplaces, and to have people call them rabbi" (*Matthew 23:6–7*). Jesus said to his followers:

> *But you are not to be called rabbi, for you have one teacher, and you are all students. And call no one your father on earth, for you have one Father—the one in heaven. Nor are you to be called instructors, for you have one instructor, the Messiah. The greatest among you will be your servant. All who exalt themselves will be humbled, and all who humble themselves will be exalted.*
>
> ✝ Matthew 23:8–12

Recent Church Pronouncements

The Church recognizes the need to include concern for women as part of its message of justice. Pope John Paul II, for example, saw the Gospel message about women to be hopeful and liberating:

> Transcending the established norms of his own culture, Jesus treated women with openness, respect, acceptance and tenderness. In this way he honored the dignity that women have always possessed according to God's plan and in his love. . . .
>
> Yes, it is time to examine the past with courage, to assign responsibility where it is due in a review of the long history of humanity. Women have contributed to that history as much as men, and more often than not they did so in much more difficult conditions. I think particularly of those women who loved culture and art, devoted their lives to them in spite of the fact that they were frequently at a disadvantage from the start, excluded from equal educational opportunities, underestimated, ignored and not given credit for their intellectual contributions.
>
> Pope John Paul II, "Letter to Women," *Origins* vol. 25, no.9

It's important to realize that while the Church takes a stand on social issues when they relate to the dignity of the human person, she does not necessarily support or condone all the political or social movements that espouse some similar beliefs. Because the Church is universal, she cannot be tied to any one civic movement of any one government. That being said, the Church and her members have continued to stand up for the rights of those who are neglected, oppressed, or treated unequally.

The Church and Women's Rights

1963, Pope John XXIII stated that one of three distinctive characteristics of our day is that "women are becoming ever more conscious of their human dignity." He affirmed his support for women when they "demand rights befitting a human person both in domestic and public life" (*Peace on Earth* 41). Considering that Pope John was speaking before the beginning of the modern women's movement, his recognition of women's rights was certainly prophetic.

1965, The Second Vatican Council noted that "with respect to the fundamental rights of the person, every type of discrimination, whether social or cultural, whether based on sex, race, color, social condition, language, or religion, is to be overcome and eradicated as contrary to God's intent" ("The Church in the Modern World" 29).

1971, The world's Catholic bishops declared that "women should have their own share in the responsibility and participation in the community life of society and likewise of the Church" (*Justice in the World* 42).

1994, The U.S. Catholic bishops wrote: "We can say with certainty that discrimination against women contradicts the will of Christ.

. . . We reject sexism and pledge renewed efforts to guard against it in church teaching and practice" (*Strengthening the Bonds of Peace*).

1995, Pope John Paul II called for "equal pay for equal work, protection for working mothers, fairness in career advancements, equality of spouses with regard to family rights and the recognition of everything that is part of the rights and duties of citizens in a democratic state. This is a matter of justice but also of necessity" ("Letter to Women" 4). He also said: "Women have a full right to become actively involved in all areas of public life, and this right must be affirmed and guaranteed also, where necessary, through appropriate legislation" (*World Day of Peace Message* 9).

1999, As the jubilee year began, Pope John Paul II said: "Among the many aggressions against human dignity, there is a widespread violation of the dignity of woman that manifests itself with the exploitation of her person and body. Every practice which offends woman in her liberty and femininity must be vigorously opposed" ("Woman as Masterpiece of God's Creation" 2).

GROUP TALK

1. What do you think it would be like to be a member of the other gender? What thoughts, feelings, and images immediately come to mind? What would make you most angry? What joys would you experience? Would young people who are members of the other gender typically answer these questions the same way you do? If you have a chance, try to find out.

2. Do you believe that full-time parenting (not working outside the home) is an economic or social option for many families in your community? Explain.

3. Write an essay describing how women and men could best collaborate together to create mutually nourishing relationships and a more just world.

Homosexual Persons

FAITH ACTIVITY

Christian Attitudes Consider the statements, "An act of homosexuality is a sin," and, "Homosexual persons suffer from injustice in our society." How does the Church expect homosexuals to behave? What should be our attitude toward homosexuality?

Even today, when popular TV sitcoms don't hesitate to include homosexual persons as part of their story lines, the topic of homosexuality often brings on such a flood of emotions that concern for the people involved gets lost. Church teaching states that homosexual sexual activity violates the intended purpose of sex which is rooted in being created as male and female to participate in God's work of creation and which finds its proper expression only in a marriage built on love and open to children. The immorality of homosexual practices not withstanding, justice demands that we look for possible ways that the lives and dignity of homosexual men and women may be threatened.

Snapshot of a Homosexual Young Person

Cindy is sixteen. She feels close to her family. She is especially close to Kevin, her twenty-two-year-old brother. Since he went away to college four years ago, Cindy has seen little of her brother. Yet when they have been together on family vacations, she has always shared with Kevin all the important concerns of her life. She would chatter on about school and boyfriends, and he would listen. When she was upset, he always seemed to understand. She would clown around and he would be the first to join in. All in all, she felt that Kevin was everything that an older brother should be.

On one of Kevin's weekend visits home, he told Cindy that he wanted to talk about himself for a change. Hesitantly, he revealed what was shocking news to her: he believed that he was homosexual. Confused, Cindy at first thought he was joking. She had many images of homosexual men in her mind, none of them flattering. What she knew of Kevin simply didn't fit these images. He was the brother who loved her and was always there for her. How could this be?

Kevin asked Cindy not to tell their parents just yet. He also reassured her that he was still her big brother and that he would not go out and do anything wrong.

Since their conversation, Cindy has not changed her life, but her view of life has changed drastically. She still jokes a lot and enjoys watching movies with her friends. But now she notices and feels uncomfortable when jokes are about homosexuals. Maybe the same jokes were told before, but she had never paid much attention to them. Now they hold new meaning. Now they touch her deepest self. Now they are about her brother.

GROUP TALK

1. If you were Cindy, what would you say to someone who said: "There's nothing wrong with joking about people being homosexual. It doesn't mean anything"?

2. How can you give a broader, Christian interpretation to the last sentence of the story?

3. Name possible ways that the following themes of Catholic social teaching could be applied to Cindy's brother as he continues on in his life:

   - life and dignity of the human person
   - family, community, and participation
   - rights and responsibilities
   - care for the poor and vulnerable
   - the dignity of work and the rights of workers
   - solidarity

The Current Situation

Homosexuality is a very emotion-charged topic, and perhaps no group suffers more from popular stereotypes and jokes than do people with a homosexual orientation. Since adolescence marks a time of developing sexual identities, teenagers especially can be particularly nervous about and cruel toward people who are homosexual or whom they imagine to be homosexual. This fear and anxiety can even apply to themselves, sometimes with devastating results. A large number of teenage suicides are linked to a fear of being homosexual. Within the blanket category *homosexual* exist flesh-and-blood persons who find themselves victimized in many ways. Often in a hostile environment, they are called to be creative, true-to-themselves, and loving persons, as we all are called to be.

It's important again to note that Catholic teaching restricts physical-sexual intimacy to the loving and life-giving context of marriage between a man and a woman. The Catechism states that homosexual acts are closed to the gift of life and "do not proceed from a genuine affective and sexual complementarity" (*CCC* 2357). Homosexual persons are called to live virtuous lives of self-mastery, as we all are, as they strive for the goal of Christian perfection.

However, in line with Catholic social teaching, the way we view and treat people who either are or appear to be homosexual is a matter of justice. The widespread negative attitudes toward people with a homosexual orientation and the harmful actions aimed against them that can result are deplorable. For instance, in their 1976 pastoral letter on morality, the U.S. bishops speak out against prejudice toward people who are homosexual:

> Homosexuals, like everyone else, should not suffer from prejudice against their basic human rights. They have a right to respect, friendship, and justice. They should have an active role in the Christian community.
>
> National Conference of Catholic Bishops, *To Live in Christ Jesus*, 51

This condemnation of unjust treatment of homosexual persons is stated again in the Catechism of the Catholic Church:

> [Homosexuals] must be accepted with respect, compassion, and sensitivity. Every sign of unjust discrimination in their regard should be avoided.
>
> *CCC* 2358

The number of men and women who have deep-seated homosexual tendencies is not negligible. This inclination, which is objectively disordered, constitutes a trial for most of them. They must be accepted with respect, compassion, and sensitivity. Every sign of unjust discrimination in their regard should be avoided.

Homophobia is a strong and destructive force at work in our society. Sometimes homophobia leads to acts of discrimination or even violence against people suspected of being homosexual.

Homosexual persons do not necessarily fit the stereotype painted of them by popular culture. Similarly, not all heterosexual men and women fit a particular stereotype of heterosexual persons. For a variety of reasons, some homosexual persons do mirror social stereotypes. The percentage who do is comparatively small. Unfortunately, all homosexual persons suffer because of society's stereotypes. As with any stereotyping, when we define people solely according to one dimension of their personality, then we lessen their individuality. We run the risk of treating them as objects and of treating them with less than the respect demanded by their being made in God's image, sharing the dignity that all possess from God, and by Catholic teaching on justice.

Loved Equally by God

Being homosexual is often cast in a negative light. In fact, people who are homosexual can live happy, loving, fulfilling lives. Many people whose sexual orientation is homosexual have made outstanding contributions to education, sports, politics, the entertainment industry, and all other aspects of society. Nonetheless, homosexual persons frequently struggle against hatred. School is often the first place young people experience discrimination and at times vicious mistreatment. School should not be a dangerous place. Unfortunately, for many young people who exhibit even the slightest possibility that they may be homosexual, school halls and lunch rooms are fearful, threatening places.

Some people's actions against homosexual persons have resulted in physical injuries and even death. But emotional and psychological abuse can be just as damaging as physical abuse. Even seemingly harmless demeaning comments can offer support to those ready to harass people who appear to be homosexual.

In *Always Our Children*, a statement from one of the U.S. Catholic Bishops' committees, we read that "God does not love someone any less simply because he or she is homosexual. God's love is always and everywhere offered to those who are open to receiving it." We stand side by side in the bright light of his love when we do justice, love kindness, and walk humbly with God. (See *Micah 6:8*.)

FAITH ACTIVITY

Decreasing Homophobia In the newspaper, research cases of violence against people because they are homosexual. How widespread is the problem? Is there evidence of an increase or decrease in such incidents? Discuss with the class how each person can help decrease homophobia.

The Catholic bishops' statement, *Always Our Children,* should serve as a guideline for dialogue between parents and children who need them.

Recommendations to Parents from *Always Our Children,* statement from the bishops who were part of the committe on Family and Marrige

Accept and love yourselves as parents in order to accept and love your son or daughter. Do not blame yourselves for a homosexual orientation in your child.

Do everything possible to continue demonstrating love for your child. However, accepting his or her homosexual orientation does not have to include approving of all related attitudes and behavioral choices. In fact, you may need to challenge certain aspects of a lifestyle that you find objectionable.

Urge your son or daughter to stay joined to the Catholic faith community. If he or she has left the Church, urge him or her to return and be reconciled to the community, especially through the sacrament of penance.

Recommend that your son or daughter find a spiritual director/mentor to offer guidance in prayer and in leading a chaste and virtuous life.

Seek help for yourself, perhaps in the form of counseling or spiritual direction, as you strive for understanding, acceptance, and inner peace. Also, consider joining a parents' support group. . . . They can share effective ways of handling delicate family situations such as how to tell family members and friends about your child, how to explain homosexuality to younger children, and how to relate to your son or daughter's friends in a Christian way.

Reach out in love and service to other parents struggling with a son or daughter's homosexuality. Contact your parish about organizing a parents' support group. Your diocesan family ministry office, Catholic Charities, or a special diocesan ministry to homosexual persons may be able to offer assistance.

As you take advantage of opportunities for education and support, remember that you can only change yourself; you can only be responsible for your own beliefs and actions, not those of your adult children.

Put your faith completely in God, who is more powerful, more compassionate, and more forgiving than we are or ever could be.

1 Are you or is someone you know homophobic? Explain.

2 Why do you think that homophobia is so strong in our society?

3 If a clear case of injustice occurred against homosexual persons in your community, would you speak out against it? Explain.

4 Is your school a welcoming or hostile environment for people who appear to be homosexual? Explain.

5 Would you join an organization at your school whose mission is dialogue and mutual support between heterosexual and homosexual students?

6 Why do you think the U.S. Catholic bishops believe it is important to remind parents to love and cherish their children regardless of their sexual orientation? Which, if any, of the bishops' recommendations to parents would you find hard to accept? Explain.

7 If you had a homosexual son or daughter, do you think he or she would more likely face injustices than if he or she were heterosexual? Explain.

8 Jesus gave his life to remind us that God loves us and that we are to love ourselves. Do you think this Christian message would be harder to realize if you were homosexual? Are there obstacles to experiencing God's love faced by homosexuals that hetersexuals typically don't face?

Faith in Action

Just Youth

Sponsored by: The Spiritan Campus Ministry

College life at Duquesne University in Pittsburgh, Pennsylvania, is more than classes, study groups, and career planning. A sophomore at Duquesne hit the core vision of how universities should see their ministry on campus when she said, "Before I came to Duquesne, my faith (Roman Catholic) was something I just did; now my faith is something I live." These words describe the new collaborative vision that has been growing at Duquesne since 2000, engaging all students, faculty, staff, administration, and faith traditions.

> "Just Youth has helped me to see the problems that are truly present in our world, to judge the source of these problems, and to act with compassion. Once involved in Just Youth, you are no longer 'just a youth' aimlessly wondering what life holds in store for you; rather, you are sent on a mission, compelled to work for justice and peace everywhere."

—Livia Montone, Duquesne University student
Spiritan Campus Ministry's Just Youth

A part of this collaborative vision called Just Youth is the social justice element of this broader notion of mission and ministry. Through Just Youth, student groups come together for responsible actions on campus and beyond

and work to make systemic changes in the community. Just Youth is about participation, not joining a specific group or organization, but the notion that, no matter what type of volunteer work you are doing promoting justice and peace, you are in effect working in collaboration with Just Youth.

Just Youth was adapted from the religious order of the Spiritans from the English province to fit the needs of the students at Duquesne and is dedicated to raising the consciousness of the university community on issues of peace and justice, offering short and long-term volunteer opportunities

Opportunities for students, faculty, and staff include: Way of Peace (a discussion group that explores the practice of non-violence), Amnesty International (advocacy work), St. Vincent de Paul (outreach to the local homeless population), Students for Life (concerned with life issues from conception to natural death), and Evergreen (an environmentally conscious organization that works to safeguard our natural resources).

Outreach opportunities include: Holy Family Institute, a residential facility for marginalized children; the Allegheny County Jail, where students provide a ministry of hospitality to families; Family House, a residential facility for families with loved ones going through long-term medical care; Shepherd's Wellness, a bi-weekly gathering of people infected and affected by AIDS and HIV; and homeless outreach to persons in downtown Pittsburgh.

Just Youth offers three cross-cultural mission trips: Appalachian Experience, where students work to improve housing conditions in the Appalachian community; Immokalee Florida, where students spend their spring break working alongside migrant workers; and Urban Challenge, where students spend a week in Camden, New Jersey, working in Headstart programs, medical clinics, food banks, drop in centers for persons with AIDS and HIV, and several other sites.

Wherever they are giving their time and talent, students, faculty, and staff at Duquesne are learning to "do justice, and to love kindness, and to walk humbly with . . . God" (*Micah 6:8*).

Visit www.harcourtreligion.com to learn more about Spiritan Campus Ministry's Just Youth and for a link to its site.

Begin by praying the Sign of the Cross.

Leader: Let us pray to the Lord, our Sovereign, who created us in his image and likeness.

Reader 1: When I look at your heavens, the work of your fingers, the moon and the stars that you have established; what are human beings that you are mindful of them, mortals that you care for them?

Reader2: Yet you have made them a little lower than God, and crowned them with glory and honor. You have given them dominion over the works of your hands.

Reader 3: You have put all things under their feet, all sheep and oxen, and also the beasts of the field, the birds of the air, and the fish of the sea, whatever passes along the paths of the seas.

All: O Lord, our Sovereign, how majestic is your name in all the earth!

Psalm 8:3–9 from *The New Revised Standard Version* of the Holy Bible

End by praying the Sign of the Cross.

›Review

1. Explain Church teaching on male-female difference.

2. Explain the terms *nature* and *nurture* as they apply to men's and women's identity.

3. What is Church teaching on the equality of women and men?

4. Define *sexism*.

5. Define *patriarchy*.

6. To what does the feminization of poverty refer?

7. Name an attitude that underlies relationship violence. Name an attitude that underlies wholesome relationships.

8. What does it mean to say that a home is meant to be a "domestic Church"?

9. What does the fourth commandment call for in relationships between generations?

10. Describe Jesus' attitude toward women. How was it different from the attitude prevalent at the time?

11. Name three characteristics of a society in which collaboration between men and women would flourish.

12. Name three provisions called for in 1995 by Pope John Paul II directed toward improving conditions for women in society.

13. What is the Church's teaching on homosexual sexual activity?

14. Define *homophobia*.

15. In essence, what have the U.S. Catholic bishops recommended to parents who discover that their child is homosexual?

›Key Words

domestic violence (p. 265)—Physical or psychological abuse within a family setting.

feminization of poverty (p. 262)—The trend that results in more women and dependent children living in poverty than men.

homophobia (p. 273)—the fear of being homosexual or of people with a homosexual orientation.

patriarchy (p. 260)—A society in which the dominant power is in the hands of a select group of men.

relationship violence (p. 264)— physical or psychological abuse that occurs in the context of a relationship such as dating or marriage.

sexism (p. 259)—Discrimination and injustice based on gender differences.

>Our Challenge

In this chapter we looked at what it means to be made in God's image as male and female and about the attitudes and behaviors that undermine the harmony and equality of women and men. Just action toward both genders requires acknowledging the uniqueness of each while maintaining the dignity of both. Also, we considered the unjust treatment of those marginalized because of their sexual orientation. A compassionate community does not let vulnerabilities and differences prevent people from helping one another. Christ invites everyone to his banquet table and wants all people to share their gifts with everyone else.

EARTH JUSTICE

CHAPTER 10

NURTURING NATURE, OUR HOME

CHAPTER GOALS

In this chapter you will:

* explore the link between concern for the person and concern for the earth.

* consider how environmental misuse has taxed the earth.

* learn that care for the earth reflects the grandeur of God.

* examine how stewardship can counteract environmental degradation.

Ecology: Making Our House a Home

According to the Bible, God created the earth to be a garden that, with the cooperation of humans, would sustain life. In the quoted passage on the next page, the U.S. Catholic bishops catalog ways that this garden has become depleted and endangered. The biblical vision of the earth as a garden and the bishops' concerns about the environment echo the message we have received from the science of **ecology**. The Greek word *oikos* from which ecology is derived means "house." In fact, nature is our house, the dwelling place that we share with other creatures. In this chapter we will "explore the links between concern for the person and for the earth, between natural ecology and social ecology" (*Renewing the Earth*).

Justice and Nature

We read stories about poisons seeping up from the ground near chemical waste dumps. Every summer, people living near or visiting beaches wonder whether ocean water will be safe for swimming. Numerous species of animals are in danger of extinction. Because of pollution in the air, the healing rays of the sun are now also more likely to produce cancer. Water we depend on for drinking must undergo more and more treatment to be safe. As human waste piles up, communities struggle to figure out what to do with all the garbage we produce. Automobiles continue to pollute the air while alternatives to the internal combustion engine receive little industry or public support.

The problems we face reflect the choices we make. For a long time, at least in Western culture, people believed that nature and the earth offered unlimited resources. Harnessing the earth's resources to benefit humanity was the goal. Pollution was a necessary side effect. Long-term depletion of resources was not a particular concern.

More recently, the language of environmental concern has become an important part of public discussion. Today, from

GROUP TALK

Have you ever participated in an organization or an activity whose goal was improving the environment? Describe the experience.

In the day that the LORD God made the earth and the heavens, when no plant of the field was yet in the earth and no herb of the field had yet sprung up—for the LORD God had not caused it to rain upon the earth, and there was no one to till the ground; but a stream would rise from the earth, and water the whole face of the ground—then the LORD God formed man from the dust of the ground, and breathed into his nostrils the breath of life; and the man became a living being. And the LORD God planted a garden in Eden, in the east; and there he put the man whom he had formed. Out of the ground the LORD God made to grow every tree that is pleasant to the sight and good for food, the tree of life also stood in the midst of the garden, and the tree of the knowledge of good and evil . . . . The LORD God took the man and put him in the garden of Eden to till it and keep it.

✝ **Genesis 2:4–9, 15**

Two Visions of Creation The effects of environmental degradation surround us: the smog in our cities; chemicals in our water and on our food; eroded topsoil blowing in the wind; the loss of valuable wetlands; radioactive and toxic waste lacking adequate disposal sites; threats to the health of industrial and farm workers. The problems, however, reach far beyond our own neighborhoods and work-places. Our problems are the world's problems and burdens for generations to come. Poisoned water crosses borders freely. Acid rain pours on countries that do not create it. Greenhouse gases and chlorofluorocarbons affect the earth's atmosphere for many decades, regardless of where they are produced or used.

Opinions vary about the causes and the seriousness of environmental problems. Still, we can experience their effects in polluted air and water; in oil and wastes on our beaches; in the loss of farmland, wetlands, and forests; and in the decline of rivers and lakes.

U.S. Catholic Conference, *Renewing the Earth*

GROUP TALK

1 Describe the contrasting vision of creation portrayed in these two passages.

2 What is the vision of humanity's role in creation that is shared by the passages?

3 What emotions do these two passages evoke in you?

an early age, school children hear the message about taking care of the earth. Grade schools celebrate Earth Day and sponsor tree plantings. Children do reports on endangered species. One way to measure the degree to which positive attitudes, behaviors, and policies have actually taken root in our society is to look at nature in terms of the Catholic vision.

Ethical Treatment of the Environment Western culture has tended to be anthropocentric. That is, it has centered on the human (in Greek, *anthropos*). **Anthropocentrism** gets distorted when other expressions of nature such as redwoods and cheetahs are seen as deserving no more respect than what we would give television sets and candy bars. They are important only insofar as they serve humans. In other words, redwoods and cheetahs are creatures beautiful for us to look at, interesting for us to study, valuable for us to learn from, and profitable for our use.

> Faced with the widespread destruction of the environment, people everywhere are coming to understand that we cannot continue to use the goods of the earth as we have in the past.
>
> Pope John Paul II, *The Ecological Crisis*, Introduction.

The very beginning of the Bible offers an alternative viewpoint on nature. It reminds us that all creatures have inherent value. During the creation account, the refrain is regularly interjected: "And God saw that it was good." As the Catechism points out, "God willed the diversity of his creatures, and their own particular goodness, their interdependence, and their order." Humans play a unique role in the natural order. They alone are created in the image of God, "called to share . . . in God's own life" (*CCC* 356). Therefore, they are to serve as God's representatives in taking care of the rest of creation. All creation is intended for the glory of God, and humans are responsible for making good use of all that God has given.

Humans are the centerpiece of creation, and all other creatures are to assist humans in reaching their end in God. No other creature can either destroy the earth and everything on it or nurture the earth for the benefit of all. However, along with our power, our unique relationship with God, and our self-awareness comes a unique responsibility to set standards for ethical treatment, not only of humans but of nonhuman creatures as well. As we will see later in this chapter, the Seventh Commandment guides us in our responsibilities as stewards of God's creation. When we are careful with all of God's creatures, we help to sustain a healthy environment in which all people can live out their God-given dignity.

FAITH ACTIVITY

Time With Nature Write a short paragraph about the effect that your time spent with nature has had on you. Include the amount of the day spent in a natural setting, the percentage of your diet that consists of foods in their natural state, and the amount of time spent in interaction with animals and plants.

Environmental Scenarios,

★ The owner of a large parcel of rich farmland is offered a great price by a developer who wants to build a mall on it.

– Should the owner be free to do whatever he or she wants to do with the land?

– Who should be involved in making the decision?

– Should the land itself be taken into consideration in the decision?

★ A strip of land serves as a nesting ground for the endangered California condor.

– Should the federal government restrict development around the area in order to preserve the condor's nesting ground?

– Upon what basis could you make a case for or against this action?

★ A company, the major employer in its area, has been dumping chemicals into a nearby stream for decades–a practice it claims is necessary for it to stay in business. Recently, citizens in a community downstream have petitioned the state government to require the company to stop this practice.

– Make a case on behalf of the company; on behalf of the citizens.

– Then, make a case on behalf of the stream and the wildlife which live in or near it.

★ The spotted owl uses only the forests of the northwestern United States as its habitat. The forests are also a rich source of lumber.

– Should the lumber industry be denied access to forests in order to protect the spotted owl? Make a case both for and against your position.

★ A complaint is lodged against a group of teenagers for abusing a stray cat in a neighborhood park. They tell police officials that the cat belongs to no one, and, therefore, no crime was committed.

– Should the teenagers be punished for their actions? If so, decide on an appropriate punishment. If not, explain why.

★ A hotel chain wants to build a lodge in the middle of a national park. The hotel chain would put in paved walking trails in order to make the park and lodge accessible to more people. Another group wants to keep the national park as primitive and natural as possible, even though this means only hardy travelers can enjoy it.

– Make a case both for and against each position.

– Where do you stand? Why?

Debate the issues involved in the environmental scenarios.

GROUP TALK

Make a case for or against each of the following statements:

1. Today's young people are more aware than earlier generations of the need to preserve the environment.

2. Today's young people treat the environment more carefully than earlier generations did.

Environmental Concerns

Concern for Social Structures

Public policies and practices, expressions of social structures, are an important sign as to what degree the earth matters in a society. On the following pages we will explore policies and practices that relate to six different aspects of nature: (1) farmland, (2) wilderness and rainforests, (3) air, (4) water, (5) animals, plants, and natural habitat, and (6) waste.

Farmland   If we travel through the western half of the United States, we might assume that land is plentiful enough. However, land that is best for farming is also best for development. In most cases, selling land for housing developments, shopping malls, and rural business centers can be more profitable for the landowner than farming the land. Maintaining land for farming is a primary land issue facing the United States.

A second issue related to land is the way farming is done. One important difference is between **inorganic farming** and **organic farming**. For many years, larger farms have relied heavily on inorganic farming. More recently other farming methods, such as **low-tillage farming**, have been developed. With low-tillage farming, narrow slits are cut in the sod, and seed and fertilizer are placed in the slits. With this method, the sod remains relatively undisturbed and erosion problems are reduced. Those using this method seek to avoid the deficiencies of both organic and inorganic farming.

Making choices about how crops are planted, which crops are planted, and how often they are planted can make the difference between protecting and enriching the land or destroying its productivity for future generations. Agricultural experts and farmers dedicated to efficient land use are making life-sustaining contributions through their efforts. Government policies can help ease financial risks that farmers take and can also support healthy land use.

Wilderness and Rainforests Another issue closely related to land is preservation of wilderness areas. Anyone who has visited one of the great national parks, especially in the western states, knows the precious resource that a Grand Canyon or a Yosemite National Park can be. Conflicts related to wilderness lands are between public versus private ownership and between development versus maintaining areas as close to a natural state as possible. Development makes wilderness areas more accessible for people but also affects the animal and plant life in the area.

Only 2 percent of the earth's surface is covered by rainforests, but more than half the earth's plant and animal species find a home there. Worldwide weather patterns and the earth's fresh water supply are directly related to the extent and health of the rainforests. Many products used for medicine, industry, and agriculture come from the rainforests. But over half of the earth's original rainforests are no more; between four and five million square miles of tropical forestland have been burned away, converted to farmland, or paved over for housing and industry. The present rate of deforestation will bring about the almost total destruction of the rainforest ecosystem in less than thirty years.

FAITH ACTIVITY

Land Use Interview someone over forty. Ask the person how he or she has seen land use in your area change over the past few decades. Has there been a vast decrease in the amount of farmland or wilderness area? If so, what has taken its place? What effect have these changes had on human life in the area? Report on your findings to the class.

FAITH ACTIVITY

Plight of Rainforests Research to find out more specific details on the plight of the world's rainforests. Share your information in small groups, and present the group's findings to the class. Do research on the national parks of the United States or Canada. What are the problems? What is being done to address the problems? Share your information in small groups (perhaps each person in the group could study a different park), and present the group's findings to the class.

While much of this destruction is due to multinational and other large companies, a good deal of deforestation results from other justice problems, especially large numbers of people who are poor and landless who use the forests for wood fuel and products to sell in order to survive. In many cases, then, the proper use of rainforests depends on land reform that will benefit people with few resources. The Vatican's Pontifical Council for Justice and Peace summarized the issue:

> There is an obvious need for more serious and responsible approaches to the use of the earth's natural resources, but ones that do not neglect the greatest of resources, the human person. We are called to make the best use of our God-given talents and abilities; in this case, by measuring the scope and extent of our social, economic and environmental problems and taking concrete steps for the increased protection of threatened forests and biological species. The Holy See therefore encourages all to develop a renewed consciousness of humanity's special vocation place in the world and relationship to the environment.
>
> *Note on Use of the Environment*

GROUP TALK

1. What steps should the world community, perhaps through the United Nations, take to protect wilderness areas? Rainforests?
2. What steps do you think our country should take to protect wilderness areas? Rainforests?
3. What can individuals do to protect wilderness areas? Rainforests?

Air If people were stuck in an elevator, it wouldn't be long before all the passengers would have exchanged at least once the air they breathe. In fact, we are still breathing in air molecules breathed at the time of Jesus. What we add to the air today will stay with us long into the future. Already there are indications of global warming, caused in part by the greenhouse effect.

Vehicles account for the greatest amount of air pollution in the world today. The haze covering major cities comes mostly from car exhaust fumes. There are basically two schools of thought about how best to cut down on automobile pollution. One group wants manufacturers to create more fuel-efficient cars. Another group fears that this is merely a stopgap measure. They believe the real solution lies in alternatives to the gasoline engine, such as electric cars and improved public transportation.

World Pollution Levels

How would you rate the United States in terms of its commitment to protecting the environment?

Compare levels of nitrogen-dioxide particle emissions of select, highly-populated cities worldwide.

Tokyo, Japan, **68** (population: 26.4 million)
Mexico City, Mexico, **130** (population: 18.1 million)
New York City, U.S., **79** (population: 16.7 million)
Mumbai, India, **39** (population: 16.1 million)
Beijung, China, **122** (population: 10.8 million)

Source: World Almanac 2005.

In addition to automobiles, factories, power plants, and waste-disposal units pollute the air. In the past few decades, the public outcry for cleaner air has led to stricter anti-pollution regulations, and many communities and companies have developed creative ways to cut down on pollution and to use waste products effectively. Nonetheless, the environment still often loses out to the economy and to politics.

Water We all know about endangered animal species. However, clean water could be classified as an *endangered resource*. Water exists in such large quantities on our planet that we find it difficult to imagine a shortage of it. Yet experts agree that the lack of clean, drinkable water creates more problems worldwide than the lack of farmable land. Those of us used to having water available at the turn of a faucet overlook the importance of this endangered resource. Even in some communities of the United States, the demand for fresh water is beginning to grow beyond its availability.

FAITH ACTIVITY

Air Pollution In small groups, look through automobile and truck magazines or books about motor vehicles. Look for evidence that air pollution is a major health concern related to motor vehicles. How much space is given to this issue? If air pollution is mentioned at all, how is it treated? Report on your findings.

When we think of water pollution, we probably imagine the streams, rivers, and lakes that chemical pollutants have made unsafe for drinking, swimming, or fishing. Due to the spreading problem of acid rain, when air pollution and moisture in the air mix, even turning our faces skyward to drink falling snow or rain is a questionable practice. Much has been done to curb water pollution, but the threat to all forms of water supplies remains. Even more importantly, as a society we have not seriously faced the fact that all of our resources need much more careful handling if they and we are to remain lively and healthy.

GROUP TALK

1. What are your water-use habits? Do you let water run while you brush your teeth? How long is your shower? Do you live in a residence where the lawn is sprinkled whether it needs it or not?

2. What other questions would help people evaluate their use of water?

Animals, Plants, and Natural Habitat The earth is increasingly inhabited by humans. If we tame much more of the earth, we may lose the unique beauty of wilderness places and the creatures that live in them.

Inhumane treatment of animals occurs in the name of real or imagined human benefit. Two areas of concern here are **animal experimentation** and **corporate farming**. Few people demand ending all experimentation on animals. There is an obvious difference between experimentation for the sake of testing medicines and experimentation with chemicals to test their effects in cosmetics. In addition many questionable practices are performed in laboratories in the name of scientific research. For instance, animal-rights groups call for the end to or stricter regulation of vivisection, the practice of performing experiments on live animals.

Many small family farms are being purchased by large corporations that then hire others to plant, cultivate, and harvest the crops. The corporate office's main purpose in buying the land is to make a profit. Since the corporate offices do not have the personal interest in the land that the family farmer had, they are less concerned with care for and future use of the land—when it is depleted, it can always be sold to a developer.

Sometimes these corporate farms become "farm factories" where cattle, pigs, chickens, and other animals are raised in large numbers and treated like mere products. Most egg-laying chickens spend their lives confined to small cages, never seeing the light of day. Their eggs are carried away on conveyor belts, and food and water are distributed through automatic machinery. The production of veal, pork, and beef can result in similar confinement for calves, pigs, and cattle; the advertised tenderness of meat is often due to the fact that the animal never had a chance to exercise or perhaps even live outdoors. In addition to the "farm factory" treatment of the animals and land, the disposal of the animal waste from such confinement-lot or feed-lot operations causes yet another danger to the environment.

FAITH ACTIVITY

If you had a parcel of land available to you, would you plant a vegetable garden? Do you think the experience would help you appreciate land use?

Waste Concern for the environment requires being attentive to resources we are using up. It also requires being attentive to what we put back into the environment. Just because the trash that we wrap in a plastic bag and place on the curb disappears on trash day does not mean that it no longer concerns us. We are surrounding ourselves with our own garbage, and the earth is choking from an overdose of waste left at the curb by people. Certain items that we may use for only a few seconds will remain with us for centuries. They are easy and inexpensive to produce but ultimately difficult to dispose of. We tend to emphasize **recycling** as the primary way to take care of our waste problem. However, cutting back on creating trash in the first place is more effective than recycling the trash that we produce.

Hazardous waste, waste from medical facilities, and waste from nuclear power plants are particularly disturbing problems. Plutonium waste from nuclear power plants, for example, will remain radioactive for half a million years. Every community wants easy access to unlimited electrical power, but no community wants nuclear waste stored in its backyard.

Environmental Misuse

Clearly, since all of us are of the earth, all of us suffer from its misuse. Two groups are particularly hard hit by environmental problems—people who are poor and people yet to be born. People who are poor suffer the most from nature's misuse. When crop production decreases because of a reduction in available farmland, people who are poor are the ones who go hungry. While those who can afford it walk around with bottled water, people who are poor and live in underdeveloped countries scramble to find drinkable water. Very often people who are poor live in areas most subject to poor air quality or work where toxic chemicals or pesticides are a hazard. Migrant farmworkers, for instance, work in fields where harmful pesticides are often used.

Second, future generations must contend with the effects of current environmental misuse. The way we treat the environment today is borrowing from the future. When we weigh the costs and benefits of our overuse of resources and of the waste we produce, we seldom think about the impact such use will have on coming generations. That is, the cost of gasoline is not just the price we pay at the pump. Because of our gasoline use, our children will inherit environmental problems that they will have to address, both in terms of depleted resources and of the effects of air pollution. For example, the plastic cup we use today is being left for future generations to deal with. Therefore, the true cost of items we make and of resources we use is not just the expense of current production. Plastic toys and trinkets may be inexpensive to buy, but their true cost includes the effect they have on the environment now and in the future.

GROUP TALK

1 Choose a natural resource or manufactured product. Calculate the true cost of the item. Include in your calculation: depletion of resources, pollution that occurs in manufacture and use, and problems related to disposal of the item after its use.

2 An attempt is being made to recycle plastic into new products. Go to three stores and make a list of products made from recycled plastic. In each store calculate the percentage of plastic products made from recycled materials.

Nature and War

"Clearly, war represents a serious threat to the environment, as the darkened skies and oil soaked beaches of Kuwait clearly remind us. The pursuit of peace—lasting peace based on justice—ought to be an environmental priority because the earth itself bears the wounds and scars of war."

U. S. Conference of Catholic Bishops, *Renewing the Earth*

War scars every natural setting that it encounters. In Vietnam, sections of otherwise lush tropical forest lie barren due to the destruction heaped upon the country forty years ago. Landmines used during warfare are a hazard to civilian travelers and local farmers, now and far into the future. Use of nuclear weapons, of course, represents the ultimate environmental crisis. What we have seen of nuclear weapons already warns us that their use can wipe out the delicate ecosystem that sustains life on our planet. Biological weapons could destroy entire species and forever alter the delicate balance of life on earth. And the majority of people on earth do not know or have a clue about what other weapons of mass destruction are being planned and developed.

One of the main reasons that war is harmful to the environment is that it distracts people from working together to make the earth a healthier environment for everyone. We face an environmental crisis. War greatly adds to the crisis and prevents us from taking steps to address the crisis.

FAITH ACTIVITY

War and the Environment Consider the environmental damages caused by wars in Kuwait and Vietnam. Keep these in mind as one factor when thinking about whether or not a military action is necessary.

GROUP TALK

1. After housing, the item people in the United States typically spend the largest chunk of their income on is a motor vehicle. As a people we are known for having a love affair with cars/trucks/SUVs. Is this true for you? If public transportation were improved in your area, would you forego buying a car? Explain.

2. Respond to the following statement of a government official in an underdeveloped country: "Your country is already wealthy, but we are poor. It is more important for us to increase industrial production cheaply than it is to be concerned about whether we are harming the environment." How might a government official from a wealthy country respond to this statement?

A Christian View of the Earth

> Man's dominion over inanimate and other living beings granted by the Creator is not absolute: it is limited by concern for the quality of life of his neighbor, including generations to come; it requires a religious respect for the integrity of creation.

CCC 2415

Think back on all the groups already discussed in this course. In all cases respect for their God-given dignity underlies justice for them. In their analysis of justice and the environment, the U.S. Catholic bishops point out that respect for human life "extends to respect for all creation" (*Renewing the Earth*). When the dignity of people is overlooked, exploitation often results. Similarly, exploitation occurs when we do not display the respect for the rest of creation that it deserves. Careful use of the goods of the earth does not diminish us as human beings. In fact, by doing so we are truly manifesting the exalted role God has given us.

Respect for Nature

The opposite of treating others with respect is **exploitation**. Exploitation means viewing the natural world as a commodity to be bought and sold, used and used up: "I own it; therefore, I can do with it whatever I want." Exploitation dismisses the divine mystery manifest through creation and is concerned solely with what can be gained from it. Exploitation of created things flows from humanity's arrogance and acquisitiveness that the Bible says has led to alienation from nature. By way of contrast, the U.S. Catholic bishops remind us that "every creature shares a bit of the divine beauty," and that we are not free "to use created things capriciously" (*Renewing the Earth*).

If exploitation seeks to exert power over nature in an unjustified way, then respect means working with nature. Exploitation represents a careless approach to nature. On the other hand respect is a care-filled treatment of nature. It flows from a spirit of nurturing rather than of abusing or carelessly using nature. Note that respect for nature does not rule out the use of nature but its abuse. Science, technology, experimentation, and human inventiveness can be respectful and nonexploitive in the interplay between the human and the nonhuman world. The goodness and beauty of creation do not cease when transformed by human hands in an appropriate way.

FAITH ACTIVITY

Respect for Nature Compose a story or poem or create a poster or art work that illustrates respect for nature. You might try composing from the perspective of a nonhuman creature.

The Web of Life God has created humans as the summit of creation. However, while there is a hierarchy of creatures with humans clearly above other creatures, there is also a solidarity and interdependence among all God's creation. The Catholic bishops of the United States have described this solidarity and interdependence as "the web of life:"

> The web of life is one. Our mistreatment of the natural world diminishes our own dignity and sacredness, not only because we are destroying resources that future generations of humans need, but because we are engaging in actions that contradict what it means to be human. Our tradition calls us to protect the life and dignity of the human person, and it is increasingly clear that this task cannot be separated from the care and defense of all of creation.

Renewing the Earth

FAITH ACTIVITY

Concern for the Earth Write an action plan that would demonstrate your concern for the earth. Use ideas from these action plans to write, as a class, an action plan for your school. Present it to the student council.

Stewardship

In a few Gospel stories Jesus refers to stewards, chief servants of a landowner charged with taking care of the owner's possessions. The same word is used of humans in Genesis when God commands: ". . . let them [humans] have dominion [that is, be stewards] over the fish of the sea, and over the birds of the air, and over the cattle, and over all the wild animals of the earth, and over every creeping thing that creeps upon the earth" (*Genesis 1:26*). In other words, Scripture acknowledges God's rule over creation:

The earth is the LORD'S and all that is in it, the world, and those who live in it.

✝ Psalm 24:1

Second, humans have been assigned to be God's stewards over the rest of creation. They are to cultivate and care for the earth. (See *Genesis 2:15*.) The term for this human role in the order of creation is **stewardship**.

Pope John Paul II and the Natural Order In the early days of his papacy, Pope John Paul II began his many pilgrimages to the countries of the world by descending a plane and kneeling down to kiss the ground. This symbolic gesture fittingly demonstrated his plea to Christians to reverence the earth. In his 1987 encyclical *On Social Concern*, the pope pointed out that misuse of nature violates the dignity of creation and the mutual connection that exists in the world. Second, he alerted us that certain resources are not renewable, which is a danger in particular for future generations. Finally, he warned that the "direct or indirect result of industrialization is, ever more frequently, the pollution of the environment, with serious consequences for the health of the population" (34).

> The Book of Genesis describes a world in which human beings are not above and apart from creation but instead exercise a special role as overseers of the rest of creation. The biblical notion of stewardship names the commission given by God to humanity to take care of his creation in all its manifestations. As any farmer or gardener knows, stewardship requires constant vigilance to maintain the delicate balance of the earth's ecosystem.
>
> Anne M. Clifford CSJ, "Foundations for a Catholic Ecological Theology of God,"
> *And God Saw That It Was Good*, 1996, p. 28

Jesus himself certainly demonstrates an appreciation for nature. People in need in his community are clearly the focus of his concern. Nevertheless, in his sayings and stories, he constantly includes references to animals, plants, and other creatures of the earth. The U.S. Catholic bishops describe Jesus' sensitivity to his natural environment in these words:

> God's grace was like wheat growing in the night (see Mark 4:26-29); divine love like a shepherd seeking a lost sheep (see Luke 15:4-7). In the birds of the air and the lilies of the field, Jesus found reason for his disciples to give up the ceaseless quest for material security and advantage and to trust in God (see Matthew 6:25-33). Jesus himself is the Good Shepherd, who gives his life for his flock (see John 10). His Father is a vineyard worker, who trims vines so that they may bear more abundant fruit (see John 15:1-8). These familiar images, though they speak directly to humanity's encounter with God, at the same time reveal that the fundamental relation between humanity and nature is one of caring for creation.
>
> *Renewing the Earth*

FAITH ACTIVITY

Where Does It All Go? Research how much trash tonnage has been collected annually in your community for the past few years. Find out where your community's trash goes. Find out what recycling programs the community offers. Report your findings to your class.

A Sacramental Vision Catholicism has a theology that supports an appreciation for nature. The sacramental life of the Church uses earthy things such as water, oil, bread, and wine to help us encounter God. A sacramental vision recognizes that nature points to God, that created things are signs of God's glory and presence. In fact, a sacramental vision affirms that: "The whole universe is God's dwelling" (*Renewing the Earth*). In other words, by its rich tradition of sacramentality, Catholicism keeps us in touch with God not through isolating us from the rest of nature but through holding up the things of nature as signs of God's presence.

Two saints who modeled the sacramental vision of Christianity are Saint Francis of Assisi and Saint Benedict. Statues of Francis frequently found in gardens and on birdbaths attest to his association with nature. He had a strong sense of his own creatureliness and of God's presence in the world. He listened intently to birds and crickets. According to legend, at one point Francis even befriended a troublesome and dangerous wolf.

Changing Personal Practices

Perhaps more than any other justice-related issue, our society says in regard to nature, "We'll worry about that tomorrow." We feel secure that lush forests and bountiful farmlands will continue to exist, even though we see them more frequently on television than in real life. We breathe the air freely, and only occasionally do the fumes remind us of potential danger. We drink water and swim in lakes and oceans, hoping that the latest pollution scare proves to be exaggerated. We continue to dispose of waste without thinking where it is going.

To cherish nature does not mean to avoid changing it. In the spirit of stewardship, we are called upon to be co-creators with God. We might think that technology is necessarily hostile to nature. In fact, although technology has at times been harmful to nature, it need not be destructive. To be effective, technology must work with nature now and in the future. Solar energy and windmills are good examples of nature-friendly technology. However, all products and appliances can be more or less nature friendly.

To change the direction of environmental decay, we need to remember:

- The foods we eat have an impact on nature.

- What we build and where we build affect land, water, air, plant and animal life.

- Use of the automobile affects the quality of our surroundings.

- Easily accessible driving and parking facilities, labor-saving devices, fast foods, packages wrapped in layers of plastic, disposable diapers and containers, and other modern conveniences leave their mark on the environment.

- Every time we throw a bottle or can into the trash, we are adding to the garbage that the earth must absorb.

Rather than having the vastness of the problem sap our energy, it can be energizing to know that we can make a difference. On environmental issues, we need not wait for government policies to change. We can make conscientious lifestyle changes—especially in the use of resources that are environmentally friendly rather than destructive.

A quick guideline for conscientious consumption is *refuse*. Our primary focus should be on refusing—resisting the pressures of our consumer society to accumulate things. When possible, resist buying or using materials that cause damage to the environment. Second *reuse*—for example, reusable grocery store bags save paper and plastic. We help the environment more when we reuse items rather than recycle them. The third dimension to conscientious consumption is recycling. *Recycle* newspapers, cardboard, wrapping paper, aluminum and tin cans, glass, grass and leaves, and plastic containers.

FAITH ACTIVITY

Cutting Back For a week, try to cut back on purchases you make, the amount of resources you use (for example, food, water, electricity), and the waste that you produce. Keep a diary of all the ways you conserved things during the week. When the week is over, write about how it felt to be a more conscientious consumer. Compare notes with other students to share experiences and to discover other possible ways to restrict using and wasting resources.

Ways to Decrease the Waste, Problem

Refuse: Cut back on purchasing waste-producing products, including the use of electrical energy.

Reuse: Use products that are reusable, recyclable, or otherwise environmentally friendly.

Recycle: Come up with environmentally sound ways to dispose of or use the waste that we produce (recycle).

Change is Possible During the summer of 2003 power plants accidentally shut down over much of northeastern United States. A quick-thinking scientist decided to use the occasion to study air quality during the shutdown compared to air quality when all the power plants were up and running. He found that even during the short break from polluting power plants, the air quality improved considerably. This experiment suggests that non-polluting sources of energy and less polluting vehicles and other products can improve the air we breathe. Keeping land fertile and water safe are possible. Species extinction can be prevented. None of these life-saving changes will occur unless we as a world community take seriously our role as stewards of creation.

Public discussion of environmental issues tends to get lost in the midst of other issues. Actually, other concerns—health care, the economy, wars—cannot be separated from concern for the environment. And since damage to the earth knows no boundaries, improving the quality of the environment is a project that needs to be undertaken both locally and universally. In this work we are acting as the human family God intends us to be.

›Faith in Action

Crown Point Ecology Center's Programs

Sponsor: **The Sisters of Saint Dominic of Akron**

How do activities like growing vegetables and tending bees help to create just social systems and preserve Earth? Each year teenagers who participate in earth camps, farm-based environmental education programs, and youth service projects at Crown Point Ecology Center in Bath, Ohio, discover that they are all part of the Web of Life, part of what happens to everyone else.

Sponsored by the Sisters of Saint Dominic of Akron, Crown Point supports justice for the human-Earth community by reaching out to the poor and advocating for environmental restoration. Since 1997 Crown Point has donated more than 140,000 pounds of its Certified Organic produce to the Akron-Canton Regional Foodbank and its Community Supported Agriculture (CSA) program involves 90 families in a local food system.

In partnership with the Summit Akron Solid Waste Management Authority in 2005, Crown Point offered a cultural exchange program called "Searching for a Sense of Place." It paired inner-city children from the Hispanic community of St. Bernard Parish in Akron with teenagers from Revere High School in Richfield, Ohio.

During the school year, Crown Point staff members introduce high school students to ecology concepts in the context of the global community. Students then volunteer with younger children during summer earth camps at Crown Point. Here they experience a sense of community, learn sustainable farming methods, and better ways to care for themselves, their neighborhoods, and all of creation. Through art, music, games, hands-on activities, and daily farm chores everyone learns about various cultures, soil types, and the diversity of seeds, plants, and animals

> "Growing fresh produce and helping to fill food banks is a great way for me to connect with and help others."
>
> —Alan W.

Introducing teenagers to organic farming at Crown Point Ecology Center and its related service projects and camps invites students to use materials and practices that enhance the ecological balance of natural systems. In addition, young people see a tangible way to support hungry families with nutritious produce.

Crown Point is gently raising awareness of other issues such as green space, green building, alternate energy sources, and sustainability. Its mission to "reconnect humans to the sacredness of the Earth while challenging society to live with simplicity and mindfulness" connects with other Dominican Congregations of Sisters that promote justice through ecology in places like Great Bend, Houston, Columbus, Kentucky, New Orleans and Springfield.

◄ Volunteers for Crown Point Ecology Center.

GO ONLINE

Visit www.harcourtreligion.com to learn more about the Crown Point Ecology Center's programs and for a link to its site.

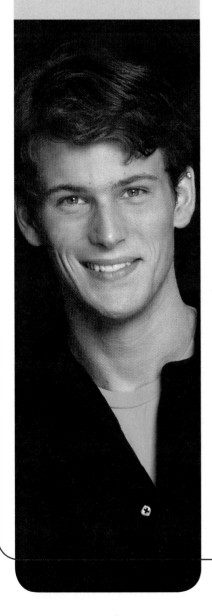

Silently reflect on the words of the psalmist.

Bless the Lord, O my soul.

    O Lord my God, you are very great.

You are clothed with honor and majesty,

    wrapped in light as with a garment.

You stretch out the heavens like a tent . . .

you make the clouds your chariot . . .

you make the winds your messengers,

    fire and flame your ministers . . .

From your lofty abode you water the mountains;

    the earth is satisfied with the fruit of your work.

You cause the grass to grow for the cattle,

    and plants for people to use,

to bring forth food from the earth,

    and wine to gladden the human heart,

oil to make the face shine,

    and bread to strengthen the human heart.

May the glory of the Lord endure forever;

    may the Lord rejoice in his works. . . .

    Psalm 104: 1–2, 3, 4, 13–15, 31

⟩Review

1. Define *ecology*. What does the Greek root of the term mean?

2. Define *anthropocentrism*.

3. What role does the Bible lay out for human beings in relation to the rest of nature?

4. Describe differences among *inorganic*, *organic*, and *low-tillage* farming.

5. What conflicts typically occur related to wilderness areas?

6. Why is the extent and health of rainforests important to people who live thousands of miles away?

7. Define the terms *global warming* and *greenhouse effect*.

8. What does it mean to say that, in much of the world, water is an endangered resource?

9. Name three ways to diminish the waste problem.

10. What would be an exploitive approach to nature?

11. Describe a sacramental vision.

12. Name two saints who modeled a sacramental perspective on nature. Describe the unique approach to nature taken by each one.

13. Define *stewardship*.

14. How can technology contribute to nature?

15. What three practices make up the guideline for conscientious consumption?

⟩Key Words

animal experimentation (p. 290)–Scientific research on animals, including some questionable practices.

anthropocentrism (p. 284)–Literally "centering on the human," viewing the rest of nature as solely for human use and not for the glory of God.

corporate farming (p. 290)–Ownership of a large number of acres and animals by persons or organizations that oversee production but do not actually work with the land or the animals.

ecology (p. 282)–Study of the environment and the relationships among the elements of creation.

exploitation (p. 294)–Using other living creatures for our purposes without respecting their God-given dignity.

inorganic farming (p. 287)–Farming dependent on chemical fertilizers and pesticides; produces immediate high-crop yields but in the long-term depletes topsoil.

low-tillage farming (p. 287)–Farming that disturbs topsoil as little as possible, leaving some ground cover to prevent erosion, but still allowing some use of fertilizer and pesticides.

organic farming (p. 287)–Farming without the use of toxic chemicals; can create topsoil.

recycling (p. 291)–Converting waste products and other goods we throw away into usable products instead of putting them into a landfill.

stewardship (p. 296)–Humanity's role, designated by God, to protect, care for, and sustain the rest of creation.

>Our Challenge

We face an environmental crisis. Recently, the human assault on the rest of nature has raised the question: How far do we extend the hand of compassion and justice? Do we stop with the human community or do we include the nonhuman as well? Applying the principles of justice to the earth does not mean caring for nature out of selfishness. Rather, in a spirit of justice and compassion, we proclaim that all creation reflects the grandeur of God.

Church leaders admonish us to take seriously our God-given responsibility to care for the earth. Inspired by the biblical refrain, "and God saw that it was good," by our gratitude for life, our care for all beings, and our sacramental vision, we can take steps, as individuals and as a society, to cooperate with God in the cultivation of his "garden."

THE CHALLENGE OF PEACE

CHRISTIAN RESOLUTION OF CONFLICT

CHAPTER GOALS

In this chapter you will:

★ identify three levels of violence used in response to conflict.

★ explore the just-war doctrine.

★ look at alternatives to violence that can be applied to conflict.

★ examine the teachings of Jesus and the Church regarding war and peace.

Approaches to Resolving Conflict

what's your opinion?

Answer **agree, disagree,** or **uncertain** to the following statements. Choose statements that you believe are most significant. Explain your answers.

1. Every possible means of resolving a conflict should be tried before resorting to warfare.

2. My country has been a leading advocate for resolving international conflicts nonviolently.

3. Warfare is an acceptable means of peacemaking.

4. Christians should lead the way in speaking out against war.

5. Nonviolent means of resolving conflict would not help prevent terrorism.

6. If my country's leaders called on me to engage in a war they considered just, I'd serve.

In our private lives and in our imperfect world, conflicts abound. The use of war to resolve group conflicts has been around for all of recorded history. Today we hear of a "war on terrorism," which refers to taking military action not against a particular nation but against various groups of people intent on using methods condemned by the international community to achieve their ends. Is warfare an acceptable means of resolving conflicts? Are there guidelines to help nations determine whether the use of war is just? Are there rules that should be followed during a war? Are there viable alternatives to warfare that we might consider?

Different opinions exist in answering the above questions. At one end, some see war not only as an accepted means to resolving a conflict but as actually considered the preferred method. On the other end of the spectrum, some people consider war an evil in itself that is always to be rejected. Only nonviolent techniques for resolving conflicts are acceptable. In between these two extremes, there is a range of attitudes toward using war to resolve conflicts. The line from glorification of war to its total rejection can be termed the **continuum of conflict resolution**. We can identify three prominent standpoints on the continuum of conflict resolution.

1. Militarism: the glorification of war

2. The just-war doctrine

3. Pacifism

A World in Conflict

On March 19, 2003, the U.S. government began its largest military operation since the Vietnam War. The objectives were to remove from power the president of Iraq, Saddam Hussein; to eliminate Iraq's weapons of mass destruction; and to end Iraq's perceived support of people responsible for the September 11, 2001, attacks on the United States. Although the United States sought support from the United Nations, that body did not sanction the war. At the time, the primary rationale for the war was the elimination of weapons of mass destruction. The United Nations had a team of inspectors searching Iraq for these weapons, and the consensus was to continue these inspections. President Hussein agreed to cooperate fully with U.N. inspections. The U.S. government believed that President Hussein was not being truthful about weapons of mass destruction and that U.N. inspections were ineffective. To achieve their objectives the United States and a few allies decided to use military force against the Iraqi government, dubbed "Operation Iraqi Freedom."

Soon after the events of September 11, 2001, most American Muslims condemned the acts as evil. However, a few teenagers from a Muslim school interviewed on TV remarked that the men who crashed planes on that day, killing so many people, were in fact martyrs. They believed that since the men acted in God's name and for a righteous cause, they were now in heaven with God. In the eyes of these students, when perceived injustice exists in the world, then violence—even extreme—is right and honorable. Those who give and take lives to confront evil deserve to be rewarded by God.

Following World War II, Germany was divided into East (communist) and West (capitalist and democratic). To prevent the flow of skilled workers from East to West, the East German government erected a concrete barrier extending over one hundred miles and right through the former capital city, Berlin. In 1989 East German citizens held a series of peaceful demonstrations calling for reforms, including freedom to travel to the West. Under constant nonviolent pressure from its own people, the government relented. Within two years, most of the Berlin wall was removed. Following this action, about 5,000 disgruntled lower-ranking party members protested outside of the headquarters where a Communist Party conference was taking place. These demonstrations and protests signaled the beginning of the end of the Cold War that had existed between Western nations and Communist nations for nearly half a century.

GROUP TALK

1. In regard to Operation Iraqi Freedom:
   * If you were a representative to the United Nations at the time, what criteria might you have used to decide whether or not to support the proposal to go to war against Iraq? Explain the decision you would have made and why.
   * Are there criteria that all nations should follow to determine whether a war is justified?

2. In regard to the scenario about the September 11, 2001, terrorist attack, if you were to engage the students from the Muslim school in a debate:
   * What arguments would you offer to counter the students' beliefs?
   * Is violence acceptable simply because someone's intentions are honorable and he or she believes a cause to be just? What other factors should be considered?
   * The students suggest that the hijackers' motives were religious, that they were doing God's will. What response would you make to this statement?

3. In regard to the third scenario:
   * Would violence have been as effective as the nonviolent tactics employed by the East Germans? Explain.
   * Could similar nonviolent tactics be used in other national or international conflicts? Explain.
   * What are possible nonviolent tactics that people might use in conflict situations?

Militarism and the World

★ The top five nations in active troop strength: China, **2.3 million;** United States, **1.4 million;** India, **1.3 million,** North Korea, **1.1 million;** Russia, **1.0 million**

★ The top five nations in military expenditures: United States, **$330 billion;** China, **$48.4 billion;** Russia, **$48.0 billion;** France, **$38.0 billion;** Japan, **$37.1 billion**

Source: *World Almanac 2005.*

FAITH ACTIVITY

Where Do You Stand? Draw a horizontal line across a sheet of paper. On the left side, write *glorification of war,* on the right side, write *rejection of war.* Add the numbers to your continuum. Place an X on the line where you see yourself in terms of the use of violence in resolving conflicts. Now think about the three standpoints introduced in this chapter. From their names, where do you think each of them falls on the continuum?

Any discussion of armed conflicts must take place within the context of right to life issues and the Church's presentation on the Fifth Commandment. The dignity of the human person requires that we respect and protect all human life, and that includes a state protecting the common good and the safety and security of its citizens. As we consider this continuum, it's paramount to remember that, as Catholics, we honor life as sacred and a gift from God. What the Church teaches about war is based upon the sacredness of life. While we look to the Church for direction on how to respond to this crisis of war in our world, we also rely on the Holy Spirit prompting our conscience to know what is right and just. As with all legal matters, we are obliged to follow the law of God and not civil directives when they contradict the moral law.

Militarism

In common usage, militarism can refer to anything having to do with the military and war. Here the term is being used to name the position on one end of a continuum of conflict resolution. An advocate of this position would propose the following: *Despite the death and destruction it causes, war is as acceptable as any other means to resolve a conflict. In fact, war is generally the best means to achieve one's goals. We need to be realistic: might makes right. Through war we defeat the enemy, which is the goal in a conflict. For this reason it is important to foster the attitude that warfare is a gallant and glorious endeavor that should not be shied away from. The killing and dying that accompany war only reinforce how noble it is.*

It's hard to imagine anyone actually holding this extreme position today. However, parts of this opinion still seep into public discussion about war. Therefore, it is important to distinguish between "war is good" and "war is regrettable but at times justified," and between "war is a first resort" and "war is a last resort" in resolving a conflict. As it is described here, militarism holds that warfare is natural, unavoidable, and even glorious. It implies that we'll always have wars and therefore trying to prevent them or to find other means of achieving goals is useless. It sees war as more often than not the "realistic" way to achieve goals. Other approaches are idealistic, impractical, and out of touch with corrupt human nature. War is a noble act; to do it well is glorious.

The Catechism, on the other hand, reminds us that evils and injustices accompany all war and that all citizens and governments are obliged to work for the avoidance of war. It states that "the Church insistently urges everyone to prayer and to action so that the divine Goodness may free us from the ancient bondage of war" (*CCC* 2307). The Catechism also states that, "All citizens and all governments are obliged to work for the avoidance of war" (*CCC* 2308).

FAITH ACTIVITY

Conflict Resolution Describe two conflict situations that exist in our world today. What approaches to resolving each conflict would you recommend? Explain why you believe the approaches you recommend would be successful in resolving the conflicts justly.

GROUP TALK

1 Do you believe that militarism is evident in the world today?

2 Do you believe that wars are "natural and unavoidable"? Can you imagine a future in which war would be unthinkable in the international community?

3 Is it possible to honor people serving in the military without a glorification of war?

The Just-War Doctrine

According to the just-war doctrine: *When all other means of resolving a conflict have been exhausted and injustices remain, then war may have to be employed. Resorting to warfare is regrettable and certainly should never be glorified, but in certain limited circumstances it may prove to be a lesser evil than not going to war. When and how warfare is used must be strictly regulated, always with an eye toward restricting to the barest minimum the harm that it produces.*

At least since the era of Saint Augustine in the fourth century, the standard position of the Catholic Church has been that wars are in certain circumstances justified. Over time principles were established spelling out how to decide if a war is justified and also what restrictions should be maintained in carrying out a war. In other words, wars were to be both (a) restricted and (b) regulated. The Catechism quotes Vatican Council II about why resorting to war may be justified in our world today: "as long as the danger of war persists and there is no international authority with the necessary competence and power, governments cannot be denied the right of lawful self-defense, once all peace efforts have failed" (*CCC* 2308). In fact, "Legitimate defense is a grave duty for whoever is responsible for the lives of others or the common good" (*CCC* 2321). It is the right and duty of the state to protect its citizens, even to the point of taking up arms. On a personal level, someone defending his or her own life or that of another does not commit murder if in the process an aggressor is killed. This "double effect" was described in Chapter 5 in connection with the treatment of other Fifth Commandment justice issues.

▼ Pope Paul VI addressing the U.N. General Assembly, October 4, 1965.

"The strict conditions for legitimate defense by military force require rigorous consideration. The gravity of such a decision makes it subject to rigorous conditions of moral legitimacy. At one and the same time:

- the damage inflicted by the aggressor on the nation or community of nations must be lasting, grave, and certain;

- all other means of putting an end to it must have been shown to be impractical or ineffective;

- there must be serious prospects of success;

- the use of arms must not produce evils and disorders graver than the evil to be eliminated. The power of modern means of destruction weighs very heavily in evaluating this condition.

The evaluation of these conditions for moral legitimacy belongs to the prudential judgment of those who have responsibility for the common good" (*CCC* 2309).

Articulation of just war principles varies slightly depending on the source consulted. A list of traditional just war principles can be found in the U.S. Bishops' pastoral statement, *The Challenge of Peace*. In this statement, the bishops have taken the universal doctrine and interpreted them for the Church in our county so that Catholics can better understand and apply the Church's teachings.

The following scenario provides a concrete example with which to examine the questions that need to be asked with each principle and to examine the difficulties involved.

Principles of the Just-War Doctrine

A group of terrorists hijack a plane carrying citizens from country *A*, intending to use the plane to kill its passengers and destroy certain prominent facilities of country *A*. Although not representatives of any government, the terrorists had trained for a time in country *B*, the leaders of which are sympathetic to their cause. Members of the terrorist organization continue to reside in country *B*.

As you examine each principle, ask the question: Based on this principle, would country *A* be justified in going to war against country *B*?

▲ Satellite view of a terrorist training camp in Garmabak Ghar

1. Just Cause Does a real and imminent threat exist?

When the U.S. Catholic bishops addressed the issue of war and peace in the 1980s, they stated: "War is permissible only to confront a 'real and certain danger,' i.e., to protect innocent life, to preserve conditions necessary for decent human existence, and to secure basic human rights" (*The Challenge of Peace* 86). According to this principle, warfare is permitted only when life or justice is clearly and immediately endangered. This mirrors the "lasting, grave, and certain" criteria articulated in the *Catechism*. (*CCC* 2309)

- Because terrorists continue to reside in country *B*, is country *A*'s government justified in waging war against that nation?

- Is self-defense the only just cause for engaging in war?

- Can a nation go to war with another nation even though it is not an immediate threat but could likely become one in the future?

2. Competent Authority Are recognized leaders following accepted rules in declaring war and in overseeing how it is carried out?

Who is responsible for addressing a conflict? In the case of the hijacking, the government of country *A* has responsibility for the welfare of its citizens. The issue of competent authority is not always as clear-cut as this. Today neither the boundaries nor the rightful rulers of some nation-states are necessarily clearly defined.

Who would be the competent leaders in countries *A* and *B*?

- Can a group ever use violence independent of a legitimately recognized government?

- Can you name a scenario in which "competent authority" could be questioned or unclear?

FAITH ACTIVITY

Using Violence Give pros and cons of the following statement: *People who wish to overthrow or influence the government of their own country should never use violent means to do so.* State your position on this issue. Use examples to illustrate why you do or do not support this statement.

3. Right Intention Are self-defense and justice the intended outcome of the action?

Even if a just cause exists, actual intentions for going to war must also be in order. For example, country *A* cannot use country *B*'s harboring of terrorists as an excuse to gain economic advantage in the region through the war. When a conflict builds, original intentions that led to declaring war in the first place can get lost. For instance, as a war progresses and emotions flare, initial intentions such as "free hostages" or "arrest suspected terrorists" can become "overthrow their government" or "kill the enemy." The principle of *right intention*, then, requires that warfare be used only to serve justice and for self-defense.

- Describe a declaration of war on the part of country *A* in terms of right intentions.

- Give examples of how this principle could be violated.

- In the early 1990s the United States joined with the United Nations in a war against Iraq because Iraq had taken over its neighboring nation, Kuwait. When the United Nations achieved its stated objective, restoration of Kuwaiti sovereignty, it withdrew its troops and ended the war. Some people criticized U.S. and U.N. leaders for not overthrowing the Iraqi government at the time, which was recognized as a repressive and brutal dictatorship. Debate the U.N. decision based on the principle of right intentions.

4. Last Resort Have all other means of resolving the conflict been tried?

This reflects the teaching in the Catechism that all other means of resolving a conflict "must have been shown to be impractical or ineffective" (*CCC* 2309). "Other means" of addressing conflict besides warfare will be discussed later in this chapter.

- What steps besides outright warfare could country *A* use to deal with terrorists residing in country *B*?

5. Probability of Success "[T]here must be serious prospects of success" (*CCC* 2309).

This principle cautions that at times warfare is still not acceptable, even when a just cause and the right intention exist. A clear application of this principle would be a prohibition against sending troops into a battle that would only lead to their slaughter. However, government leaders must also deliberate whether a war has a good chance of achieving intended goals. For instance, in the above scenario "success" would mean eliminating or diminishing terrorism. If the leaders of country *A* believed that war with country *B* would not likely stem terrorist attacks against their nation, then war would not be justified.

- Can you give another example of a situation in which prospects for success would call for not going to war?

- Can you imagine a situation in which "winning a war" would not make a country more secure?

6. Comparative Justice Do the rights and values involved justify killing?

Comparative justice requires that any country contemplating war should not presume that the other side doesn't have legitimate concerns or that there are no limits to how it can wage war. Comparative justice has two parts to it. First, a nation must be very clear that it is right about the threat posed by the nation or group to be attacked. Secondly, the reasons for a given war must be so important that they override the presumption against it.

- What are some of the "rights and values" that country *A* should consider when assessing whether or not to go to war with country *B*?

- If you were to make a case against country *A* going to war from the perspective of country *B*, how might you do that?

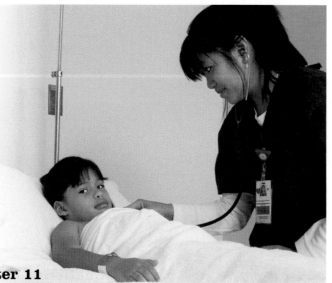

7. Noncombatant Immunity Will people not directly involved in fighting be spared becoming victims?

Noncombatants are those persons not directly involved in the manufacture, direction, or use of weapons. In an earlier era when the just-war doctrine was taking shape, the distinction between combatants and noncombatants was much clearer. In medieval Europe, knights fought knights, while others went about their business undisturbed. In many modern wars, it has not always been easy to identify who are combatants and who are noncombatants. Modern weaponry makes it possible to pinpoint targets with some degree of accuracy, but it can also cause great amounts of destruction and **collateral damage**. Destroying a country's water supply system, filling hospitals with wounded persons, causing loss of limbs or eyesight to a large number of civilians, and leveling cities can demoralize a country as well as perhaps hasten conclusion to a war. For example President Harry S Truman largely justified dropping atomic bombs that killed civilians in two Japanese cities because it could hasten the end of World War II. Are such attacks that harm noncombatants ever justified? Traditional just-war teaching states that no military action may be aimed directly at noncombatants.

- Would a loosening of this principle provide justification for terrorism since terrorist attacks typically target noncombatants?

8. Proportionality Will the foreseeable good resulting from the military action outweigh the probable damage caused?

The principle of **proportionality** asks: Does the good likely to result from using violence outweigh the probable damage caused? War obviously causes great harm. We see some of the immediate harm done when the faces of soldiers who have died are shown on evening news broadcasts. However, wars have long-term negative consequences that are more difficult to measure. Weighing the cost of warfare in human life and suffering is difficult but crucial in determining whether or not war is justified. We again see the connection to the traditional elements of just war doctrine as stated in the Catechism, "the use of arms must not produce evils and disorders graver than the evil to be eliminated" (*CCC* 2309).

- In the plane hijacking scenario, would country *A* be justified in causing the deaths of thousands of people in country *B* in order to kill or capture terrorists hiding there?

- What are some probable long-term negative consequences that would result from a war between country *A* and country *B*?

FAITH ACTIVITY

Research to find the number of civilian deaths in recent wars. Are these death tolls easier or more difficult to find than military fatalities? Are civilian deaths more, less, or equally important? Discuss your answers and reasons with your class.

Use of Violence Make a case for or against the following action as a just use of violence: After the French government surrendered to Germany during World War II, some French people, calling themselves the Resistance, continued to fight the German occupying forces by using guerrilla warfare tactics. In one incident, Resistance troops posed as farmworkers working in a field as a contingent of German soldiers marched by. Since the location was far from the front, the soldiers were not battle-ready. The Resistance fighters picked up guns hidden in the field and fired on the soldiers, killing a number of them.

▼ Column of German troops marching down the Champs Elyssees towards the Arc de Triomphe shortly after the Nazi occupation of France

Applying Just-War Principles

Two observations are in order regarding the application of the just-war doctrine. On the one hand, it provides important principles to evaluate when nations consider war:

> Just-war theory has always played a part in official arguments about war. No political leader can send soldiers into battle, asking them to risk their lives and to kill other people, without assuring them that their cause is just—and that of their enemies is unjust. And if the theory is used, it is also, inevitably, misused. Sometimes it serves only to determine what lies our leaders tell . . . . It is important not to give up the theory just because of its misuse—no more than we would give up our ideas about friendship just because they are exploited by false friends.

Michael Walzer, *Just and Unjust Wars*
(New York: Harper Collins, Basic Books, 1977), xi-xii

On the other hand, it is necessary for governments to exercise legitimate authority, using morally acceptable means, for the common good of society. So debate on its application should be welcome:

> People of good will may differ on how to apply just war norms in particular cases, especially when events are moving rapidly and the facts are not altogether clear.

U.S. Conference of Catholic Bishops, "Statement on Iraq"

The Just-War Doctrine Applied After a Conflict

In the face of every war, we are all called to ponder our responsibilities, to forgive and to ask forgiveness.

Pope John Paul II, Message marking the 50th anniversary of the end of the Second World War in Europe, May 16, 1995 (quoted in Luigi Accattoli, *When a Pope Asks Forgiveness* [Boston: Pauline Books, 1998], p. 143)

In 1994, theologian Michael J. Schuck wrote an article about a dimension of the just war that has been overlooked. He noted that the doctrine offers principles to help us determine when war is permitted and how war is to be conducted. Schuck suggested that we should also think about how the concept of a just war can be applied after a conflict. Here are three principles that reflect the spirit of the just-war doctrine following resolution of a war.

1. Sorrow The end of a war is certainly cause for celebration. Nonetheless, a victory celebration need not be an angry or humiliating display toward the former enemy. In a real sense, any war is a defeat for all humanity. Along with celebration that peace is restored, there should be regret that war occurred at all. No sin is incurred by engaging in a just war. However, sorrow about the death and destruction resulting from any war can forge the way for cooling of anger and hatred and begin a healing process.

2. Honorable Surrender History affords us examples of victors using victory to humiliate and degrade the defeated and also examples of victors saluting and honoring the vanquished. The aim of a just war is justice, not the shaming of enemies. Therefore, an appropriate just-war principle following a war is attempting to preserve the honor and dignity of those who are surrendering.

FAITH ACTIVITY

Concern for Justice Research the atmosphere that surrounded the end of a war that has occurred within the past century. Write a report on whether or not there was concern for justice on the part of the victors. Share it with your class.

3. Restoration A defeated country is a ravaged country. The land itself cries out for restoration, and many innocent victims will continue to suffer long after guns are silent. Perhaps the thought of working as hard to restore a defeated country as armies had worked to destroy it sounds unrealistic. If so, then the idea of a just war is unrealistic. As stated earlier, the only rightful intention for entering into warfare in the first place is restoration of justice. The goal of restoration cannot end when the shooting stops.

GROUP TALK

1. Name three film characters who you believe represent the attitude of militarism. Then, name three film characters who you believe represent a rejection of militarism. What is the attitude toward war or conflict resolution held by each of these characters?

2. The three principles of a just war after a conflict are sorrow, honorable surrender, and restoration. Do you believe that these principles are usually followed after modern wars? Do you think following these principles would have a positive effect? Are there other guidelines you would recommend for nations after a war has ended?

Pacifism: Rejection of Violence

Pacifism belongs on the opposite end from militarism on the continuum of conflict resolution. It means a complete rejection of warfare and reliance solely on nonviolent methods for resolving conflicts. The pacifist position can be stated in these terms: *Using war to achieve peace is like eating to lose weight—only peaceful means can achieve true peace. Believing that warfare solves problems is shortsighted and unrealistic. Wars are a breeding ground for further violence. If pacifism appears unrealistic it is only because it has so seldom been tried. Given the destructive power of weapons today, complete rejection of war is the only hope for human survival.*

Pacifism is not the same as **passivity**. *Passivity* means not getting involved, not attempting to resolve conflicts, being detached. On the other hand, *pacifism* literally means making peace. It involves conflict resolution through nonviolent means. These distinctions are important to keep in mind. We might picture a pacifist as standing on the sidelines while innocent people are getting hurt. However, the two most famous modern pacifists—the Hindu Mohandas K. Gandhi of India and the Baptist minister Martin Luther King Jr. of the United States—could never be accused of being passive. They rejected violence and in the process opened themselves to violence perpetrated by others. Both were assassinated. Gandhi believed that pacifism meant fighting—nonviolent fighting, fighting for peace and justice through nonviolent means. He even said: "Where there is only a choice between cowardice and violence, I would choose violence."

FAITH ACTIVITY

Ultimate Sacrifice During World War II, many Catholics sacrificed their lives to resist Nazism—Titus Brandsma, Franz Jagerstatter, and Karl Leisner are three. Research one of these men and present an oral report to the class on a Catholic conscientious objector.

Two of the most famous American Catholic pacifists were Dorothy Day of the Catholic Worker Movement and Gordon Zahn, who was a **conscientious objector** during World War II. A contemporary American Catholic pacifist is the Jesuit priest John Dear. He has written and spoken out against war while visiting many of the world's greatest trouble spots. After the September 11, 2001, terrorist attacks on the United States, Father Dear volunteered to be a chaplain for the Red Cross, counseling some 1,500 family members of victims as well as police and fire fighters. Even after that experience he continued to advocate nonviolent approaches to dealing with the deep-seated problems we face worldwide.

GROUP TALK

After September 11, 2001, a number of people who lost family members in the attacks formed a group calling for nonviolent responses so that others would not experience the great suffering that they did. Some even went to Afghanistan to help people when the United States went to war with that country soon after the September 11, 2001, attacks.

1 Do you think that personal tragedy influences people to be more compassionate toward others and less tolerant of violence?

> Non-violent means of resistance to evil deserve much more study and consideration than they have thus far received. There have been significant instances in which people have successfully resisted oppression without recourse to arms.
>
> National Conference of Catholic Bishops, *The Challenge of Peace*, 222

A pacifist approach to armed conflict can shed much light on how to avoid war, which is one of the goals of the Church's just war doctrine. We need to continually strive to ensure that these principles are implemented appropriately and completely before war is waged and during the course of armed conflict.

Two categories of pacifists exist. *Absolute pacifists* believe that violence, in principle, is always wrong. In their view any use of violence would violate their religious or humanitarian principles. On the other hand, *practical pacifists* believe that nonviolence is a better way than violence to resolve conflicts. Practical pacifists would point to the wars and bloodshed of the past few centuries to make the case that violence has proved to be much more destructive than constructive.

> I am against war, against violence, against violent revolution, for peaceful settlement of differences, for nonviolent but nevertheless radical changes. Change is needed, and violence will not really change anything: at most it will only transfer power from one set of bull-headed authorities to another.

Thomas Merton

Catholic Teaching on Pacifism

Although the Catechism states that: "Public authorities . . . have the right and duty to impose on citizens the *obligations necessary for national defense*" (*CCC* 2310), it also points out that "Public authorities should make equitable provision for those who for reasons of conscience refuse to bear arms" (*CCC* 2311). There is even a patron saint of conscientious objectors—Saint Marcellus the Centurion, who, at the end of the third century, was killed when he renounced his position in the Roman army and became Christian.

In 1969 the U.S. Catholic bishops commissioned a statement on conscientious objection in which they call upon citizens to insist on principles of nonviolence for regulating conflicts. In 1993 the U.S. Catholic bishops once again called for the nation to take up the challenge of seeking nonviolent means of addressing conflict:

> Christian nonviolence . . . consists of a commitment to resist manifest injustice and public evil with means other than force. These include dialogue, negotiations, protests, strikes, boycotts, civil disobedience, and civilian resistance. Although nonviolence has often been regarded as simply a personal option or vocation, recent history suggests that in some circumstances it can be an effective public undertaking as well. Dramatic political transitions in places as diverse as the Philippines and Eastern Europe demonstrate the power of nonviolent action, even against dictatorial and totalitarian regimes . . . . These nonviolent revolutions challenge us to find ways to take into full account the power of organized, active nonviolence . . . . As a nation we should promote research, education, and training in nonviolent means of resisting evil. Nonviolent strategies need greater attention in international affairs . . . . In some future conflicts, strikes and people power could be more effective than guns and bullets.

U.S. Catholic Bishops, *The Harvest of Justice Is Sown in Peace*

Pacifism Before Conflict

As the just-war doctrine has principles that apply both before and during a conflict, so does pacifism. People don't have to be pacifists to try to resolve conflicts through nonviolent means. In fact, one of the key principles of a just war is that other, nonviolent, means are to be used first, and only when these fail may violence be employed as a "last resort." True pacifists, of course, also reject war and violence even as a last resort. Here are two principles of pacifism before a conflict escalates and two principles of pacifism that can be applied in the heat of conflict.

Creating a Climate of Peace A first principle of pacifism is to work on creating a climate of peace. Local news programs often emphasize violence, which leads to an atmosphere of fear, mistrust, and possibly retaliation. Reports on violence in our neighborhoods add to our fear of "the other." In fact, most violence occurs at the hands of people who are part of the family or social network of their victims. We create a climate of peace or violence through our speech, our interaction with others, the way we drive our cars, the television programs we watch, and the time we spend reducing or adding to stress.

A climate of peace does not exist when leaders, media, or even private citizens blame people in another country for the world's problems. When people constantly find fault with others, insulting and belittling them, and generally view them

as evil, then clearly a climate of peace is wanting. Creating a climate of peace requires first of all examining attitudes toward others, especially toward potential enemies. When countries are in conflict, their citizens can view enemies as either subhuman and therefore not worthy of respect or as possessing superhuman prowess or determination. In either case, the enemy is to be feared and not reasoned with. Small groups within countries, such as politicians and talk-show hosts, and even groups within small communities, such as schools, can stir up violence by voicing attitudes toward the "enemy."

Second, creating a climate of peace implies examining ourselves. We can have as distorted an image of our own goodness and right-mindedness as we do of the faults and evil intentions of people in a country with which we are in conflict.

Finally, creating a climate of peace means placing a higher priority on peacemaking than on war making. In other words, the resources of a nation—financial, educational, governmental, and economic—can be used for peaceful efforts, or they can be used for preparing for war. A climate of peace supports efforts aimed at creating and maintaining peace, such as student exchanges between nations, rather than warmongering.

Put things in order, listen to my appeal, agree with one another, live in peace; and the God of love and peace will be with you.

✝ 2 Corinthians 13:11

FAITH ACTIVITY

Pacifism Advocate Research one of the following advocates of pacifism. Write a report describing the person's position on violence and conflict resolution: Leo Tolstoy, Mohandas Gandhi, Martin Luther King Jr., Dorothy Day, Thomas Merton.

GROUP TALK

1. Review the words of a politician, a talk-show commentator, or a newspaper editorial. Does the person speak about others in a way that promotes peace or violence? Explain.

Rooting Out the Causes of Conflict A second principle of pacifism is determining and working to remove the causes of conflict, which is sometimes called a **spiral of violence.**

- Injustice itself is a first level of violence.

- If victims of injustice respond violently under the weight of their oppression, then second-level violence occurs.

- Authorities who forcefully crack down on second-level violence are engaging in a third level of violence, and the spiral of violence continues.

In other words, injustices described earlier in this book (such as poverty or racism) are in fact forms of violence—specifically, first-level violence. When certain people or members of a particular ethnic group feel as though other ways are unavailable to them, they may respond to what they consider to be an injustice with either organized or spontaneous violence. This second level of violence is more likely to make the headlines of newspapers than the daily grind of poverty or oppression that victims of injustice experience. Attempts to "restore peace," putting down second-level violence without addressing the injustices that helped lead up to it, do not end the spiral of violence. When we are truly concerned about peacemaking, then we seek to uproot unjust conditions boiling below the surface of potential conflicts that might explode into visible violence. The spiral of violence reminds us that the pain and frustration of injustice are violence even before they reach the boiling point. Pacifism tries to end violence at each level of its spiral, thus it addresses more than armed conflict or war.

Pacifism During Conflict

Pacifism before conflict seeks to prevent violence. When serious conflicts occur, however, as they will, then pacifism demands at least as much energy, creativity, strength, wisdom, and courage as violence does. What exactly does nonviolent conflict resolution look like? Gandhi is the modern era's greatest apostle of nonviolence. He applied his strategies of nonviolent conflict resolution to a situation that has frequently led to violence—a colony, India, seeking independence from a colonial power, Britain. Therefore, Gandhi serves as a valuable model for pacifism in action.

Gandhi called his approach to nonviolence **satyagraha**. With this term Gandhi was proposing that "right makes might" rather than the other way around. Gandhi and his followers practiced a wide variety of techniques to achieve their goals, sometimes altering plans in highly imaginative and unexpected ways. For instance, during World War II Gandhi called off protests against England because he felt that England was rightfully preoccupied with fighting Germany. He didn't want to take advantage of its moment of weakness. Throughout, Gandhi held to two principles that guided his approach to resolving conflicts. First, both sides in a conflict possess some truth. Second, a conflict is not resolved until both parties agree to a common solution.

Seeking Truth on Both Sides Gandhi believed that both sides in a conflict always possess some truth, even though not always equally so. He regarded *satyagraha* as an attempt to discover the truth of each position in a conflict and then to act according to that truth. He felt that violent ways of resolving a conflict led to false resolutions.

Simply put, domination by one party reveals only which side of the conflict is physically stronger. Domination does not reveal where truth lies. Since truth is not served by domination, the underlying problem remains for future generations to resolve. In addition, the use of violence creates new conflicts between the two groups.

Interestingly, Gandhi held the same reservations about compromise as he did about domination. He saw compromise as each side winning a little, but each side losing a little as well. Likewise, when a judge or court of law decides which side is right, Gandhi believed that the losing side would feel that the truth in their position has been overlooked. The losing party might also feel humiliated and thus cooperate only reluctantly. For Gandhi neither compromise nor appeal to law truly resolves a conflict.

FAITH ACTIVITY

Increased Violence Look through recent news magazines for stories about conflict. Look for evidence that the spiral of violence was or was not at work in these conflict situations. For instance, is there evidence that injustice or violence of a sort existed in Northern Ireland, parts of Africa, and the Middle East before the violence that makes newspaper headlines erupted? Write a report on your findings.

GROUP TALK

1. Name three conflict situations—interpersonal, communal, or international. Identify as many truthful claims as possible that each side is making. Then, for each conflict, describe a resolution that would represent truth rather than selfish interests. Based on this exercise, do you agree with Gandhi that each side in a conflict possesses truth, although not equally so, and that it is possible to find common truth? Explain.

2. Do you want your country to be recognized for its military strength or for its advocacy of peace in the world? Are the two contradictory? Explain.

Civil Disobedience Citizens are obliged by conscience to "obey God rather than man." That is, we are to discern when the directives of civil authorities are contrary to the demands on moral order. Do you believe that it is justified for a group of protesters to chain themselves to the doors of a local abortion clinic? If you believed that airplanes equipped to carry weapons used against civilian targets are immoral, would you break into an air force base and pound one of these planes with a hammer while pouring blood on it in a gesture meant to symbolize its destructiveness? Would you attempt to disrupt whaling ships from killing whales, even if you had to break a law to do so? If your government decided that everyone who reaches age eighteen must register for a military draft, would you refuse to do so?

Practices such as these have come to be associated with nonviolent protests. Clearly some methods go beyond the acceptable bounds of nonviolence. For instance, it would be legal for a group of residents in a graffiti-filled neighborhood to carry signs in front of a store protesting the sale of spray paint to children. It would be another matter if this same group spray painted the store's outside walls; some people might label such an action a form of violence.

Seeking Truth in Common

An opponent is not always bad simply because he opposes.

Mohandas Gandhi

Gandhi rejected the word *enemy* because its use gets in the way of the search for truth. For Gandhi, an opponent in a conflict was not an enemy. The pacifist's first task is to see the conflict from the points of view of each of the combatants. One side may have the greater weight of truth, but that does not mean that the other side has no rightful claims and concerns. Gandhi taught that combatants are not enemies. In a conflict, the real enemy is falsehood.

Gandhi believed that a conflict is not resolved until opponents agree to a solution. In other words, true resolution of conflict occurs only when two parties formerly on opposite sides of an issue occupy the same side. Seeking to resolve differences calls for constant bargaining. When one party refuses to bargain in good faith or dismisses the concerns of the other party, then the opponent may need to engage in some form of nonviolent campaign. A nonviolent campaign might include activities such as we have come to associate with nonviolent protests: demonstrations, boycotts, strikes, sit-ins, fasting, and civil disobedience.

For Gandhi these activities do not involve using force—either physical or psychological. Instead of attacking an opponent, Gandhi taught non-cooperation. That is, Gandhian fighters would not cooperate with falsehood but would act according to their understanding of the truth. For instance, when the British issued a tax on salt in India—which he considered unjust—in open defiance of British law, Gandhi organized a great march to the sea where salt was available.

In the early days of the civil rights movement in the United States, some black and white students in southern states went to lunch counters marked "whites only" and sat down together. The moral force of their action eventually led to laws making such discrimination illegal. In the 1970s, when gasoline prices suddenly skyrocketed, a large group of truckers drove their trucks to Washington, D.C. There they obstructed traffic by driving slowly around the capitol building, thus drawing national attention to their problem.

Civil disobedience has become a major form of nonviolent confrontation. Civil disobedience does not entail breaking laws randomly. For instance, a young person who believes that the high cost of movies is unfair and therefore sneaks into a theater without paying is not practicing civil disobedience. Practiced as a form of nonviolent protest, civil disobedience normally involves:

1. Breaking only those laws considered morally unjust

2. Accepting the legal penalties for breaking the law

3. Making a clear, public statement of intentions

4. Ensuring that no harm is caused to persons

Some of the protests against the racial segregation laws that existed in the United States half a century ago illustrate classic civil disobedience. Martin Luther King Jr. himself spent time in jail for violating laws he considered unjust.

In the United States during the era of the Vietnam War, some antiwar protesters went beyond breaking laws that they considered unjust. Instead, they also broke laws that they considered moral in order to bring to light what they saw as a grave immorality—specifically, the Vietnam War itself. For example, a group of protesters broke into a draft office near Baltimore and burned some files housed there.

GROUP TALK

1 Name five ways that a climate of peace, exists or could be encouraged exists within your school community. If you can identify ways that you believe a climate of violence exists within your school, list those as well and suggest how that climate could change.

2 Name five ways that a climate of violence exists within your country; within the world community. Suggest ways that such a climate could change.

3 Name five ways that a climate of peace exists or could more strongly exist, within your country and within the world community.

4 When you visualize peace, what images come to mind?

5 One alternative to warfare sometimes recommended in international conflicts is a blockade, or "economic sanctions." The aim of a **blockade** is to prevent certain goods–perhaps all goods–from entering a country.

- Would restricting everything but food and medical supplies from entering a country be nonviolence? Explain your response.

- Would you consider a blockade of all goods to be a form of nonviolence? Explain.

Catholicism and Peacemaking

In the Old Testament, many heroes—for example, Joshua, Samson, and David—employed violence without a hint of disfavor on the part of God. We can also find other passages from Scripture that denounce violence. The books of the prophets provide us with images of a reign of peace and the melting of ill will between enemies. Here is one passage that ever since biblical times has stirred the imagination of those who long for peace.

> The wolf shall live with the lamb,
> —the leopard shall lie down with the kid,
> the calf and the lion and the fatling together,
> —and a little child shall lead them.
> The cow and the bear shall graze,
> —their young shall lie down together;
> —and the lion shall eat straw like the ox.
> The nursing child shall play over the hole of the asp,
> —and the weaned child shall put its hand on the adder's den.
> They will not hurt or destroy
> on all my holy mountain;
> for the earth will be full of the knowledge of the LORD
> —as the waters cover the sea.
>
> Isaiah 11:6–9

FAITH ACTIVITY

Visualizing Peace Write a "peace poem" or create some other artistic depiction of peace.

Jesus, Prince of Peace

Pope John Paul II stated that, "the language of arms is not the language of Jesus Christ" (Discourse at Heldenplatz, Vienna, September 12, 1983 [quoted in Luigi Accattoli, *When a Pope Asks Forgiveness* [Boston: Pauline Books, 1998], p. 140).

Much in popular culture—our sinful tendencies as well—glorifies violence. A frequent theme in movies portrays otherwise peaceful people driven to their breaking point. When they finally repay with violence, the music rises in pitch and the audience cheers. Typically, when a U.S. president declares war on another country, his approval rating goes up. Politicians and judges who promise to "get tough" win votes.

The culture of Jesus' day also was in some ways attracted to violence. Armed Roman soldiers patrolled Israel, and some Jews, called *sicarii*, carried knives hidden in their sleeves, ready to attack unsuspecting soldiers. In the face of such violence, Jesus comes across as a person of unmistakable peace. Jesus constantly advocated peace and refused to resort to violence. Some readers interpret the incident when he cleared the temple area and derided the moneychangers gathered there to be an endorsement of violence on the part of Jesus. The actions of Jesus can also be viewed as a nonviolent demonstration to reclaim the temple for its rightful purpose—the worship of God.

Jesus met his persecutors and death on the cross nonviolently. He censured Peter in the garden of Gethsemane when Peter cut off the ear of a soldier who had come to arrest Jesus. The early Christian writer Tertullian declared, "The Lord, by taking away Peter's sword, disarmed every soldier thereafter." All Christians must come to terms with the clear teaching of Jesus: In response to violence done to you, "turn the other cheek."

FAITH ACTIVITY

Peace Efforts Research and write a brief report on Catholic peace organization.

FAITH ACTIVITY

Gospel of Peace Find five passages in the New Testament that speak to the gospel of peace. Using the five passages, make a poster on the topic.

The Gospel of Peace Paul in his Letter to the Ephesians contrasted Jesus' "gospel of peace" with reliance on military weapons and warfare. He describes the message of Jesus as one of truth, justice, and peace, replacing the old ways of violence and domination.

> *Stand therefore, and fasten the belt of truth around your waist, and put on the breastplate of righteousness. As shoes for your feet put on whatever will make you ready to proclaim the gospel of peace. With all of these, take the shield of faith, with which you will be able to quench all the flaming arrows of the evil one. Take the helmet of salvation, and the sword of the Spirit, which is the word of God.*

Ephesians 6:14-17

In the gospel of peace, all traces of a glorification of violence dissolve. Jesus preaches love of enemies, not their destruction; enduring suffering, not inflicting it. God's reign signifies forgiveness, compassion, elimination of underlying causes of violence, and expansion of the term *neighbor* to include all people—rejecting the notion of enemy. In the Lord's Prayer, we pray for God's reign to be established on earth. Through this prayer, we are reminding ourselves to cooperate with God in establishing his reign of peace.

The Church and the Gospel of Peace

In the early Church, most Christians interpreted Jesus' rejection of violence in a literal sense. Even into the fourth century, Christians refused military service. For example, Saint Martin of Tours rejected his soldierly profession in these words: "I am a soldier of Christ. It is unlawful for me to fight." However, once Christianity gained power in the Roman Empire under Constantine (306–337), Christian leaders felt that the responsibility of ruling in a sinful world required the use of force.

> The reign of Constantine represents a turning point in Christian thinking about the legitimacy of violence and war. By and large writers before him tended to be pacifist in outlook, whereas those following his rise to power argued for the legitimacy of war under certain conditions.

Louis J. Swift, *The Early Fathers on War and Military Service*
(Wilmington, DE: Michael Glazier, 1983), 27

It was at this time that Saint Augustine (d. 430) first laid out the restrictions for a just war. In other words, violence never was meant to go unchecked. Even during the Middle Ages, when violence was so much a part of the feudal system, the Church enacted strict rules governing warfare. For instance:

- According to a decree called the *Peace of God*, certain groups such as members of the clergy were not to participate in war, and excommunication was imposed upon those who used violence against noncombatants.

- The *Truce of God* prohibited fighting on Sundays and specified holy days, during Lent, in seasons of harvest (August 15 to November 15), and for a part of each week (usually from Wednesday evening to Monday morning). In its final form the truce allowed only eighty days a year for war.

- In 1139 the Second Lateran Council forbade the use of "military engines" against people.

The Modern Era Over the course of the modern era, Church leaders have frequently addressed the question of war. Often they have warned against using just-war principles to defend wars that do not meet the strict standards of the doctrine. For instance, both the pope and the U.S. bishops urged the United States not to go to war against Iraq in 2003, appealing to just-war principles. Beyond that no organization of such size has spoken more forcefully or more frequently against use of military power than the Catholic Church. Priority is always to be given to peaceful means for resolving conflicts. Any use of violence falls short of the ideal, must meet strict standards, and, at the very least, requires constant reevaluation.

> Peace is not just the absence of war. . . . Like a cathedral, peace must be constructed patiently and with unshakable faith.
>
> Pope John Paul II, "Homily at Baginton Airport, Coventry"
> (*Origins* vol. 12, no. 55, 198)

>Faith in Action

Archdiocese of Philadelphia's Refugee Resettlement Program

Sponsored by: **Catholic Social Services**

Isamidin, his wife Mavluda, and their three children are ethnically considered Meskhetian Turks. Because of their Muslim beliefs and their Turkish heritage, they were forced out of Georgia and into Uzbekistan, and then forced back into Russia. They were persecuted, denied permanent residency, and forced to register with the government as "visitors" every forty-five days. Isamidin and Mavluda were not allowed to work legally or lease land and their children could not attend school past the eighth grade without paying. Riding the school bus was something Isamidin's children could only dream of . . .until they were resettled into the United States.

> "Thank you, America, thank you very much."
>
> – Isamidin Lomidze

Many refugees like Isamidin and Mavluda come to the United States with little more than the clothes on their backs. Some flee their homeland as a result of persecution based on race, religion, nationality, social group, or political opinion. Others flee from war or armed conflict. Most of them go to the nearest country where they may live in camps for years while enduring harsh weather with little food or health care. Resettlement is the process though which they are permanently transferred to a third country, where they can begin a new life.

Refugees are legally admitted into the United States by the Department of State and the Office of Refugee Resettlement, and are sponsored and resettled by various voluntary agencies, including the United States Conference of Catholic Bishops. These agencies try to place refugees in areas where they may already have family members or "anchors," or where there are related ethnic communities.

The number of refugees that have resettled in the United States since the mid-1970s numbers 2.4 million. Of these, Between 90,000 and 100,000 have resettled in Pennsylvania. More than half reside in Philadelphia County and include Liberians, Sudanese, Ethiopians, Vietnamese, West Africans, Moldovans, Eastern Europeans, and Meskhetian Turks.

Isamidin and his family were sponsored by Catholic Social Services (CSS) of the Archdiocese of Philadelphia. The agency helped the family apply for their social security cards and receive public benefits. CSS assisted them with their enrollment into a Match Grant program which provided them with access to English as a Second Language classes and job placement. CSS enrolled their three children into a local school where they are learning English. CSS caseworkers provided the family with cultural orientation to their new country, teaching them how to shop at a grocery store, how to pay monthly bills, how to write checks, and how to use a bank.

CSS caseworkers build relationships with refugees like Isamidin and Mavluda, and together develop a plan that meets their clients' basic needs—from safe housing and job placement to education and healthcare referrals.

Within months most refugees are completely self-sufficient. Studies show that through their hard work and drive to succeed, refugees are usually as well off as native-born Americans within ten years.

GO ONLINE Visit www.harcourtreligion.com to learn more about the Archdiocese of Philadelphia's Refugee Resettlement Program and for a link to its site.

Prayer

Silently reflect on the words of Saint Francis.

Lord, make me an instrument of your peace.

Where there is hatred, let me sow love;
    where there is injury, pardon; where there is doubt, faith;
    where there is despair, hope;
    where there is darkness, light;
    and where there is sadness, joy.

O, Divine Master, grant that I may not so much seek to
be consoled as to console;
    to be understood as to understand;
    to be loved as to love.

For it is in giving that we receive;
    it is in pardoning that we are pardoned;
    and it is in dying that we are born to eternal life.

Amen.

– Attributed to Saint Francis of Assisi

›Review

1. What is the continuum of conflict resolution?

2. What attitude toward violence is expressed through the term militarism?

3. List the eight principles of a just war.

4. How has the principle of noncombatant immunity been clouded by modern warfare?

5. Name and explain the three principles of the just-war theory after a conflict.

6. What is the difference between pacifism and passivity, absolute pacifists and practical pacifists?

7. Name three attitudes that can foster a climate of peace.

8. Describe the spiral of violence.

9. Define civil disobedience. Name the four elements of civil disobedience.

10. What was the attitude of Jesus toward violence?

11. What did the author of the Letter to the Ephesians contrast with use of military weapons?

12. What effect did the reign of Roman Emperor Constantine have on Christian attitudes toward war?

13. Define the medieval decrees called the Peace of God and the Truce of God.

14. What view of pacifism has developed within modern Church teaching?

15. What warning is found in modern Church teaching regarding use of the just-war doctrine?

›Key Words

blockade (p. 329)–Preventing the transport of goods to a nation in order to pressure that nation to change certain practices.

civil disobedience (p. 329)–Breaking a law which is against the norm of an upright conscience or against the demands of the moral law.

collateral damage (p. 317)–Unintended death or destruction that accompany an attack on a legitimate target.

conscientious objector (p. 322)–Someone who opposes participation in war for religious or philosophical reasons.

continuum of conflict resolution (p. 308)–The degree of acceptance of war as a means of resolving a conflict, ranging from a preference for war over other means to absolute rejection of it.

militarism (p. 310)–Belief that war is natural, unavoidable, and the most effective means of resolving international conflicts.

pacifism (p. 321)–Seeking to resolve conflicts through nonviolent means without resorting to any form of violence.

passivity (p. 321)–Making no attempt to resolve conflict; not getting involved, being detached.

proportionality (p. 317)–The good that results from a war must be greater than the harm caused.

satyagraha (p. 326) Truth force; soul force; belief that right has power rather than "might makes right."

spiral of violence (p. 325)–An injustice which leads to violence and an attempt to crush that violence with more violence; violence that builds on violence.

Our Challenge

"Let us . . . find ways of resolving controversies in a manner worthy of human beings. Providence urgently demands of us that we free ourselves from the age-old bondage of war."

The Documents of Vatican II, "The Church in the Modern World," #81

Peace is not the absence of conflict but creative resolution of conflicts: "Peace is the work of justice and the effect of charity" (*CCC* 2304). True peace cannot exist without justice. That is, the only way to have a peaceful world is to have a world where justice prevails. At this point in history, we are in urgent need of discovering new methods of resolving interpersonal and international conflicts. Church teaching accepts that warfare for defensive purposes is justified. However, in the words of the U.S. Catholic bishops: "Catholic teaching begins in every case with a presumption against war and for peaceful settlement of disputes" (*The Challenge of Peace*, summary). The *Catechism of the Catholic Church* states, "Because of the evils and injustices that all war brings with it, we must do everything reasonably possible to avoid it" (*CCC* 2327). For Jesus, peacemaking was absolutely basic: "Blessed are the peacemakers, for they will be called children of God" (*Matthew 5:9*).

PEACEMAKING

CHAPTER 12

A NEW ATTITUDE

CHAPTER GOALS

In this chapter you will:

* examine peacemaking on personal and global levels.

* explore the culture of violence which leads to the breakdown of society.

* consider terrorism and modern tools of war and their impact on international peace.

* learn about the U.S. role in peacekeeping.

Becoming People of Peace

what's your opinion?

Answer **agree, disagree, or uncertain** to the following statements. Choose statements that you believe to be most significant. Explain your answers.

1. Teenagers, more than any other age group, engage in violent activities.

2. The United States is an exceptionally violent country.

3. When someone kills another person, I view it solely as that individual's problem.

4. If I had children, I would not allow them to play with toy guns or violent video games.

5. I want my country to be militarily the best equipped nation in the world.

6. I consider myself a peaceful person.

Especially since the terrible devastation of World War II, Church leaders have grappled with the question of war. Reflecting on the extent of violence that has marked our modern age and also the destructive power of modern weapons, the bishops of the Second Vatican Council made the following timely observation:

> All these considerations force us to undertake a completely fresh appraisal of war. People of the present generation should realize that they will have to render an account of their warlike behavior; the destiny of generations to come depends largely on the decisions they make today.
>
> *The Documents of Vatican II*, "The Church in the Modern World," 80

In many respects, the "new attitude" that the bishops called for is as old as the Christian Good News itself. Jesus proposes that we look at violence and enemies with a new attitude:

> *"You have heard that it was said, 'An eye for an eye and a tooth for a tooth.' But I say to you, Do not resist an evildoer. But if anyone strikes you on the right cheek, turn the other also; and if anyone wants to sue you and take your coat, give your cloak as well . . . . You have heard that it was said, 'You shall love your neighbor and hate your enemy.' But I say to you, Love your enemies and pray for those who persecute you, so that you may be children of your Father in heaven. . . ."*
>
> ✝ Matthew 5:38–40, 43–45

Two Tales of Violence

• At school Luke is often the butt of jokes. Perhaps it's his weight, his attempts to be funny (which always seem to fall flat), or just that he tries too hard to fit in. For whatever reason, many of his fellow students feel as though Luke is fair game for teasing and mocking. No one thinks of their teasing and mocking as wrong.

• Magda's mother has a way of talking to her that always leaves her angry and baffled. When Magda brought home a report card with mostly Bs, her mother said, "Those are very good grades—for you." Magda has recently started hanging out with a group that doesn't take school or anything else very seriously—a group she feels comfortable in. Magda has learned what her mother has taught her—not to expect much of herself or of life.

At first glance the stories of Luke and Magda do not seem to be about violence. In neither case is someone physically striking or abusing another person. However, isn't it true that both Luke and Magda are victims of violence of another sort?

Psychological violence refers to harming a person in ways other than through physical force. In Chapter 9, we looked at domestic violence, or violence that occurs within a family. Sometimes domestic violence is physical; more often it is psychological, or emotional. Sometimes it is both, since psychological violence within families often builds to physical violence. Whatever its form, domestic violence leaves people damaged. For example, in the above scenario Magda suffered because of emotional rather than physical abuse. Frequently, patterns of psychological violence at home carry over into violence at school or in other settings. As the story of Luke illustrates, the weapons of words, looks, and gestures can cut down a person as violently as guns can—and, as several school shootings have shown, can lead to violence on the part of the abused person.

GROUP TALK

Read the following pledge and discuss the questions:

I pledge to seek peace and to resolve problems peacefully. To the best of my ability I will:

* ★ Reject violence, physical and psychological.
* ★ Avoid rash judgments and listen to what others have to say.
* ★ Tell others my wants and viewpoints without demeaning them or their views.
* ★ Seek resolutions to conflicts, not victories over enemies.
* ★ Remain open to new ideas and possible solutions.
* ★ Rely on the power of reason, not on physical intimidation.
* ★ Focus on current problems, not on the past.
* ★ Be honest about myself and my feelings.
* ★ Search for the good in others.

Respond to these questions: Would you like to see such a petition passed around your school? Would you sign it? Explain.

FAITH ACTIVITY

Are You a Peacemaker? Consider the following question: Am I a peacemaker? List ten attitudes you have or actions you perform that would identify you as a peacemaker. Share these actions in a class discussion.

In our world, some teenagers kill teenagers with guns or baseball bats, and nations compete for the most powerful weapons. On television and in movies, bloodshed is so commonplace that it frequently plays a major role in any serious plot, and real wars come to us in vivid color. With our sophisticated communications systems, we are confronted with news from around the world about genocide, terrorism, and ethnic groups killing each other with careless disregard for life.

In light of all the violence we see, it is necessary to focus on the words "Thy kingdom come on earth." To make a beginning, we need to cultivate a personal spirituality. With the grace of the Holy Spirit, a personal spirituality of peace can help us become channels of God's peace and thus contribute to the fashioning of God's kingdom.

In the business of everyday living, we need to stop to take time to think about God, about ourselves, and about what is going on around us. How does it all connect? How do we make sense of current events? Without peace within ourselves we cannot live in peace with others. Conversely, becoming actively involved in peacemaking increases our longing for personal peace. By using our gifts and talents, nurtured through prayer and reflection, we contribute to God's reign of peace.

During conflicts, we have a tendency to reduce other individuals, groups, or nations to "the enemy." Recently we have also heard various groups of people lumped together and called "the terrorists." Using such catchall phrases carries tremendous emotional weight and short-circuits our ability to see others as human persons like ourselves. Peace can never be achieved until name-calling is put aside. In interpersonal relationships, true peace does not produce "winners" and "losers" but aims for a win-win outcome.

GROUP TALK

In the face of a culture that divides people into friends and enemies, good guys and bad guys, what are wholesome ways of relating to others with whom we don't get along or who rub us the wrong way?

A New Attitude Toward Others

One meaning of **respect** is "to look at a second time"; it is a way of looking at people. Respect is shown through our actions. In 1994, in their pastoral letter, *Confronting a Culture of Violence*, the U.S. Catholic bishops called for "a commitment to civility and respect in public life and communications—in the news media, politics, and even ecclesial dialogue." They noted that: "Violence is overcome day by day, choice by choice, person by person." The Church calls us to live lives filled with respect, truth, freedom, and justice while avoiding malice and misrepresentation.

Positive Influence In a poem, a story, a group symbolic gesture, or a drawing, illustrate how respect can influence a culture of violence in a positive way.

Sometimes respect includes confrontation, which can be mistaken for "attack," but in fact is quite different. Confrontation is a challenge but not a personal attack. It invites people close to us to examine their words or actions and the consequences of those words or actions. For instance, a young man might tell a young woman how much he cares for her and that she's the only one for him. Then, among his friends, he keeps his distance from her and doesn't communicate publicly that they are going out. An empowering confrontation on the young woman's part would be to point out to him that his words say one thing but that his actions say another. Such a confrontation shows the young woman's true feeling, as well as care both for herself and for the young man. Even if a breakup results, it is an invitation to mutual respect—honest sharing rather than unkindness and violence.

GROUP TALK

Think about concrete examples of the following violent situations. For each situation, describe whether, and if so, how mutual respect might help lessen the chance of violence and promote peace.

1. abusive boy-girl relationships or dating circumstances
2. violence between gangs or groups of teenagers
3. young children who are not getting along
4. confrontations between police officers and citizens
5. vandalism
6. automobile-related violence
7. sports-related violence
8. family violence

Confronting a Culture of Violence

> " The United States is a violent country. Episodes of violent crime . . .
> are not exceptions to the rule. Indeed, comparative statistics among
> nations . . . indicate that the United States outranks most other nations
> of the industrial world in violent crimes like assault, rape, and robbery.
> In the category of murder, we are far and away the most violent indus-
> trialized nation on earth. "
>
> Raymond B. Flannery, *Violence in America* (New York: Continuum, 1997), 18

Nightly news reports and newspaper headlines regularly remind us of our culture of violence. Studies about violence in the United States consistently arrive at two conclusions: the United States is particularly violent, and violence increases when there is a **breakdown in community**.

Breakdown of Community

Many factors contribute to violent behavior in society. Some studies even suggest a genetic tendency toward aggressive behavior in some people. However, if such a gene exists, it is a human gene, not a national one. Therefore, it does not account for the higher level of violence in the United States. According to psychologist Raymond B. Flannery, who studied patterns of violence in America over the past fifty years, a breakdown in community underlies the persistence of violent, antisocial behavior that plagues the United States.

> " The network of stable family life, consistent schooling, and supportive
> services from other adults in the community was not a part of the lives
> of these offenders, and it is reasonable to assume that this absence
> of community may have contributed, at least in part, to their violent
> lifestyle. "
>
> *Violence in America*, 22

The U.S. Catholic bishops have expressed great regret over teen violence, as well as any violence. In their examination of the culture of violence, they too detected a link with the breakdown of community:

FAITH ACTIVITY

Culture of Violence List as many social factors as you can that you believe contribute to a culture of violence. Number these factors in terms of importance. Compare your list with those of other students, seeking to arrive at agreement on factors influencing violence in society.

If a breakdown in community contributes to violence, then it stands to reason that building up community serves as an antidote to violence. The chart on the following page lists the risk factors that, according to Flannery, lead to violence. The next quote addresses the last item in the chart: the media. If these factors ignite violence, then eliminating or changing them in healthy ways kindles peace.

Brandon Centerwall, an epidemiologist at the University of Washington, studied the relationship between TV violence and the growth of violence in various communities. His conclusion: TV violence is a public health problem deserving measures as practical as nutrition, immunization, and bicycle helmet programs. He cites such studies as one from a remote Canadian community that in 1973 was due to acquire television. [Previously television service was unavailable to them.] Social scientists seized the opportunity to investigate the effects of television on this community's children, using for comparison two similar towns that had long had television. Before television arrived, they monitored rates of inappropriate physical aggression among 45 first- and second-graders. After two years of television, the rate increased 160%, in both boys and girls, and in those who were aggressive to begin with and those who were not. The rate in the two communities that had television for years did not change.

John W. Glaser, *Three Realms of Ethics* (Kansas City, MO: Sheed & Ward)

Factors that lead to violence

poverty

domestic violence

discrimination

inadequate schooling

substance abuse

easily available weapons

the media

FAITH ACTIVITY

Induced violence Which of these factors have you seen in your school, community, and city? What steps can you and your classmates take to help break the spiral of violence..

Institutional violence

- Sabrina cleans houses for a living. Due to the uncertain nature of her work, Sabrina is not always sure she can support herself and her two children. During a recent public transportation strike, she was unable to get to two houses, so the homeowners hired another person for the job, someone who owned a car. Sabrina was left with a drastic reduction in her weekly income. She receives some food and clothing for the children from a neighborhood church. She tries to remain optimistic, but it is hard for her not to feel trapped in poverty.

- Darnell, who lives with his grandmother and three other children, has skipped school for a number of days. The school counselor has spoken to him about the importance of his attending school, but she fears going to Darnell's home because of the violence on his block. She has spoken to the school reading specialist, who informed her that space is not available for all who need personalized assistance with reading. Darnell has not received help.

Isn't it accurate to say that both Sabrina and Darnell are experiencing violence? This kind of violence should not be overlooked simply because its portrayal would not be the subject of a blockbuster action-adventure movie. If someone locked Sabrina in her home so that she could not get to work, we would immediately identify that as violence. If reading textbooks were handed out to students, and Darnell's was snatched from his hands, we would call that violence. However, Sabrina and Darnell are suffering a similar fate because of less direct, less obvious expressions of violence. The perpetrator of the violence seems to be society itself.

In cases such as these, a major thesis of this course comes full circle: justice, created by a compassionate community and open to the movement of the Holy Spirit, brings peace. That is, only a just community is truly a peaceful one. Therefore, a principal way to confront violence in society is to work for justice. Violence resulting from injustice within a society is **institutional violence**, that is, violence that does harm to people through the structures of a society. This includes the way that public utilities and businesses operate, the way that schools and hospitals are funded, the types of programs made available for different age groups, the methods in place for helping families, and the way that law enforcement and the criminal justice system works. Insofar as an institution operates in an unjust way, it is violent. Injustices within the very fabric of society are institutionalized violence. On the other hand healthy and just institutions foster peace.

GROUP TALK

Think about characteristics of contemporary society.

* Make four lists naming strengths, weaknesses, opportunities, and threats that you perceive in society today.

* Based on your lists, identify key changes that could lessen societal or institutional violence.

Nurturing Global Peace

> Every gun that is made, every warship launched, every rocket fired signifies, in the final sense, a theft from those who hunger and are not fed, those who are cold and are not clothed.
>
> This world in arms is not spending money alone. It is spending the sweat of its laborers, the genius of its scientists, the hopes of its children.

President Dwight D. Eisenhower

The above words were spoken in the 1950s by President Dwight D. Eisenhower, a man who was himself a former army general. It voices a concern that remains with us today. Nations have limited funds. They can build either tanks or tractors, either warships or low-cost housing. The pie that symbolizes a nation's budget can be sliced only so many ways. For a majority of countries, including the United States, military spending accounts for a large piece of the pie. President Eisenhower knew that money spent on expensive weapons systems meant that less money was available for education, health care, and other social programs.

Afghan children play on the turret of anabandoned Soviet tank north of Kabul ▼

But doesn't the armaments industry create jobs? In the first place, military spending actually creates fewer jobs than almost any other form of government expense. Second, most jobs created by military spending are positions for highly skilled labor. Consequently, the defense industry employs few of those people most in need of work—those who are unskilled and poorly educated and who therefore make up the majority of the ranks of unemployed.

If justice leads to peace, then an unequal amount of time, energy, technology, research, and money given over to military matters takes away from applying these same resources to working for justice. In other words, the following question demands an answer: Which is more likely to bring peace—preparedness for war or working for justice? Unfortunately, given limited resources, "both" is not a realistic answer.

The Tools of War

In the last hundred years, the nations of the world have taken war to new appalling depths. Never before in the history of humankind has such an array of new weapons been imagined and created.

FAITH ACTIVITY

Take the time to go by yourself to a quiet place where you can think about and create a journal entry in response to the following questions:

• Where in my life am I experiencing a lack of peace?

• Who or what is causing me not to be at peace?

• What actions can I take to find peace?

▼ This atomic bomb, named Fat Man, is located at the White Sands Missile Test Site's Rocket Park in southern New Mexico

Nuclear Weapons A common scene in cartoons shows a character trying to kill a pesky fly with a hammer or a shotgun. The end result is a large hole in a wall or a painfully throbbing bump on a friend's head—and a fly that keeps on buzzing. The joke is straightforward: if we use high-tech weapons in a situation that calls for a more low-tech response, we end up making matters worse.

For over forty years, the focus of the U.S. military was on winning or preventing an all-out nuclear war with the other superpower of the time, the Soviet Union. Since the beginning of the 1990s, there has been no Soviet Union. Nonetheless, the United States continues to maintain a stockpile of nuclear weapons aimed at targets in the former Soviet Union.

In the decades from the 1950s to the 1980s, many people in the United States feared that they would die in a nuclear holocaust. Since then that fear has greatly diminished. While people's fear of nuclear destruction has lessened, the risk of nuclear destruction remains. The U.S. Catholic bishops addressed the question of nuclear weapons most directly in their 1983 pastoral letter, *The Challenge of Peace*. There they stated that use of nuclear weapons is wrong and can never be justified. They applied traditional just-war principles to the unique nature of nuclear weapons to arrive at this conclusion: "In simple terms, we are saying that good ends (defending one's country, protecting freedom, etc.) cannot justify immoral means (the use of weapons which kill indiscriminately and threaten whole societies)" (332).

While the bishops condemned the use of nuclear weapons, they do not outright condemn possession of nuclear weapons. At the time, possessing nuclear weapons was thought to serve the purpose of **deterrence**. In other words, if a country has nuclear weapons available for use, then other countries would risk their own destruction if they used nuclear weapons against it. The bishops accepted this reasoning, but only hesitantly. For one, they agreed with what President Eisenhower had said: money spent on nuclear weapons is taking money from much needed social programs. Second, they noted that "The political paradox of deterrence has also strained our moral conception. May a nation threaten what it may never do? May it possess what it may never use?" (137) Third, nuclear deterrence is justified only so long as there is progress toward nuclear disarmament.

Since the breakup of the former Soviet Union, the reasoning for keeping nuclear weapons has become even more clouded. For instance, what justification exists for targeting sites in a country that is no longer considered either a threat or "the enemy"? In effect the United States is spending money to maintain the capacity to destroy a nation to whom it now sends aid. One general, formerly in charge of the U.S. Strategic Command, believes that nuclear weapons become an addiction. Once we have them, it's hard to give them up—even when their reason for being is unclear. This addiction is very expensive. Nuclear weapons cannot simply be stored somewhere. They require constant maintenance and updating, the cost of which is very high. In the meantime, nuclear capabilities continue to spread to new countries. The bishops counter:

> Diverting scarce resources from military to human development is not only a just and compassionate policy, but also a wise long-term investment in global and national security. Concern for jobs cannot justify military spending beyond the minimum necessary for legitimate national security and international peacekeeping obligations.

Administrative Board, U.S. Catholic Conference, *Political Responsibility*

Land Mines: The Residue of Wars Past Peter Bell is president of CARE, the world's largest international relief and development organization. In thirty-nine of the sixty-three countries where CARE works, land mines are still in place. According to Bell, the United Nations estimates that 110 million land mines are planted around the world. Each year, 26,000 people are killed or hurt by land mines. Besides this direct human suffering from mines, whole communities are effectively paralyzed by them. An organization such as CARE, which tries to help people in need, cannot work effectively where land mines exist. Staples of life—farmland, water, and trade—are cut off where mines dot the landscape.

FAITH ACTIVITY

Modern War Create a political cartoon or poster about some aspect of modern warfare.

▼ Holding an amputee child in her lap, Princess Diana meets victims of landmines

Few soldiers actually die from land mines during wartime. Mines do their damage after the fighting stops, when children and farmers try to resume some sort of normal life even though unseen danger is present. In 1996 fourteen retired generals, including Norman Schwarzkopf, who headed U.N. troops during the 1991 Persian Gulf War, wrote President Bill Clinton to say that a ban on land mines would not lessen the effectiveness or safety of U.S. troops or those of other nations.

FAITH ACTIVITY

Jesus on Peace. In an essay, imagine that Jesus addresses the United Nations on land mines. What do you think he would say?

The Administrative Board of the U.S. Catholic Conference repeated what many recent Church documents have stated:

"The United States should take a leadership role in reducing reliance on, ending export of, and ultimately banning anti-personnel land mines, which kill some 26,000 civilians each year" (*Political Responsibility*).

> No less than 25 percent of landmine victims are children . . . mothers in Somaliland are forced to tie their children to trees so they will not wander innocently into one of the more than one million laid haphazardly in that country during the last decade. . . . I spoke with Andrew Cooper, land mines researcher for the Human Rights Watch Arms Project in Washington, D.C. . . . A total of 4.4 million anti-personnel mines, he commented, were exported by the United States from 1969 to 1992 to countries in Asia, the Middle East and South America.

Regina Griffin, "The Land Mine Menace," *America* (July 19-26, 1997), 14

GROUP TALK

Research the topic of land mines, and report on their impact on "the state of the world."

Terrorism—A Transnational Threat

◀ A fireman after the terrorist attacks of September 11, 2001.

"On April 19, 1995, around 9:03 A.M., just after parents dropped their children off at day care at the Murrah Federal Building in downtown Oklahoma City, the unthinkable happened.

A massive bomb inside a rental truck exploded, blowing half of the nine-story building into oblivion.

A stunned nation watched as the bodies of men, women, and children were pulled from the rubble for nearly two weeks. When the smoke cleared and the exhausted rescue workers packed up and left, 168 people were dead in the worst terrorist attack on U.S. soil."

Cable News Network "The Bombing," 1996

Terrorism is a unique category of violence. On the one hand, it is not what we normally think of as crime, since crimes are typically committed for personal gain. On the other hand, it doesn't fit what we normally think of as war either. Terrorism targets nonmilitary personnel or soldiers apart from a field of combat.

The bombing of a federal building in Oklahoma City in 1995 was the most destructive terrorist act in U.S. history up to that time. Then on September 11, 2001, four planes were hijacked and three of them were used as weapons, while the fourth crashed before reaching its target when passengers rushed the terrorists. This dire event elevated terrorism to the number-one fear of people in the United States in regard to violence. Following close on its heels, threats of biological and chemical weapons compounded the fear.

World Response to Terrorism

World leaders universally condemn acts of terror. The question is, how best to prevent them. Soon after these attacks, many religious leaders of the world joined Pope John Paul II at Assisi, Italy, to reflect together on peace in light of the disaster. They condemned terrorism, reminding everyone that the ways of violence never lead to genuine solutions to the world's problems.

The religious leaders gathered also produced a declaration, listing ten commitments that they as religious leaders pledged to the rest of the world as their response to terrorism:

1. To do everything possible to eliminate the root causes of terrorism

2. To educate people to mutual respect and esteem

3. To foster a culture of dialogue

4. To defend the right of everyone to live a decent life

5. To move beyond differences and to use diversity as an opportunity for greater understanding

6. To forgive one another for past and present errors and prejudices

7. To take the side of people who are poor and helpless

8. To take up the cry of those who refuse to resort to violence

9. To encourage efforts to promote friendship among peoples

10. To urge world leaders to create and consolidate a world of solidarity and peace

In a world with ever more open borders, shrinking distances, and better relations, as a result of a broad network of communications, we are convinced that security, freedom, and peace will never be guaranteed by force but by mutual trust.

Pope John Paul II and Religious Leaders of the World, "Final Declaration of Representatives of the Religions of the World" (January 24, 2002)

GROUP TALK

1. What type of terrorist attacks threaten the world today?

2. Do you believe that the ten commitments of the world's religious leaders are an effective agenda for counteracting terrorism? Would you add to or subtract from the declaration in any way? Explain.

3. Do you agree that developing mutual trust is more effective against terrorism than use of force?

U.S. Role in Global Peace and War

> The virtue of patriotism means that as citizens we respect and honor our country, but our very love and loyalty make us examine carefully and regularly its role in world affairs, asking that it live up to its full potential as an agent of peace with justice for all people.
>
> National Conference of Catholic Bishops, *The Challenge of Peace*, 327

The U.S. Catholic bishops encourage Catholics to be active in politics. They encourage Catholics to ask the country's leaders and citizens to make peace always a primary concern in policies and practices. At the Second Vatican Council, the world's Catholic bishops gave a fuller description of the virtue of **patriotism**:

> Citizens should cultivate a generous and loyal spirit of patriotism, but without narrow-mindedness, so they will keep in mind the welfare of the entire human family which is formed into one by various links between races, people, and nations.
>
> *Documents of Vatican II*, "The Church in the Modern World," 75

This description of patriotism differs greatly from **nationalism**. According to the bishops at the council, patriotism is a positive virtue; nationalism is a selfish, narrow-minded vice. Patriotism includes identifying oneself as a world citizen, not just a citizen of one's particular country. A true patriot seeks to find out how one's country can contribute positively to making the entire world a better place. On the other hand a nationalist spirit places the good of one's own country above the needs of every other country, as if one nation can exist apart from and independent of all others.

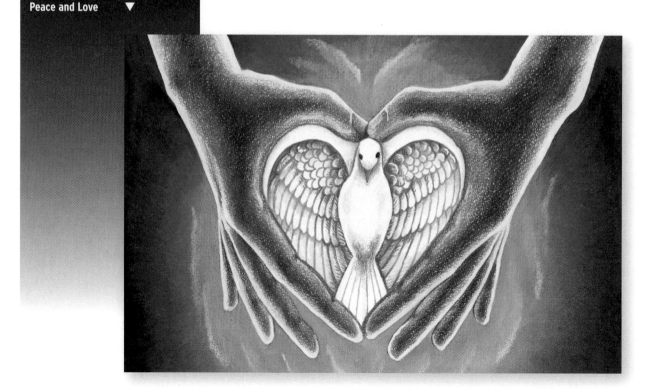

Peace and Love ▼

1 Evaluate the following activities from the view of nationalism and patriotism. When you have finished, describe the types of activities you would like to see the United States engaged in that would show "The United States at its best."

★ U.S. companies are the world's largest suppliers of military weapons.

★ A school run by the U.S. Army trains military leaders from Latin American countries. Some graduates of this school have been directly responsible for repression, torture, and human rights abuses. Sometimes their victims have been U.S. citizens doing missionary work in underdeveloped countries.

★ The U.S. government sends its military into a civil strife occurring in a country that is strategically important to U.S. interests. It voices concern but provides no military or economic assistance to a country experiencing civil war, but which is not strategically important.

★ If the United States grants "most favored nation" status to a particular country, it would benefit some U.S. companies. However, the country is known for its human rights abuses.

★ The U.S. government supplies economic aid to countries based on their benefit to the United States rather than based on their need.

★ A group of U.S. missionaries to a Latin American country are killed by a paramilitary death squad. The U.S. government does not pressure the country's leaders to investigate the murders for fear that they might involve government officials friendly to the United States.

★ A professional athlete refuses to stand during the playing of "God Bless America" because he views it as a statement in support of a war he opposes.

2 Debate the pros and cons of the position on land mines presented by the U.S. Catholic bishops.

3 Apply the teachings of the bishops to the manufacture and use of chemical and biological weapons.

>Faith in Action

Teens Acting for Peace (TAP)

Sponsored by: **The Institute for Peace and Justice**

"Preach the Gospel at all times and when necessary use words," St. Francis of Assisi said. Teenagers in schools from Pennsylvania to California are doing just that. Modeling peace and teaching peace in elementary schools, Teens Acting for Peace (TAP) show younger students how to respect each other, to be good listeners, to forgive others when they are hurt, and to act with courage, even when it's not popular.

> "TAP is a life changing experience and will overwhelmingly change the way you view life. It has helped me grow and become a better person. This program is so important to pass on to our younger youth."
>
> Rachel Norris, Kansas City, Kansas

TAP, the national youth violence prevention program initiated by the The Institute for Peace and Justice, trains college, high school and middle school students as peace educators to help reduce violence in schools and to equip younger children with the skills and values they need to confront injustices in their world.

The Teens work in teams to teach the Pledge of Nonviolence. By telling their own stories based on the seven principles of the Pledge, the Teens teach children that making peace starts from within themselves and within their schools. They use skits, music, crafts, and discussion groups to enhance their interaction. One elementary school class buried their "grudges," complete with pall bearers and a funeral procession. Another class received balloons with hurtful words written on them. After talking about how words could be verbal violence, they popped the balloons to find affirming words inside.

Teens at Notre Dame de Sion High School in Kansas City, Missouri, and Bishop Miege High School in Shawnee Mission, Kansas, have taken leadership of their programs, organizing and coordinating TAP in their own schools, and in the local elementary schools. In 2005, reacting to a continuing national climate of war and terrorism, students in the Kansas City TAP elementary schools were encouraged to act courageously for peace by gathering peace messages written on hearts to be sent to Iraqi children caught in the midst of war.

By pledging to "eliminate violence, one school at a time," starting with their own, these students are forming more peaceful schools, more peaceful communities, and a more peaceful world.

The Institute for Peace and Justice is an independent, interfaith, not-for-profit organization that creates resources, provides learning experiences, and advocates publicly for alternatives to violence and injustice at the individual, family, community, institutional, and global levels.

GO ONLINE Visit www.harcourtreligion.com to learn more about The Institute for Peace and Justice's and for a link to its site.

Prayer

Begin by praying the Sign of the Cross.

Leader: God our Father, giver of life, from the beginning you planted within us the seeds of an earth on which people care for one another and where peace reigns. Your Son, Jesus Christ, is our hope and our salvation.

All: Because of him we can dream dreams of a just and peace-filled world.

Leader: With him and united with the Holy Spirit, we can add our voices, our eyes, our ears, our hands, and our feet to building your reign.

All: Because of him we can dream dreams of a just and peace-filled world.

Leader: In him and through him we proclaim that justice and peace are possible, that people who are poor or otherwise needy will be satisfied, and that those who are suffering now will be comforted.

Leader: *Lord Jesus Christ, you said to your apostles:*
I leave you peace, my peace I give you.
Look not on our sins, but on the faith of your Church,
and grant us the peace and unity of your kingdom
where you live for ever and ever.

All: Amen.

"Sign of Peace," *The Sacramentary*

❯Review

1. Describe the "new attitude" toward war that Vatican II called for.

2. What is the literal meaning of respect?

3. Why is confrontation different from an attack?

4. How does creating a personal spirituality of peace affect the greater community in which we live?

5. Name seven factors that contribute to violence.

6. Define *psychological violence*. What are possible effects of psychological violence?

7. In what setting does psychological violence frequently occur?

8. Define *institutional violence*.

9. How is terrorism defined in today's world?

10. How did world leaders respond to the September 11, 2001, attack on the United States?

11. What caution was voiced by President Eisenhower about a military buildup?

12. Define *deterrence* in relation to nuclear weapons.

13. Which group receives more injuries from land mines: soldiers or civilians?

14. Besides killing and maiming civilians, how do land mines disrupt areas where they remain?

15. Explain the difference between patriotism and nationalism.

❯Key Words

breakdown in community (p. 345) Lack of a stable family life, regular schooling, and support services from other adults.

deterrence (p. 352) Discouraging use of weapons for fear of retaliation in kind.

institutional violence (p. 349) Violence that results from injustices within a society.

nationalism (p. 358) Love of country regardless of its actions, and refusing to recognize or trying to change its flaws; placing one's own country above the needs of the rest of the world; a "my country right or wrong" attitude.

patriotism (p. 358) Love of country that admits its shortcomings and tries to right them.

respect (p. 343) Appreciation and value of persons as they are.

terrorism (p. 356) Violence to achieve political ends perpetrated by a group lacking legal status.

>Our Challenge

On the president's chair in Independence Hall in Philadelphia is a carving of half a sun on a horizon. After the signing of the Declaration of Independence there, Benjamin Franklin reportedly remarked that "only time will tell whether the sun is setting or rising." Today, the world finds itself facing an even larger crisis. Modern weapons have ever-increasing accuracy and destructive capabilities. Modern technologies have created a world that is more a global village than a collection of isolated nations. Terrorism is an international problem calling for a global response. The decisions we make and the actions we take, individually and collectively, will determine whether our sun is rising or setting. Ultimately, only justice built on charity and compassion will make the world a more peaceful place.

How do we achieve a world of peace? How do we get there? We get there by asking God to lead us there. We get there by following the way of Jesus. We get there by being open to God's grace given to us through the Holy Spirit. We get there through living Christian charity and through the difficult, challenging work of justice. When we embrace the new life in the Spirit made possible by Jesus and respond to God's love by working for justice, we live out our true identity as images of God.

A

ageism—Discriminatory attitudes and practices toward people based on their age.

Alzheimer's disease—A progressive disease that may occur in older people, leading to confusion and impaired judgment.

Americans with Disabilities Act—Act passed by Congress in 1990 initiating changes to ensure that the rights of the disabled are not violated because of a disability.

animal experimentation—Scientific research on animals, including some questionable practices.

anthropocentrism—Literally "centering on the human," viewing the rest of nature as solely for human use and not for the glory of God.

B

Basic rights—Rights that all people possess because of their very nature as humans; inalienable rights.

Beatitudes—Jesus' teachings about the meaning and path to true happiness, teachings which depict the attitudes and actions that followers of Christ should have and the way to live in God's kingdom today. They describe the way to attain the eternal holiness or blessedness to which God calls all people.

blockade—Preventing the transport of goods to a nation in order to pressure that nation to change certain practices.

breakdown in community—Lack of a stable family life, regular schooling, and support services from other adults.

C

capitalism—Individual ownership and administration of the production and distribution of goods.

cash crops—Crops grown to be exported in order to raise money.

Catholic Social Teaching—The body of official Church documents written by Church leaders in response to various social, political, and economic issues.

Church—The community of the faithful who through holy Baptism are nourished by and become the Body of Christ (See *CCC* 777.)

civil disobedience—Breaking a law which is against the norm of an upright conscience or against the demands of the moral law. (See *CCC* 2242.)

collateral damage—Unintended death or destruction that accompany an attack on a legitimate target.

colonialism—The political and economic system by which one country controls and exploits another, holding it in a subservient role.

common good—A long-standing Christian concept advocating that society should be organized so that, as much as possible, all people, either in groups or as individuals, are given the opportunities to reach their fulfillment more fully and easily.

communities of resistance—Groups that take a unified stand against an area of injustice.

conscience—The capacity to make good judgments involving a process of discernment about right and wrong as well as judgment itself.

conscientious objector—Someone who opposes participation in war for religious or philosophical reasons.

Consumerism—The distorted desire to possess things out of proportion to our needs or normal wants.

continuum of conflict resolution—The degree of acceptance of war as a means of resolving a conflict, ranging from a preference for war over other means to absolute rejection of it.

corporate farming—Ownership of a large number of acres and animals by persons or organizations that oversee production but do not actually work with the land or the animals.

covenant—a solemn promise, or agreement, made between two parties; another word for testament.

creation—the act by which God began all that exists outside of himself.

crimes against persons—Killing or physically hurting someone.

crimes against property—stealing or damaging property.

Crisis of limits—The finite and irreplaceable nature of essential resources, such as oil and rainforests.

culture of death—Culture that fosters values and practices harmful to life.

culture of life—Culture that values all human life.

decision-making power— Ability to make choices regarding an institution or one's life.

deterrence—Discouraging use of weapons for fear of retaliation in kind.

Dignity—The respect owed to all humans because they are made in God's image.

domestic violence—Physical or psychological abuse within a family setting.

ecology—Study of the environment and the relationships among the elements of creation.

economic colonies—Poorer countries dependent on a few wealthy countries to purchase their limited selection of crops or products.

encyclical—An official letter to the whole Church written by a pope.

energy-intensive—Large-scale farming that depends more on heavy machinery, chemical fertilizers, irrigation systems, and pesticides than on people.

euthanasia—The deliberate killing of sick, suffering, or disabled people intended to "end their suffering."

Exodus—liberation of the Israelites from Egyptian slavery under the leadership of Moses, who was led by God.

exploitation—Using other living creatures for our purposes without respecting their God-given dignity.

Fatalism—The belief that the world is out of the control of humans and in the hands of blind fate.

feminization of poverty—The trend that results in more women and dependent children living in poverty than men.

fixed income—The income that remains much the same year after year, such as Social Security or pension payments.

food crops—Crops grown to feed the people within a country.

global warming—An increase in the temperature worldwide.

graced social structures— Structures of society that encourage and strengthen life, dignity, and the development of community.

greenhouse effect—A warming of the earth's surface and lower atmosphere that tends to intensify with an increase in atmospheric carbon dioxide.

homophobia —the fear of being homosexual or of people with a homosexual orientation.

Hope—The theological virtue by which we desire and expect from God eternal life and the grace necessary to attain it. Hope envisions a better world and affirms that, with God's help, a better world is possible.

Incarnation—the singular and unique mystery whereby the Son of God, while not ceasing to be God, assumed a human nature and became man, so that he might accomplish our salvation.

income levels—Comparative amounts of money earned annually by individuals or families.

Individualism—A way of being and acting that emphasizes personal independence and the rights of individuals over interdependence and concern for the common good.

inorganic farming—Farming dependent on chemical fertilizers and pesticides; produces immediate high-crop yields but in the long-term depletes topsoil.

institutional racism—Racist actions and attitudes ingrained and operating in organizations of a society.

institutional violence—Violence that results from injustices within a society.

Interdependent—Reliance on one another for survival and well–being.

Justice and Peace   365

Jesus—name that means "God saves"; Jesus of Nazareth is the Savior God sent to redeem people from sin and eternal death.

jubilee year—The Old Testament law stating that debts should be canceled and land restored to its original owners every fifty years.

justice—the constant and firm will to give God and other people what is their due. Justice is a virtue (a dimension of one's character), a process (the work of justice), and a goal (a just world).

kingdom of God—God's reign of justice, love, and peace.

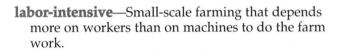

labor-intensive—Small-scale farming that depends more on workers than on machines to do the farm work.

life choices—Decisions about living made by an individual or group.

long-term solutions—Changes that provide ongoing resolutions to problems.

low-tillage farming—Farming that disturbs topsoil as little as possible, leaving some ground cover to prevent erosion, but still allowing some use of fertilizer and pesticides.

magisterium—The living, teaching office of the Church by which it gives authentic interpretation of the word of God.

malnutrition—A state resulting from a diet lacking the nutrients vital to good health.

Messiah—the Anointed One, the Christ. As Messiah, Jesus restored all people to communion and friendship with God through his life, death, and Resurrection.

militarism—Belief that war is natural, unavoidable, and the most effective means of resolving international conflicts.

nationalism—Love of country regardless of its actions, and refusing to recognize or trying to change its flaws; placing one's own country above the needs of the rest of the world; a "my country right or wrong" attitude.

natural law—We find order and design all through creation. The sciences and our human powers manifest a plan that discloses harmony and order. This harmony exists also in humans, where certain laws govern not only our bodies, but what is right and wrong.

oligarchy—A country ruled by a few members of an elite group clearly distinct from the vast majority of the population.

organic farming—Farming without the use of toxic chemicals; can create topsoil.

original sin—the decision by the first humans to disobey God. Thereafter, all people (except Jesus and Mary) began life with a wounded human nature, drawn to selfishness and sin and in need of redemption by Christ.

pacifism—Seeking to resolve conflicts through non-violent means without resorting to any form of violence.

passivity—Making no attempt to resolve conflict; not getting involved, being detached.

patriarchy—A society in which the dominant power is in the hands of a select group of men.

patriotism—Love of country that admits its shortcomings and tries to right them.

Pentecost—The event, fifty days after Easter, when the Holy Spirit appeared as fire and wind to Christ's Apostles. As a result, the Apostles began actively to proclaim the Gospel. The feast is celebrated each year to mark the ongoing presence of the Holy Spirit in the Church.

personal causes—Individual actions that lead to problems.

physical quality of life index—The combination of a country's average infant mortality, life expectancy, and literacy rates.

plea bargaining—Pleading guilty to a charge or to a lesser crime in exchange for a recommendation of a lighter sentence than one usually given for the offense.

prejudice—Narrow-minded opinion based on a false premise.

prophet—one who has a close relationship with God and communicates a divinely inspired message.

proportionality—The good that results from a war must be greater than the harm caused.

psychological violence—Harming someone through nonphysical means.

racial prejudice—A strong negative feeling that a person holds toward members of another race.

racism—Subordination based on race; discrimination or oppression based on race.

recycling—Converting waste products and other goods we throw away into usable products instead of putting them into a landfill.

relationship violence—Physical or psychological abuse that occurs in the context of a relationship such as dating or marriage.

respect—Appreciation and value of persons as they are.

satyagraha—Truth force; soul force; belief that right has power rather than "might makes right."

senility—Irreversible brain damage that may occur in the aging process.

sexism—Discrimination and injustice based on gender differences.

Simple living—A way of life in which a person buys and uses only what is needed, out of respect for people and resources.

sin—"a deliberate thought, word, deed, or omission contrary to the eternal law of God" (*CCC* Glossary).

sinful social structures—Structures of society that discourage and weaken life, dignity, and the development of community.

single-export economies—Budgets based on one product as the main source of income.

social action—Steps taken to change society's structures.

social sin—A term referring to sinful social structures resulting from the effects of personal sin and leading to social conditions and institutions that do not embody God's goodness; "structures of sin" (John Paul II, *Reconciliatio et paenitentia* 16). (*CCC* 1869.)

socialism—Government ownership and administration of the production and distribution of goods.

Solidarity—A spirit of unity and mutual concern; the quality of justice that breaks down barriers between people.

spiral of violence—An injustice which leads to violence and an attempt to crush that violence with more violence; violence that builds on violence.

stereotyping—Generalizing about an entire group of people and limiting our view of members of a group to narrow preconceptions.

stewardship—Humanity's role, designated by God, to protect, care for, and sustain the rest of creation.

terrorism—Violence to achieve political ends perpetrated by a group lacking legal status.

Throwaway society—A social group in which it is acceptable to squander usable materials and products.

triage—The practice of placing people into one of three groups based on their likelihood of survival and treating first the two groups most likely to survive.

underlying causes—Ways society is structured that affect people.

undernourishment—Amount of food is less than what can sustain life.

works of mercy—Charitable actions aimed at meeting the physical and spiritual needs of others.

Index

A

Abortion, 124–127, 128–129, 204
Act (of ART), 116
Adam and Eve, 9, 11
Ageism, 134, 139–141
Air Pollution, 282–283, 289
Alzheimer's disease, 135
America/Americans, 52
    African, 52, 169
    Native, 52, 169
Americans with Disabilities Act, 145
Amos the prophet, 20–22
Animals, 290–291
    Experimentation, 290
Anthropocentrism, 284
ART (Act, Reflect, Transform), 116

B

Baptism, 5, 42
Basic human rights, 67, 175, 186, 272, 314
Beatitudes, 32, 33, 46
    Special beatitudes, 147
Benedict, Saint, 298
Blockade, 329
Body of Christ, Members of, 50
Breakdown in community, 345
Brothers and Sisters to Us, 51

C

Capitalism, 56, 57
Capital punishment, 157–159
CARE, 353
Cash crops, 204
Catholic Social Teaching, 55, 58–59, 66–68
    Seven themes of, 69–76
Catholic Workers Movement, 57
Charitable justice, 96
Charity, 96, 111–113
Chávez, César, 184–185
Christians/Christianity, 48–50, 52, 243
    And the call to justice, 48
    Communities, 49–50
    Social teaching, 53
Christianity and Social Progress (Mater et Magistra), 67
Chronic fatigue syndrome, 115
Chronic malnutrition, 197–198
Chrysostom, Saint John, 43
Church, 42
    And racism, 243–244
Global, 59
God's call to, 42
Growth of, 49
History of Early, 48–49, 242
Response to justice, 53, 211–212

Unity of, 42
Civil disobedience, 327, 329
Civil rights, 14
    Movement, 107, 231, 328
Claver, Saint Peter, 53
Close–mindedness, 229
Collateral damage, 129, 317
Colonialism, 52
Common good, 47, 67, 71–72, 167
Communities, 43
    Immigrant, 182
    Multicultural, 244
    Of compassion and charity, 114
Of resistance, 115
Compassion, 33, 109–110, 112–114
Compassion fatigue, 115–116
Conscience, 44, 45
Conscientious consumption, 82, 86
Conscientious objector, 322
Consumerism, 83–85
Contemplation, 129
Continuum of conflict resolution, 308
Covenant, 12
Creation, 8, 10, 14, 73, 283
Crimes against persons, 150
Crimes against property, 150
Criminal justice system, 150–154
Crisis of limits, 83
Culture of death, 127
Culture of life, 127
Culture of violence, 345

D

Day, Dorothy, 57, 59, 322
Decision-making power, 104
Declaration of Independence, 363
Deterrence, 352
Dignity, 6, 50, 53, 70, 142–147
Disabilities/Disabled people, 142–147
    Americans with Disabilities Act, 145
Distribution of power, 104
Divine law, 46
Domestic violence, 265
Drexel, Katharine, 52
Drought, 199
Drugs, 140, 151, 170
Drunk driving, 150

E

Ecology, 282
Economic colonies, 202
Economic Justice for All, 68
Economic migrants, 186
Economy, 74, 182, 206
Eisenhower, Dwight D., 350
Employment, 72, 170–171, 178–179, 182
Encyclical, 55

Environmental misuse, 291–292
Excessive consumption, 84
Exile, 50
Exodus, 13–14
Exploitation, 184, 294
Eucharist, 25, 43, 214
Euthanasia, 124, 127, 137

F

Faith, 57, 88
Famine, 199–200
Farming, 286–287
    Corporate, 290
    Energy-intensive, 218
    Inorganic, 287
    Labor-intensive, 218
    Low-tillage, 287
    Organic, 287
Fatalism, 87–88
Fear, 181
Feminization of poverty, 262
Figurative language, 9
Fixed income, 136
Food crops, 204
Food references in the Bible, 213
Frances, Saint (of Assisi), 51

G

Gender differences, 256–259, 261
Generalizations, 226, 228
Genesis, 8–12
Ghandi, 326–328
Global interdependence, 82
Global warming, 288
God, 4, 6
    And poverty, 176
    And the Covenant, 12
    Creation of the heavens and the earth, 10
    Defends the innocent, 128
    His promise, 23, 221
    His promise to Abraham, 8, 12
    His reign, 30
    His will, 21
God is Love (Deus Caritas Est), 67
Golden Rule, 247
Good Samaritan, 26–27, 29
    Story of, 26–27
Gospels, 87, 211
    Influence of, 54
    Of Peace, 332
Graced social structures, 103
Green-house effect, 288
Gross National Product, 207–208

H

Hate groups, 230
Health
    Mental, 134–135
    Physical, 134
Holy Spirit, 4, 6, 8, 24–25, 30, 88
    Inspiration of, 19
Signs of, 48
Homelessness, 172–173
    Economic factors of, 173
    Statistics about, 173
Homophobia, 273
Homosexuality/Homosexuals, 270–274
Hope, 88
Hosea the prophet, 20–22
Hundredth Year (Centesimus Annus), 67
Hunger, 197–198
    Causes, 199
    Material problem, 205
    Moral problem, 205

I

Immigrants/Immigration, 181–187, 244
    Communities, 182
    Deportation, 182
    Hostility towards, 181
Incarnation, 24
Income levels, 194
Individualism, 80
Industry, 55–56
Inequality, 15, 49
Injustice, 14, 56, 89
Institutional racism, 239
Interdependent, 81
Israelites, 13, 16, 241

J

Jeremiah the prophet, 20–22
Jesus, 24
    All as one in, 49
    And the Holy Spirit, 25, 59
    And women, 267–268
    As a healer, 35
    As a Jewish peasant, 28
    As the "bread of life", 212
    As the word of God, 24
    Gift of, 8, 24
    Justice, 26–27
    Mission of, 50
    Prince of Peace, 330
Jews, 27, see also, Israelites
John Paul II, Pope, 67, 74, 84, 89
John XXIII, Pope, 67
Jonah, 241
Jubilee year, 210

Justice, 4, 5–8, 26, 48–49, 96, 109
    And nature, 282–285
    As a virtue, 4
    Economic, 55–56
    Global, 58–59
    Racial, 239–240
Just-war doctrine, 312–313
    Applied after a conflict, 319–320
    Principles, 314–317

K

Kingdom of God, 28
King, Jr., Martin Luther, 14, 107, 248

L

Land mines, 353–354
"The Law", 46
Leo XIII, 55–56, 67
Liberation, 14–15
Life choices, 113
Long–term solutions, 101
Lord's Prayer, 30

M

Magisterium, 66
Malnutrition, 197–198
Marillac, Louise de, 52
Marx, Karl, 55
Mary, 209
Media, 79, 174, 266
Messiah, 24
Mexico/Mexican,
    Americans, 182–183
    Conquered territory, 184
    Exploitation of laborers, 185–186
    Immigrants, 183–184
    Opportunity, 184
    Stereotypes, 184
Migrant workers, 185, 186
Migration/migrants, 181, 186
    Stereotypes, 184
Militarism, 310–311
Military spending, 217
Milleret, Marie Eugenie, 54–55
Minimum wage, 169, 171, 182
Missionaries, 52–53
Missionaries of Charity, 100
Montgomery bus boycott, 107
Moses, 15, 21
Moral compass, 44
Mother Teresa of Calcutta, 100

N

Nationalism, 348
Natural law, 6, 9, 46
Near homeless, 173
New Law, 46
New Testament, 8–9
Nobel Peace Prize, 100, 107
Nuclear weapons, 351

O

Oklahoma City Bombings, 355–356
Old Law, 46
Old Testament, 8–9, 46, 210
Oligarchies, 207
On the Conditions of Workers (Rerum Novarum), 56, 67
On the Development of Peoples (Populorum Progressio), 67
Original sin, 11
Overconsumption, 216–217

P

Pacifism, 321, 323–324, 326
    Absolute pacifists, 323
    Practical pacifists, 323
Parables, 26
Parks, Rosa, 107
Patriarchy, 260
Patriotism, 358
Passivity, 321
Paul, Vincent de, 52
Peace, 324, 332, 350
Peace on Earth (Pacem in Terris), 67
Pentecost, 41–42
Personal causes, 98
Physical quality of life index, 194
Pius XII, 185
Plea bargaining, 152–153
Pollution, 288–289
Pope Benedict XVI, 67
Poverty, 166–180, 194, 197, 203
    And the environment, 291–292
    As a scandal, 178
    Children in, 177
    Effects of, 166–168
    Elimination of, 178
    Global, 194
    Government policy, 177–178
    Guidelines, 171
    Images of, 167
    Impoverished countries' characteristics, 202
    Indicators of, 194
    Myths about, 168–169
Power, 104–105

Photo Credits